FAITH ESTABLISHES THE LAW

SOCIETY OF BIBLICAL LITERATURE

DISSERTATION SERIES

Howard C. Kee, Editor

Number 55
FAITH ESTABLISHES THE LAW
by
C. Thomas Rhyne

C. Thomas Rhyne

FAITH ESTABLISHES THE LAW

Scholars Press

Distributed by
Scholars Press
101 Salem Street
P. O. Box 2268
Chico, CA 95927

FAITH ESTABLISHES THE LAW

C. Thomas Rhyne

Th.D., 1979
Union Theological Seminary
Richmond, Virginia

Advisor:
Paul J. Achtemeier

© 1981
Society of Biblical Literature

Library of Congress Cataloging in Publication Data

Rhyne, Clyde Thomas.
  Faith establishes the law.

  (Dissertation series / Society of Biblical
Literature ; no. 55) (ISSN 0145-2770)
  Thesis—Union Theological Seminary.
  Bibliography: p.
  1. Law (Theology)—Biblical teaching. 2. Bible.
N.T. Romans—Criticism, interpretation, etc.
3. Christianity and other religions—Judaism.
4. Judaism—Relations—Christianity. I. Title.
II. Series: Dissertation series (Society of Biblical
Literature) ; no. 55
BS2655.L35R49   234   81-1794
ISBN: 0-89130-483-5   AACR2

Printed in the United States of America
1 2 3 4 5 6
Edwards Brothers, Inc.
Ann Arbor, Michigan 48106

To Elizabeth Ann, my faithful companion,
    for more reasons than I can count.

To Anna Elizabeth, our daughter,
    for that added dimension.

To Fred and Margaret Rhyne, my parents,
    for bringing me to the Scriptures.

To Gilbert and Minnie Geren, my parents-in-law,
    for giving me Elizabeth Ann.

TABLE OF CONTENTS

Page

ACKNOWLEDGMENTS vii
LIST OF ABBREVIATIONS ix
INTRODUCTION 1
Chapter
I. THE STATUS OF THE LAW *POST CHRISTUM* 5
    Introduction 5
    Paul's Approach to the Status of the Law
      in Christianity 7
      Discontinuity 8
      Continuity 13
      Mediating Positions 19
    Conclusion 23
II. ROMANS 3:31 AS A *CRUX INTERPRETUM* 25
    Introduction 25
    Romans 3:31 in Relation to Its Context . . . 26
      Romans 3:31 as the Conclusion to Romans
        3:21-30 26
      Romans 3:31 as the Introduction or
        Transition to Romans 4:1-25 30
    Paul's Use of Rhetorical Questions 32
      Introduction 32
      Epictetus 34
      Paul 41
      Conclusion 58
    Conclusion 59
III. THE EXEGESIS OF ROMANS 3:21-4:25 63
    Introduction 63
    The Exegesis of Romans 3:21-30 63
    The Exegesis of Romans 3:31 71
    The Exegesis of Romans 4:1-25 75
    Conclusion 89

Chapter	Page
IV. ROMANS 10:4 ONCE MORE	95
Introduction	95
The Exegesis of Romans 9:30-10:21	98
The Exegesis of Romans 9:30-33	98
The Exegesis of Romans 10:1-21	102
Conclusion	112
CONCLUSION	117
NOTES	123
SELECTED BIBLIOGRAPHY	175

ACKNOWLEDGMENTS

Of the many persons who have contributed in some way to the production of this dissertation, I gratefully acknowledge indebtedness to the following:

My supervisor, Dr. Paul J. Achtemeier, whose insight and understanding greatly enhanced my ability to complete this task.

My readers, Drs. Mathias Rissi and W. Sibley Towner, who made valuable criticisms and suggestions in the course of the writing.

The administration and staff of the Library of Union Theological Seminary and especially Mrs. Martha B. Aycock, whose genuine interest and help exceeded the call of duty.

Union Theological Seminary and its supporters for the various fellowships and other funds which made this venture an accessible goal.

My wife, Elizabeth Ann, whose support and patience have been the sustaining factor during seven years of concentrated effort.

LIST OF ABBREVIATIONS

AnBib	Analecta Biblica
BEvT	Beiträge zur evangelischen Theologie
BJRL	*Bulletin of the John Rylands University Library*
CBQ	*Catholic Biblical Quarterly*
ÉtBib	Études Bibliques
EvT	*Evangelische Theologie*
FRLANT	Forschungen zur Religion und Literatur des Alten und Neuen Testaments
HNT	Handbuch zum Neuen Testament
HNTC	Harper's New Testament Commentaries
HTKNT	Herders theologischer Kommentar zum Neuen Testament
HTR	*Harvard Theological Review*
HUT	Hermeneutische Untersuchungen zur Theologie
ICC	International Critical Commentary
IDB	*Interpreter's Dictionary of the Bible*
Interp	*Interpretation*
JBL	*Journal of Biblical Literature*
KExKNT	Kritisch-exegetische Kommentar über das Neuen Testament
LXX	Septuagint
MT	Masoretic Text
MüTZ	Münchener theologische Zeitschrift
NICNT	New International Commentary on the New Testament
NT	New Testament
NTA	Neutestamentliche Abhandlungen
NTS	*New Testament Studies*
OT	Old Testament
RSV	Revised Standard Version
SJT	*Scottish Journal of Theology*
SNTS	Society for New Testament Studies
TDNT	*Theological Dictionary of the New Testament*

THkNT	Theologischer Handkommentar zum Neuen Testament
TLZ	*Theologische Literaturzeitung*
TZ	*Theologische Zeitschrift*
WMANT	Wissenschaftliche Monographien zum Alten und Neuen Testament
ZNW	*Zeitschrift für die Neutestamentliche Wissenschaft*
ZTK	*Zeitschrift für Theologie und Kirche*

INTRODUCTION

Concluding his recent comparison of Paul and Palestinian Judaism, E. P. Sanders asserts: "In short, *this is what Paul finds wrong in Judaism: it is not Christianity.*"[1] Given Sanders' understanding of Judaism and Pauline Christianity, it is easy to nod assent to this statement. However, what interests us in Sanders' concluding assertion (and in his entire monograph) is that he raises again the question of the continuity between Judaism and Christianity. Is Judaism in any way continuous with Christianity? Or, to put the question from the Christian standpoint, is Christianity in any way continuous with Judaism? In particular, does Paul regard the connection between the church and the synagogue as totally discontinuous? Or does he in some way view the church and the synagogue as continuous with each other?

Within the confines of his own work Sanders can reasonably answer this question in the negative. But, for reasons which will become evident in the first chapter of the present study, we intend here to reopen this question. Suffice it to say at this point that it is the scholarly stalemate over Paul's attitude toward the law which propels us in this direction. Thus, we are not primarily concerned with challenging the validity of Sanders' conclusions but with the crucial issue he raises in his work.

Though we could approach this question from several angles, we propose to limit our inquiry to Paul's[2] understanding of the status of the law as one of the basic elements of continuity between Judaism and Christianity. By "status" we mean the law's continuing role as a way of salvation, as a norm for living, as a standard of divine judgment, as a witness. One aspect of the status of the law in the church is spotlighted in the apostle's question about the relationship between the law and faith (Rom 3:31), a text not mentioned by Sanders: "Do we then overthrow the law by this faith?

By no means! On the contrary, we uphold the law."[3] Precisely what does Paul mean by the statement that he upholds the law by faith? What does this verse teach about Paul's estimation of the status of the law in the church? Hence, what does Rom 3:31 reveal about the continuity between church and synagogue? It is to the resolution of these questions that we are devoting the major part of this study.

To provide a background for our inquiry, we will survey recent scholarly discussion about Paul's conception of the status of the law in the church (Chapter I). Here it will become evident that, in their interpretation of Pauline texts on the status of the law in Christianity, scholars may follow three general approaches: discontinuity, continuity and mediating positions. The apparent scholarly impasse over Paul's understanding of the status of the law in the church which comes to light in this survey should in part justify the necessity of our own research. Because of this impasse we intend to concentrate our efforts on the exegesis of Rom 3:31, one Pauline text which speaks unequivocally of the continuing validity of the law in the church.

With this survey as a background we can proceed to describe the two opposing ways in which scholars construe Rom 3:31 in the context of the epistle along with the resultant interpretations of this verse (Chapter II). To break this deadlock we will appeal to Paul's use of rhetorical questions, especially those negated by μὴ γένοιτο (see Rom 3:31ab), as a means of unlocking the relationship of this verse to its context. Therefore, we will examine first Epictetus', then Paul's use of such questions in order to determine if a pattern is present which sheds light on the role of Rom 3:31 in its context.

Next, in conjunction with our study of Paul's use of rhetorical questions, we will conduct an exegesis of the immediate context of the verse under investigation (Rom 3:21-4:25), giving special attention to Paul's understanding of the law at crucial points in this passage, 3:21-30; 3:31; 4:1-25 (Chapter III). Our exegetical conclusions should corroborate our findings in Chapter II about the relationship of Rom 3:31 to its context. Moreover, we should now be able

Introduction

to define what this verse teaches about the status of the law in the church and, consequently, what it has to say about the continuity between the church and the synagogue.

Then we will bring the results of our investigation to bear on another key Pauline text about the status of the law in the church, Rom 10:4, in order to determine whether our understanding of Rom 3:31 is instructive for its interpretation (Chapter IV). After a brief analysis of the two main interpretations of this much debated text and of the arguments presented in their favor, we will engage in an exegesis of the entire section (Rom 9:30-10:21) so as to ascertain the significance Rom 10:4 has in its context and in Paul's theology of the law. In the course of this exegesis we will stress the thematic importance of Rom 9:30-33 for a proper understanding of Paul's subsequent discussion (10:1-21) and particularly of 10:4. By way of conclusion we will compare our findings from Rom 3:21-4:25 with those from 9:30-10:21.

Finally, we will summarize our insights on the continuity between Judaism and Christianity with regard to the law from the two passages we have examined (Conclusion). Hopefully, these insights will provide a basis for judging Paul's numerous other statements about the law.

CHAPTER I

THE STATUS OF THE LAW *POST CHRISTUM*

Introduction

As already indicated, this study addresses the question of the continuity between Judaism and Christianity as it relates to the matter of the law. In order to address this issue adequately we will first look briefly at the centrality of the law in Judaism, then the centrality of Christ in Christianity and finally the resulting problem of the status of the law in Christianity.

In terms of its practical dimensions, S. Safrai vividly expresses the centrality of the law in Judaism with the following words:

> The most striking characteristic of the Jewish people in the period of the Second Temple was the observance of the Law of the one God, as revealed in the written Torah and the oral tradition. That the whole life of the Jewish people, from hour to hour of its working days as well as on the solemn moments of sabbath and feast-day, was dominated by the Law is evident from talmudic tradition, Josephus and the New Testament, especially the writings of Paul.[1]

The apostle Paul, our closest datable witness, describes this observance of the law in terms of a "zeal for God" (Rom 10:2). Also, he depicts his former life in Judaism as blameless with regard to the righteousness which is in the law (Phil 3:6). In fact, he had outstripped his Jewish peers in his own zealousness for the patriarchal traditions (Gal 1:14).

In terms of its theological dimensions,[2] Paul portrays contemporary Judaism as pursuing the "law of righteousness" on the assumption that they could attain to this law by doing its works (Rom 9:31-32). Or, as he expresses it in other words, they were seeking to establish their own righteousness on the basis of the works of the law (Rom 10:3). In this manner they hoped to obtain life (Rom 10:5). For this reason they had found faith in Christ to be a stumbling block (Rom 9:32-33; 10:3).

However, with the emergence of the church the Jewish attitude toward the law underwent a reevaluation among those who became followers of Jesus of Nazareth. The Gospels show that Jesus Christ had come to assume the primary role which the law once held in the life of those who had espoused the Way. This centrality of Christ becomes apparent in the introductory words of the Gospel of Mark: "The beginning of the gospel of Jesus Christ, the Son of God (1:1)." The focus of attention has now shifted to such a degree that Mark does not even use the word "law" (νόμος) in this treatise, though questions of the law do surface at certain points in the Gospel. At some of these points the priority of Christ over the law is evident (2:28; 7:19; 10:21). A survey of the other Synoptics would yield similar results, though there the word "law" does appear.

When we move to the Gospel of John, the supremacy of Christ over the law is expressed almost from the outset: "For the law was given through Moses; grace and truth came through Jesus Christ. No one has ever seen God; the only Son, who is in the bosom of the Father, he has made him known (1:17-18)." In this statement it becomes clear that Jesus has taken the revelatory role between God and humanity which Moses and the law formerly occupied.

As for Paul, we can agree in principle with Paul Démann when he sums up the apostle's attitude toward the law with the words: *"Christus nimmt im Leben des Paulus den Platz des Gesetzes ein."*[3] That Christ has indeed assumed the place of the law in the apostle's life as far as obtaining righteousness is concerned becomes evident in Paul's description of his own Christian experience: "Indeed I count everything as loss because of the surpassing worth of knowing Christ Jesus my Lord. For his sake I have suffered the loss of all things, and count them as refuse, in order that I may gain Christ and be found in him, not having a righteousness of my own, based on law, but that which is through faith in Christ, the righteousness from God that depends on faith (Phil 3:8-9)."

In view of the prominent position attributed to Christ in the emerging church, it was inevitable the problem of the status of the law should arise. How early this question of the relationship between the law and faith in Christ became a burning issue in the church we cannot know with certainty. For the Gospel writers, it goes back into the ministry of Jesus himself as the Marcan texts mentioned above show. For the writer of Acts, it flares up again in the post-ascension period with the trial of Stephen (Acts 7-8) and receives its climactic solution at the so-called "Jerusalem Council" (Acts 15).

Actually, Paul himself represents again the earliest datable witness to the existence of this problem. On occasion he waged a life-and-death struggle over the issue of the works of the law versus faith as the Epistle to the Galatians clearly reveals. The same issue reappears in Romans, but the heat of the debate seems to have subsided. It is with the apostle's approach to this problem of the status of the law in the church that we will be concerned in the remainder of this chapter.

Paul's Approach to the Status of the Law in Christianity

Here we turn to examine Paul's understanding of the law's status as it is interpreted in recent scholarly literature.[4] As a result of our survey of this literature we have observed that scholars have adopted three general approaches to Paul's position on the status of the law in Christianity, namely, discontinuity, continuity and mediating positions. Of course, we must emphasize from the start that these three general approaches do not necessarily correspond to scholarly camps or schools. For, while some scholars may stress discontinuity against continuity and vice versa or mediate between these two extremes, others can work with combinations of or variations on these three general approaches depending on the Pauline text under discussion. We will investigate these three approaches in some detail before suggesting a Pauline text where a fundamental solution to the problem may lie.

Discontinuity

While few scholars would view Paul as Marcionite in his attitude toward the law,[5] some do emphasize the concept of discontinuity between the law and the Christian faith more forcefully than others. In this section we will mention and discuss those Pauline texts which are commonly interpreted as demonstrating this discontinuity.

More than any other text, Rom 10:4 has become the *locus classicus* for expressing the discontinuity between the church and the synagogue: τέλος γὰρ νόμου Χριστὸς εἰς δικαιοσύνην παντὶ τῷ πιστεύοντι. Understanding τέλος as "end" in the sense of termination, scholars interpret this verse to mean that Christ has ended the law as a way of salvation.[6] In fact, the expression, "Christ the end of the law," has become a widespread slogan in Pauline theology, being used in titles of books, chapters, sections and articles.

For example, in a recent essay Peter Stuhlmacher discusses the origin and beginning of Pauline theology under the rubric, "Das Ende des Gesetzes," indeed without a closer examination of Rom 10:4, the text which apparently motivated his study. He argues that the statement, Christ is the end of the law, is the quintessence of what God impressed on Paul, the zealot of the law, before Damascus in the form of the crucified, resurrected One.[7]

Moreover, this end of the law may be viewed in either historical or existential categories.[8] But many insist that it occurs only in the realm of faith.[9] Further, scholars base this abolition of the law at times on the apocalyptic notion of the two aeons,[10] at times on a rabbinical scheme of history which supposedly teaches the law will cease with the coming of the Messiah,[11] at times on Paul's conversion and his acquaintance with a particular apocalyptic conception of the law,[12] at times on Paul's borrowing from the Hellenistic church[13] and at times on the simple notion that the one way of salvation in Christ excludes all others.[14]

A text sometimes related to Rom 10:4 because of the occurrence of τέλος is 2 Cor 3:7-18.[15] The interpretation of the entire passage as well as that of τέλος (3:13) and of the important verb καταργεῖν ("to abolish," 3:11, 13, 14) remains a moot point. Nevertheless, some understand τὸ καταργούμενον (3:11), τοῦ καταργουμένου (3:13) and καταργεῖται (3:14) as explicit references to the abolition of the old covenant and thus as implicit references to the abolition of the law.[16] At the same time they draw a correspondence between this passage and Rom 10:4. In this way τέλος (3:13) receives the same connotation that the scholars already mentioned ascribe to it there.[17]

What this abolition means concretely is described in various ways. It is the end of the law as that which demands and therefore leads to death and condemnation.[18] It is the abolition of the law in the "old, legalist, sense."[19] Or it is the abrogation of the law as a system of salvation in opposition to the gospel or as "letter" in opposition to the "Spirit."[20]

Another text often interpreted to demonstrate the abolition of the law is Gal 2:18: "But if I build up again those things which I tore down (ἃ κατέλυσα), then I prove myself a transgressor." Some have seen in Paul's mention of the things which he had torn down the abrogation of certain prohibitions of the law (especially the food regulations) or the abolition of the law as a dividing wall between Jews and Gentiles (cf. Eph 2:14).[21] Others apparently find a clear reference to the nullification of the law as a way of salvation.[22]

Also, Paul's pivotal remark about the manifestation of God's righteousness (Rom 3:21) is viewed as a significant statement on the abrogation of the law: "But now the righteousness of God has been manifested apart from law (χωρὶς νόμου), although the law and the prophets bear witness to it." The short phrase, "apart from law," is taken as signaling the end of the law. Thus, in commenting on this verse, Ernst Käsemann[23] argues that, because God's eschatological salvation is valid for the creation, it excludes the law understood as a summons to righteousness by works. Similarly, Günther Bornkamm[24] states that it is the eschatological now which puts an end to human history under the law.

Furthermore, some find in the apostle's description of his conversion (Phil 3:2-11) an indication of the end of

the law: "For his sake I have suffered the loss of all
things, and count them as refuse, in order that I may gain
Christ and be found in him, not having a righteousness of my
own, based on law, but that which is through faith in Christ,
the righteousness from God that depends on faith (3:8-9)."
Hence, P. G. Verweijs[25] asserts that Paul proclaims here the
end of the law on the basis of his own experience but grounds
it by the event of salvation in Christ.

In addition to the texts just mentioned, there are a
number of texts referring to the believer's relationship to
the law which are interpreted as teaching the abolition of
the law in some sense. First, one should note those texts
which state the believer is no longer under the law (Rom
6:14-15; Gal 3:25; 4:5; 1 Cor 9:20; cf. Gal 5:18). With
regard to Rom 6:14-15, Franz J. Leenhardt writes that "the
law, considered as a system of salvation is abolished; Christ
has instituted a new régime."[26] Concerning Gal 3:25 Heinrich
Schlier[27] notes that the lordship of the law is fundamentally
and in principle broken; Christ has become its end in fact
and for the world in its entirety. Moreover, in treating
Gal 4:5, J. B. Lightfoot states: "The abolition of the law,
the rescue from bondage, was a prior condition of the universal sonship of the faithful."[28] Finally, interpreting Paul's
statement, μὴ ὢν αὐτὸς ὑπὸ νόμον (1 Cor 9:20), C. K. Barrett
asserts:

> *The law* here means the law of Moses; but if this is
> repudiated, by an *a fortiori* argument all less important
> and directly divine laws are repudiated. Paul is now
> related to God through Jesus Christ (cf. i.30), and no
> room is left for law.[29]

Again, another text speaks of the believer as having
been discharged from the law: "But now we are discharged
(κατηργήθημεν) from the law, dead to that which held us captive, so that we serve not under the old written code but in
the new life of the Spirit (Rom 7:6)." Thus Käsemann[30] points
out that our being discharged (literally "abolished") from the
law does not mean a new understanding and use of the Torah but
its end for those who have become Christians.

Further, a couple of texts refer to the believer as
having been freed from the law (Rom 8:2; Gal 4:21-5:1). In

the first text Paul explains his statement that there is now no condemnation for those who are in Christ Jesus: "For the law of the Spirit of life in Christ Jesus has set me free from the law of sin and death (Rom 8:2)." Taking "the law of the Spirit of life" as the order of the Spirit-law (*Geistgesetz*) and "the law of sin and death" as the Mosaic law, Karl Kertelge[31] asserts that in the new order of the law of the Spirit the old order of the Mosaic law is actually abolished.

In the second text (Gal 4:21-5:1) the apostle argues from the law against the Galatians' desire to subject themselves to the law. Though the law is not mentioned specifically in the discussion after 4:21, Joseph Shou-Jen Wang[32] finds it embodied in the Sinaitic covenant represented by the slave Hagar. According to Wang, the casting out of Hagar exemplifies the setting aside of this covenant and, consequently, the making non-effective of the law.

Moreover, some texts refer to the believer as having died to the law (Rom 7:4; Gal 2:19). While they differ over the interpretation of details, scholars detect in Rom 7:4 an indication of the abolition of the law: "Likewise, my brethren, you have died to the law through the body of Christ, so that you may belong to another, to him who has been raised from the dead in order that we may bear fruit for God." Thus Marie Joseph Lagrange[33] encounters in this statement about the death of Christ (= the body of Christ) the fundamental reason for the abrogation of the law. Paul's other statement is similar: "For I through the law died to the law, that I might live to God (Gal 2:19)." With regard to this text Reimer Gronemeyer[34] asserts that the law has been set aside through the law itself and led *ad absurdum*.

Finally, another text proclaims the believer has been redeemed from the curse of the law (Gal 3:13; cf. 4:5). Making a connection with Eph 2:14-18, Lightfoot concludes about this verse: "Thus the law, the great barrier which excluded the Gentiles, is done away in Christ."[35] On the other hand, Gronemeyer[36] argues that the law as a pernicious power which hinders God's blessing is set aside through the death of Christ.

Besides these passages which treat the believer's relation to the law, in two contexts Paul speaks expressly of the law as an addition (Rom 5:20; Gal 3:19, 24). In the first case, scholars focus particularly on the apostle's use of παρεισέρχεσθαι: "Law came in (παρεισῆλθεν), to increase the trespass; but where sin increased, grace abounded all the more (Rom 5:20)." Hence Egon Brandenburger,[37] who takes this verb as meaning "to come in between" in a derogatory sense (cf. Gal 2:4), holds that the law has only episodic character and comes to an end with the inbreaking of the new aeon (cf. Rom. 10:4). While agreeing over the episodic character of the law, others[38] reject the notion Paul describes the law here in a sinister fashion.

In the second case, scholars have directed their attention to Paul's use of προστιθέναι in conjunction with the ἄχρις-clause: "Why then the law? It was added (προσετέθη) because of transgressions, till (ἄχρις) the offspring should come to whom the promise had been made; and it was ordained by angels through an intermediary (Gal 3:19)." Thus, in his treatment of Gal 3:19-22, Francis Irving Fesperman states:

> There can be no question but that Paul here teaches that the law had a definite beginning and a definite ending in time: from Moses to Christ. It does not belong, as the Jews thought, to the seven things created before the world, nor is it eternal.[39]

In the matter of Gal 3:24 interpreters make much of the phrase εἰς Χριστόν: "So that the law was our custodian until Christ came (εἰς Χριστόν), that we might be justified by faith." Understanding this phrase in a temporal sense, Franz Mussner declares: "Die Funktion des Gesetzes ist eine zeitlich begrenzte; sie ist auch eine inhaltlich begrenzte."[40]

Another context in which scholars often speak of the abolition of the law embraces Paul's use of the Spirit/letter antithesis (Rom 2:27-29; 7:6; 2 Cor 3:6). Especially important is Rom 7:6 where Paul contrasts the "newness of the Spirit" with the "oldness of the letter": "But now we are discharged from the law, dead to that which held us captive, so that we serve not under the old written code but in the new life of the Spirit." In order to determine whether Paul means by the "oldness of the letter" the obsolescence of the law, one must ask whether "letter" and "law" can be directly equated in Paul's thought.

Some have made this equation and thus can speak of the abrogation of the law in this context. For example, Lagrange asserts:

> En opposition à cet état nouveau, le règne de l'Esprit et de la grâce, l' ancien était une chose désuète, la lettre, qui est déjà de sa nature une chose morte. Paul ne distingue pas entre la loi cérémonielle et la loi morale; c'est toute la Loi comme régime que est abrogée, sans detriment de la morale qui est éternelle, indiquée plus haut comme obéissance à la volonté de Dieu (vi,16).[41]

Finally, we must mention several Pauline texts thought to support the idea of a new or messianic law, thus implying at times the abolition of the old one (Rom 3:27; 8:2; Gal 6:2; 1 Cor 9:21). This conception of a new or messianic law assumes various forms. Basing his approach primarily on 1 Cor 9:21, C. H. Dodd suggests Paul conceived of the "law of God" as something more inclusive than the simple "law" in the sense of the Torah. He states: "The law of God, which at one stage and on one level finds expression in the Torah, may at another stage and on a different level find expression in the 'law of Christ.'"[42] Besides the apostle's use of the explicit phrase ὁ νόμος τοῦ Χριστοῦ (Gal 6:2), Dodd refers in particular to Paul's use of the words of Jesus to give content to this "law of Christ."[43]

Drawing on rabbinic tradition as well as Paul's own statements, Hans Joachim Schoeps[44] places alongside his view that the apostle held the law would be abolished with the coming of the Messiah (Rom 10:4), the idea that God will promulgate a new Torah through the Messiah (Rom 3:27; 8:2; Gal 6:2). However, despite these statements about the abrogation of the old law and the promulgation of a new one, Schoeps[45] notes that Paul continued to remain faithful to the Jewish Torah.

Continuity

While scholars have discovered statements in Paul's writings to the effect that the law has been abolished in the realm of the church, they have also found there indications of the continuity between the law and the Christian faith. Below we will mention those Pauline texts most commonly interpreted as showing this continuity.

Though some scholars find Rom 10:4 to be the *locus classicus* for expressing the idea of discontinuity between church and synagogue, others regard it as a classic statement of continuity. Understanding τέλος as "goal" or "fulfilment," they interpret this verse to mean that in Christ the law has reached its goal or fulfilment.[46] As a perusal of the literature reveals, these scholars generally view this attainment of the goal of the law or fulfilment of the law in Christ in terms of its requirement or promise of righteousness.

A series of closely connected Pauline statements about the law which has assumed much importance in discussing the continuity between the law and the Christian faith is Rom 3:21, 27, 31, especially the latter. With respect to the first statement (Rom 3:21) we have already noted that some regard the presence of the phrase χωρὶς νόμου as a signal of the end of the law. However, others call attention to the remainder of Paul's statement to the effect that the law and the prophets bear witness (μαρτυρεῖν) to the righteousness of God now revealed apart from the law. As the apostle explains, this righteousness of God is a righteousness which comes by faith in Christ (Rom 3:22). The point often made here is that, far from being abolished, the law along with the prophets remains as an abiding witness to righteousness by faith and affirms the continuity between God's past and present saving acts.[47]

In connection with Rom 3:21 we should also mention Rom 3:27 where Paul asks: Ποῦ οὖν ἡ καύχησις; ἐξεκλείσθη. διὰ ποίου νόμου; τῶν ἔργων; οὐχί, ἀλλὰ διὰ νόμου πίστεως. Above we discussed the approach of some scholars who view Paul's use of the expression νόμος πίστεως as evidence for a new or messianic law. But in a departure from the more common interpretation of this expression as the norm, principle, rule, system, order of faith, Gerhard Friedrich[48] understands this phrase (as well as νόμος τῶν ἔργων) in terms of the OT law (the Pentateuch, cf. Rom 3:21) as the law which announces

faith. Thus, in contrast to the law as a demand for works
("the law of works"), Paul, as in Rom. 3:21, emphasizes the
abiding character of the law as a witness to righteousness by
faith ("the law of faith") which excludes boasting. As will
become apparent later, Friedrich has recently gained support
among scholars for his approach.

However, the most important of these three statements
is Rom 3:31: "Do we then overthrow the law by this faith? By
no means! On the contrary, we uphold the law." It has become
the *locus classicus* for expressing the concept of continuity
between the law and the Christian faith. Even those scholars
who argue Rom 10:4 teaches the abolition of the law recognize
the importance of Paul's assertion that he upholds the law by
faith. With regard to the interpretation of this important
text scholarship has followed two general directions. On the
one hand, some consider Rom 3:31 as the introduction or transition to Rom 4. Analyzing this statement in the light of Rom
3:21 and sometimes 3:27, they usually understand Paul to be
saying that faith establishes the law because the law bears
witness to faith as the case of Abraham (Gen 15:6) reveals.
On the other hand, others view Rom 3:31 as the conclusion to
Rom 3:21-30. Denying any connection between this verse and
Rom 4, they usually interpret Paul's statement in the light of
the preceding or following context (e.g., Rom 3:19-20, 24-25,
27; Rom 5; 6; 7; 8:4; 9-11; 12-15). Because of this dispute
we intend to treat this decisive text in the next two chapters.

Another text thought to speak positively about the
relation between the law and faith is Gal 3:24: ὥστε ὁ νόμος
παιδαγωγὸς ἡμῶν γέγονεν εἰς Χριστόν, ἵνα ἐκ πίστεως δικαιωθῶ-
μεν. In the preceding section we saw how scholars have interpreted this verse, especially the phrase, εἰς Χριστόν, as
pointing to the temporally restricted function of the law.
Some, however, understand this phrase in a final (purposive)
sense, calling attention also to the abiding condition implied
in the perfect γέγονεν. Thus Paul Johannes Du Plessis[49] argues
that the law became and is now an agent which conducts us to
Christ in order that we might be justified by faith.

Furthermore, Paul's assertions in Rom 8:2, 4 have
become increasingly important for demonstrating the validity

of the law in the context of the church. Though some have
found in Rom 8:2 a statement about the abrogation of the law,
others have seen here an expression of its continuing validity
in the realm of faith: "For the law of the Spirit of life in
Christ Jesus has set me free from the law of sin and death."
Diverging from the usual way of understanding νόμος here as
order, rule, norm, compulsion, dominion, control, several
scholars take it as referring to the OT law in both of its
occurrences. In brief, "the law of sin and death" is the law
qualified by sin and death; "the law of the Spirit of life in
Christ Jesus" is the same law qualified by the life-giving
Spirit. To cite only one interpretation among others we may
refer to Ferdinand Hahn:

> Wie der νόμος τῆς ἁμαρτίας καὶ τοῦ θανάτου das Gesetz in
> seiner die Sünde blossstellenden und den Menschen in der
> Verlorenheit behaftenden Macht bezeichnet und damit über
> sich hinaus auf Christus verweist, so ist der νόμος
> πίστεως bzw. der νόμος τοῦ πνεύματος τῆς ζωῆς das Gesetz,
> wie es für den, der von Sünde und Tod befreit ist, ver-
> pflichtend in Erscheinung tritt.[50]

Likewise, many scholars encounter in Rom 8:4 a declaration of the continuity between the law and faith in Christ:
"In order that the just requirement of the law might be fulfilled in us, who walk not according to the flesh but according to the Spirit." Thus C. E. B. Cranfield can say:

> What the law, frustrated and abused by men's sin, could
> not accomplish, Christ has triumphantly accomplished in
> that He has dealt once and for all with our sin by taking
> upon Himself our condemnation (Rom. 8.3). But this He
> has done, not in order that the law might be done away,
> but "that the ordinance [i.e., the righteous requirement]
> of the law might be fulfilled in us, who walk not after
> the flesh, but after the spirit [so RV wrongly: "Spirit"
> is required]" (Rom. 8.4).[51]

Though all would not agree with every aspect of Cranfield's
interpretation of this verse, they do admit its importance as
an expression of continuity.[52]

Also, we should call attention to Paul's discussion of
the station in life that the Lord has assigned to each person
and several important statements made there (1 Cor 7:17-24).
For one thing, two statements about remaining in one's calling
(κλῆσις) after conversion would seem to imply that the law,

as a primary component in the Jew's calling, still retains its validity (7:18, 20). Consequently, Wilfred L. Knox asserts with regard to 7:18: "It is clear that S. Paul continued throughout his life to practice Judaism, and that he expected Jewish converts to do so."[53]

For another thing, we have the apostle's more explicit statement: "For neither circumcision counts for anything (οὐδέν ἐστιν) nor uncircumcision, but keeping the commandments of God (τήρησις ἐντολῶν θεοῦ, 7:19)." Reflecting on this verse, Wolfgang Schrage asserts:

> Entscheidend ist nun aber dies: Die justificatio impii bedeutet nicht eine Erweichung oder Aufhebung der Gebote (1 Kor 7,19). Der Kampf gegen den Nomismus ist kein Kampf gegen das Halten der Gebote, sondern dagegen, dieses Halten der Gebote zum Heilsweg und zur Heilsbedingung zu verdrehen.[54]

Or Hans Conzelmann can remark:

> οὐδέν ἐστιν, "is nothing," is related strictly to salvation . . . . This very οὐδέν ἐστιν means, of course, that the Jew continues to remain a Jew. What matters, and what is possible, is the obedience of each individual in the particular place allotted to him, that is, in the world.[55]

Moreover, several scholars underline the importance Paul's positive statements about the character of the law (Rom 7:10, 12, 14) have in supporting the thesis of the continuing validity of the law in the church. Thus these assertions about the relation of the law to life (7:10) and about the holiness, righteousness, goodness and spirituality of the law (7:12, 14) are said to bolster that interpretation of Rom 10:4 which declares Christ is the goal or fulfilment of the law.[56] Also, Georg Eichholz speaks of the entire chapter in this manner: "Röm 7 ist ein einziger Beleg dafür, dass es Paulus nicht darum gehen kann, die Tora zu annullieren."[57]

Next, it is appropriate to mention the apostle's utterances about the law and judgment: "All who have sinned without the law will also perish without the law, and all who have sinned under the law will be judged by the law. For it is not the hearers of the law who are righteous before God, but the doers of the law who will be justified (Rom 2:12-13)."

Contrary to those who interpret these verses as a remnant of Jewish theology which Paul has not yet overcome, as hypothetical in nature or as the necessary precondition for Paul's teaching on justification,[58] some find here an indication of the law's enduring validity as the standard of future judgment for Christians. Of course, they differ among themselves about how one should perceive this validity.[59]

Furthermore, scholars have given particular attention to those texts which speak of the summing up and/or fulfilment of the law in the love-command (Rom 13:8-10; Gal 5:13-14). Thus Andrew John Bandstra comments with regard to the former:

> In addition, Rom 13:8, 10 specify that the Christian activity of loving also fulfills the law. Here the concrete action in the Christian life is in mind. In this sense, also, the law does not stand opposed to the life in the Spirit; rather it finds its fulfilment there.[60]

In addition, when comparing the relation of the unbeliever and of the believer to the law in light of Gal 5:13-14, Andrea van Dülmen declares with respect to the believer:

> Auch für ihn ist das Gesetz verbindlich; aber er steht als von Christus Befreiter ausserhalb seines Machtbereiches. Die Liebe ist für ihn massgebend. In ihr ist es ihm möglich, das Gesetz zu erfüllen.[61]

Finally, we must consider two instances in which Paul refers to a "law of Christ" (Gal 6:2; 1 Cor 9:21). Previously we noted some scholars who find in these texts (among others) support for the view that Paul held the notion of a new or messianic law regarded for the most part as distinct from the OT law. However, others have come to understand these statements in terms of the OT law which Christ has possessed and in some way renewed. Here the emphasis is more on continuity. Therefore, in a belated remark on Gal 6:2, Hahn explains: "Im Sinne der Rechtsforderung und der Weisung ist der νόμος Χριστοῦ die kritische Rezeption des alttestamentlichen Gesetzes."[62] In the light of Gal 5:13-14, this critically received OT law often amounts to nothing more than the love-command.[63]

With regard to 1 Cor 9:21 scholars single out the phrase ἔννομος Χριστοῦ as evidence of the continuing validity of the law. Hence Knox argues:

> Apparently S. Paul here means that in dealing with those
> outside the Law, he behaves as if he were free from the
> Law (as indeed he claims to be in v. 20), not in the
> sense of refusing to recognize any divine Law, but as in
> fact obeying the Jewish Law in Christ, or in a Christian
> sense, as something which he is more or less bound to
> observe, but which others are not.[64]

Others interpret this phrase in a more universal Christian sense than Knox who apparently restricts its application to Jewish Christians.[65]

Mediating Positions

Above we surveyed those texts in which scholars find expressions of the discontinuity or continuity between the law and the Christian faith. Here we propose to do two things. First, we want to focus briefly on one Pauline text which has become perhaps the most important rallying point for those who would mediate between the extremes of discontinuity and continuity. Second, we will give a general survey of scholarly approaches to Paul's understanding of the law which mediate between these two extremes.

Oddly enough, the much debated text, Rom 10:4, has become the object of attempts to mediate between the extremes of discontinuity and continuity[66] or else to tone down the extremeness of one's own interpretative stance.[67] In such cases the crucial word τέλος carries simultaneously the two opposing meanings ("end" and "goal" or "fulfilment") that it receives in scholarly interpretation. Thus we often hear, on the one hand, that what has reached its end has also reached its goal or fulfilment and, on the other hand, that what has reached its goal or fulfilment has also reached its end.[68] In spite of the resulting contradiction, some, as John W. Drane,[69] argue that the ambiguity was intentional on Paul's part.

Having looked at Rom 10:4, we now turn to survey scholarly approaches to Paul's understanding of the law that mediate between the extremes of discontinuity and continuity. One of the most common approaches teaches that the law is abolished as a way of salvation but continues as an expression of God's will.[70] From this simple statement scholars move out in a variety of directions to define how and to what extent the law remains as an expression of God's will. Below we will mention several examples without pretending to have exhausted the field.

First, Schlier[71] argues that for Paul the law is restored in its original sense as "instruction" (*Weisung*) but abolished as "law" (*Gesetz*) or "legal demand" (*Gesetzesforderung*).

Richard N. Longenecker[72] asserts that the law is abolished in its "contractural obligation" but remains as the "standard and judgment of God."

By means of a detailed exposition of Paul's use of the Greek word νόμος, Ernest De Witt Burton[73] declares that the law as a "legalistic system" is abrogated but continues as "ethical principle."

For Paul Althaus[74] the law as "law" (*Gesetz*) ceases, but it is restored as "commandment" (*Gebot*), for such it was, he claims, in its original condition.

Similarly, Schrage[75] speaks of the law that is abolished as a way of salvation but remains valid as a norm for Christian living.

Stuhlmacher[76] differentiates between the Mosaic law, which for Paul is the demonic perversion of God's will, and the will of God which in the law of Christ has now become again an aid for life.

According to van Dülmen,[77] the law determined by the letter and the flesh has ended, but the law in its pneumatic essence remains.

Christoph Haufe[78] argues that Paul's statements about the abolition of the law are directed at the ceremonial and ritual law but not at the moral and ethical law.

Though adamantly insisting the law is not abolished but established in Christ, Cranfield[79] can say that the ceremonial ordinances are no longer obligatory, that the ritual regulations are valid only as witnesses to Christ and that in the moral and civil realms one must distinguish between those commandments which express the absolute will of God and those which are limited to temporal human conditions.

The Law *Post Christum*

Otto Kuss[80] thinks the law retains its validity mainly as "Scripture" and "promise."

Similarly, in his study on Paul's use of the OT Scripture, Philipp Vielhauer[81] maintains that the law as "halachah," as a way of salvation, is abolished but retains its validity as revelation, as "haggadah."

Finally, in his treatment of the various shades of meaning νόμος has in Paul, Francisco Marín[82] declares that, while the self-sufficient "law of the flesh" (to be distinguished from the Mosaic law) ceases, the law of Moses endures forever, conserving its validity even today.

Actually, when everything is said, few are willing to indicate what is the specific content of the "law" that remains. What we often have left is the Decalogue or at least the love-command.[83] Furthermore, it practically goes without saying that the ceremonial and ritual laws have been abolished in Christ.[84]

Another approach which endeavors to mediate between the extremes of discontinuity and continuity focuses specifically on the differences between Jews and Gentiles in relation to the law. Thus in the view of Albert Schweitzer[85] Paul held that on the basis of the interim period before the parousia the Jews must continue to keep the law but the Gentiles should not be obligated to it. Moreover, Charles A. Anderson Scott[86] contends that for the apostle the law as a system for securing righteousness has come to an end but that as the divine requirement with respect to character and conduct it remains valid for Jews and Christians, though not valid in exactly the same sense for both. What Scott apparently means is that, while both moral and ceremonial law are valid for the Jews, only the moral law is valid for all. Further, according to Michael Wyschogrod, the Gentiles were obligated to keep only the so-called Noachian commandments, but the Jews the entire Mosaic law. Hence, he asserts that "Paul believed in a church with two components: a Jewish one with the Torah and Christ, and a gentile one with the Noahidic commandments and Christ."[87]

In a similar direction runs the approach of W. D. Davies who proposes to explain Paul's ambivalent attitude to the law, that is, his statements about its abrogation on the one hand and its establishment on the other. It is related conceptually to the discussion of the new or messianic law above.[88] As one will remember, in certain cases the notion of a new or messianic law was set in virtual opposition to that of the old one. After a cautious assessment of the rabbinic as well as other evidence, Davies[89] concludes that the rabbis indeed spoke of a new Torah but only in the sense of a fuller explanation of the old one. Thus, according to Davies,[90] Paul regarded Jesus as a new Moses who had brought a new Torah. Yet, Jesus had remained faithful to the old Torah, demonstrating thereby universalism in belief and particularism in practice.

Consequently, Davies argues:

> In view of all this, it would be unnatural for Paul also to believe that loyalty to the new law of Christ did not involve disloyalty to the Torah of his fathers, while at the same time holding that the latter, in its full sense, had also predicted that the Gentiles should share in the glories of the Messianic Age. There was no reason why Paul should not reject the view that Gentiles should be converted to Judaism before entering the Messianic Kingdom and at the same time insist that for him as a Jew the Torah was still valid.[91]

In this way Davies' approach provides for both continuity and discontinuity, since Paul treated the old as well as the new Torah as valid for himself and Jewish Christians.

Finally, as Davies, James A. Sanders[92] sets out to explain Paul's contradictory attitude toward the law. He finds the solution in what he calls the binary nature of Torah, that is, in its dual role as both stipulation and story. First, appealing to Laurent Monsengwo Pasinya's study on the word νόμος in the Greek Pentateuch,[93] Sanders asserts that νόμος could have the full range of meaning in the Hellenistic age which the Hebrew "Torah" had. Νόμος (i.e., Torah) could mean Judaism itself, the identity symbol, over against Χριστός. Thus, Sanders argues in opposition to the approach of Wyschogrod already noted above:

> On the contrary, Paul may have viewed certain laws as abrogated for Gentile converts (and for Jewish converts), but still have viewed *Nomos-Torah* as abrogated as well,

in the limited sense that the new era had arrived, that Christ was the Torah Incarnate, the New Torah, the new identity symbol which opened God's work of election-redemption to all people who would believe. Christ as the New Torah inaugurated the messianic era and to that extent superseded the Torah era, but also to that extent did not eradicate or annul Torah. Torah was caught up in Christ in a new age.[94]

Moreover, basing himself in part on the work of Dietrich Rössler,[95] he maintains that, while some Jewish sects emphasized the stipulation aspect of Torah, others stressed the story aspect. According to Sanders, Christianity and, therefore, the apostle Paul fell heir to the emphasis on the story aspect of Torah. As a result, he concludes that

> Paul in facing his mandate (. . .) to preach the Gospel to gentiles, found it well to emphasize Torah as the story of divine election and redemption, in the eschatological conviction that God's recent work in Christ had made that election and that redemption available to all mankind, while at the same time to de-emphasize those specific stipulations which seemed to present stumbling-blocks to carrying out the mandate, and which seemed to detract from the Torah-Gospel Story of God's righteous acts which had found their culmination, goal and climax in God's eschatological act in Christ.[96]

Thus, Paul's ambivalent attitude to the law was due in part to his emphasis on story rather than stipulation.

Conclusion

In the preceding pages we presented in brief detail what amounts to a scholarly *Sic et Non* on Paul's understanding of the law's status in the church. The contradictory interpretations to which the various Pauline texts have been submitted are best exemplified in the case of the widely diverging opinions about Rom 10:4. Moreover, when two texts like Rom 3:31 and 10:4 are juxtaposed, we have what, on some interpretations of these verses, seems to be a flat contradiction in Paul's thinking: on the one hand, the law is established by faith; on the other hand, it is set aside by Christ.

Naturally, the causes for these conflicting interpretations are numerous. Apart from the ambiguity of some Pauline texts owing to our present perspective, we should first

note that the way in which scholars understand the Greek word
νόμος may at times influence their interpretative disagree-
ments. In addition, the identity of Paul's readers poses
another difficulty in reaching a consensus about Paul's
statements on the role of the law. In other words, how would
the composition of Paul's congregations affect our understanding of the texts?

Further, the way in which scholars qualify their
interpretation of a given Pauline text in its context sometimes occasions apparent contradictions. Finally, we must
also reckon with theological presuppositions which have moved
scholars in the direction of either an overestimation or,
conversely, an underestimation of the law. Nevertheless,
when we take the entire range of opposing interpretations into
account, we are faced with the dilemma of seemingly irrecon-
cilable statements about the law in Paul.

Of course, it is impossible in this study to address
all of the issues involved or to treat all of the texts mentioned above. Yet, with an eye on these contradictions, we
turn to the apostle's assertion that he upholds the law by
faith (Rom 3:31). This text makes what appears on the surface to be an unambiguous statement about the status of the
law in Christianity. However, the clarity of its message has
been marred by scholarly differences over its interpretation.
Coming as it does directly at the end of Paul's exposition of
justification by faith (Rom 3:21-30), its interpretation
should probably form the starting point for any assessment of
the apostle's attitude to the law vis-à-vis Christ.

Though it has been treated together with other texts
in articles and monographs on Paul's understanding of the law,
only two articles have been devoted entirely to Rom 3:31 in
scholarly literature.[97] By way of contrast, one should note
the more extensive literature and discussion centered on Rom
10:4. Therefore, it is to this important text that we must
turn in the next two chapters.

CHAPTER II

ROMANS 3:31 AS A *CRUX INTERPRETUM*

Introduction

The interpretation of Rom 3:31 has been a perennial problem for students of Paul, particularly for those who view Paul as antinomian in his attitude to the OT law. According to Adolf von Harnack,[1] Marcion apparently found this verse and the following chapter so intolerable for his thesis of Pauline antinomianism that he deleted it from the Epistle to the Romans.

Recent scholarship has also found Rom 3:31 to be problematic. For example, Dodd, commenting on Rom 3:31 in relation to Rom 3:21-30, says:

> The natural conclusion from all this is that *by this faith we cancel the Law*--a conclusion most distasteful to Paul's Jewish or Jewish-Christian readers. He hesitates to draw the conclusion. It would have made things clearer if he had boldly done so.[2]

Similarly, Hans F. von Campenhausen declares with respect to this verse:

> In his efforts to rebut any suspicion of hostility to the Law he is even capable of the audacity of claiming that he--with his Gospel of freedom from the Law--is in fact upholding the Law.[3]

Finally, Schoeps[4] calls Rom 3:31 a "mean concession" which alone separates Paul's denial of the permanence of the law (so Gal 3:19 according to Schoeps) from gnosis.

Indeed, no other statement in Paul poses more acutely the problem of the relationship between law and faith than this short verse. Having placed all humanity (Jew/Gentile) under sin and thus under God's wrath (1:18-3:20), Paul declares that the righteousness of God has now been revealed (3:21). This righteousness comes impartially to all those who believe

(3:22, 28, 30). Such an emphasis on faith or believing as opposed to the works of the law might suggest Paul has set aside the law altogether. So the question arises: "Do we then overthrow the law by this faith (3:31a)?" Paul promptly answers: "By no means! On the contrary, we uphold the law (3:31bc)." Immediately following this short reply the apostle asks: "What then shall we say was gained by Abraham, our forefather according to the flesh (4:1, RSV margin)?" Then he presents his midrash on Abraham in the remainder of Rom 4.

The positioning of this question adds to its importance, for it comes immediately after Paul's climactic presentation of his teaching on justification by faith for both Jew and Gentile alike (3:21-30). However, this query and particularly Paul's reply are somewhat puzzling to the mind accustomed to regard the law as totally overthrown in the Christian context. Moreover, the relation between Rom 3:31 and its context, especially 3:21-30 and 4:1-25, is still disputed. Is Rom 3:31 simply the conclusion to the previous section (3:21-30) and thus unrelated to what follows (4:1-25)? Or is Rom 3:31 actually the basis for and theme of 4:1-25? It is to the definition of this relationship that we now turn.

Romans 3:31 in Relation to Its Context

As we indicated in Chapter I, scholars have approached the question of the relationship of Rom 3:31 to its context from two directions. While some regard this verse as the conclusion to Rom 3:21-30, others view it as the introduction to Rom 4. Now we must consider these two diverging approaches in more detail.

Romans 3:31 as the Conclusion
  to Romans 3:21-30

Among those arguments advanced to support the claim that Rom 3:31 is the conclusion to 3:21-30, we mention here the following: First, some contend that Rom 3:31 stands in a more logical relation to what precedes than to what follows. Thus John Murray[5] points out that, since Rom 3:31 issues naturally and inevitably from Paul's previous statements about the law (3:20-21, 27-28), it must be the conclusion to 3:21-30. In addition, Murray[6] argues that the new question (Rom 4:1), which implies a new beginning, does not seem suitably related to the categorical declaration of 3:31c. Finally, Rom 4, it is asserted, does not answer the question raised in 3:31 but deals with other matters as, for example, the exclusion of boasting or proof of the doctrine of justification by faith.[7]

Second, in opposition to the other approach which usually understands νόμος (Rom 3:31) in the sense of the Scripture (Pentateuch or OT) as a witness (cf. Rom 3:21), these scholars hold it must refer more narrowly to the demands of the OT law rather than to the law as Scripture. So Althaus[8] argues that if νόμος meant Scripture here, then the continuity of Paul's argument from Rom 3:28 forward would break down, for there he is concerned with the works of the law not the witness of the law. In addition, Stanislas Lyonnet[9] maintains νόμος cannot mean the Scripture here, for it always has the article when it refers unambiguously to Scripture. Furthermore, Ulrich Luz[10] declares it would be pointless for Paul to speak of the abiding validity of the OT after he has unhesitatingly used it to support his argument about the sinfulness of humanity (Rom 3:10-18). Finally Günther Klein[11] rejects any presumed connection between νόμος in Rom 3:31 and νόμος in Rom 3:21 on the grounds that in the latter the expression used to signify the OT is not simply νόμος but νόμος καὶ προφῆται.

Third and finally, some appeal to stylistic or rhetorical considerations to defend the notion that Rom 3:31 concludes 3:21-30 and is not to be connected with Rom 4. Hence, Cranfield[12] asserts that the conjunction οὖν (Rom 4:1) is not the natural one to introduce the proof of an immediately preceding statement as would be the case if Rom 4 were tied directly to 3:31. Moreover, he argues,[13] the brevity of Paul's answer in Rom 3:31c is not without parallel (see Rom 3:8) and, thus, does not require the elucidation of Rom 4. Again, Lightfoot[14] contends it is not unlike Paul to throw out an objection, negate it and subsequently take it up for discussion in its proper place, as he in effect does here. Last, on the basis of his understanding of Paul's use of the rhetorical *topos* with its dual functions of argumentation and amplification, Wilhelm Wuellner[15] apparently considers Rom 4 as the amplification of Rom 3:29-30 and Rom 5-8, 9-11 as the amplification of Rom 3:31.

Once it is decided that Rom 3:31 is the conclusion to 3:21-30 and is practically unrelated to Rom 4, then the interpretation of this verse finds its basis in what precedes or somewhere in the remainder of the epistle. Of the numerous interpretations which explain Rom 3:31 initially in terms of the preceding context, we will reproduce here the more typical ones. First, understanding νόμος as the Mosaic legislation and pointing back to Rom 3:20, W. Feyerabend[16] asserts that Paul claims to establish the law in its true intention, that is, to bring knowledge of sin. However, the apostle withholds his full explanation until later (Rom 5:12-21; 6-7).

Similarly, Walter Grundmann[17] interprets Rom 3:31 in the light of Rom 3:19-20 as the establishment of the law in its conviction of sin and putting to death of the sinner.

Moreover, Bornkamm[18] expounds our verse first in relation to Rom 3:20 as indicating the confirmation of the law in its effect of making sin a practical human experience and sealing the guilt of humanity, second, in relation to Rom 3:21 as showing the establishment of the law in its witness to justification by faith. With respect to the latter he points to Rom 4, thus appearing to adopt at the same time the approach to Rom 3:31 that relates this verse to what directly follows.

In what appears to be a reflection on Rom 3:24-25, John F. Walvoord,[19] who understands νόμος as "all moral law," interprets Rom 3:31 to mean that in his death Christ met the requirements of the Mosaic law, the content of the OT and the Gentile law in one single act.

Also, Althaus[20] views the establishment of the law in the light of the death of Christ (Rom 3:25) but finds a fuller explanation of Rom 3:31 in Rom 6-8, especially 8:4.

Furthermore, Anders Nygren evidently connects Rom 3:31 with Rom 3:19, 27, as he explains:

> The righteousness of faith accomplishes what the law
> would effect: it excludes all boasting. It shows
> that the law is right when it stops every mouth.
> Thus it upholds the law and makes it effective.[21]

In addition, some, as Irene Beck,[22] associate Rom 3:31 with the expression νόμος πίστεως (Rom 3:27). This "law of faith" (also "law of Christ," Gal 6:2; 1 Cor 9:21 or "law of the Spirit," Rom 8:2) corresponds to the OT law in its pneumatic essence. It is to this specifically Christian "law" that Paul refers when he says he upholds the law by faith. Hence, he does not propose to destroy the law but to represent it as holy and valid and to establish it anew in the "law of faith."

Finally, Adolf Schlatter[23] explains our verse in a variety of ways particularly in relation to the preceding context. Thus Paul's preaching of justification by faith confirms the validity of the law by creating a community of God's people, by revealing the unity of God, by allowing the law to bring knowledge of sin, by excluding boasting, by providing forgiveness of sins and by demanding obedience to Christ.

With regard to those interpretations which explain Rom 3:31 in terms of the following context, excepting Rom 4, we will also mention here the most common ones. In this case Rom 3:31 is often regarded as an interposed thought or as an anticipatory reference to be clarified in what follows.

First, emphasizing the nature of the law as "commanding compliance and performance," Murray[24] understands Paul's answer in this verse as a rejection of moral antinomianism which the apostle further develops in Rom 6.

Moreover, Lightfoot,[25] who understands νόμος to signify the Mosaic law as "an external system of restraints," holds that Paul rejects the notion he stultifies the law in this particular role. However, the apostle gives the fuller explanation of his meaning in Rom 7.

Also, maintaining the anticipatory nature of Paul's question and response (Rom 3:31), Nils A. Dahl[26] seemingly finds the more complete development of the apostle's thought in Rom 6-7.

Similarly, Paul Schubert[27] apparently regards Rom 3:31 as a rejection of antinomianism. Yet the complete answer to Paul's question comes only in Rom 6-8.

Furthermore, several scholars[28] find the clarification of our verse in Paul's statement: "in order that the just requirement of the law might be fulfilled in us who walk not according to the flesh but according to the Spirit (Rom 8:4)." Thus in their walk in the Spirit, Christians establish the law as they fulfill its just requirement.

For Wuellner[29] Rom 3:31 apparently receives its amplification in Paul's expositions in Rom 6-8, 9-11.

Finally, Lyonnet[30] points to Rom 8:4 but also to the "moral part" of the epistle (Rom 12-15) to give content to the apostle's assertion he upholds the law by faith.

Romans 3:31 as the Introduction or Transition to Romans 4:1-25

In opposition to the approach we have just outlined, other scholars consider Rom 3:31 to be an introduction or transition to Rom 4. Indeed, so convinced are they of this fact that they sometimes alter the commonly used paragraph divisions to allow Rom 3:31 to stand apart with Rom 4. Below we will survey the principal arguments adduced to support this approach.

First, like some of the scholars mentioned above, these also feel a certain incompleteness in Paul's brief reply (3:31c). However, they seek for clarification in Rom 4 rather than in the remainder of the epistle. Heinrich August Wilhelm Meyer expresses this sentiment well when he says:

> If we should, . . . , assume that at iv.1 there is again introduced something new, so that Paul does not carry further the νόμον ἱστῶμεν, v.31, but in iv.1ff. treats of a new objection that has occurred to him at the moment, we should then have the extraordinary phenomenon of Paul as it were dictatorially dismissing an objection so extremely important and in fact so very naturally suggesting itself, as νόμον οὖν καταργοῦμεν κ.τ.λ., merely by an opposite assertion, and then immediately, like one who has not a clear case, leaping away to something else.[31]

In addition, some[32] argue that the postponement of the explanation of Rom 3:31 to a subsequent section of the epistle, as often happens in the approach previously discussed, constitutes an unwarranted break in the movement of Paul's thought.

Moreover, Joachim Jeremias[33] appeals to Paul's practice of posing and answering objections (*Einwände*) as a means for establishing the relationship between Rom 3:31 and 4:1-25. He notes how in Romans the apostle frequently raises objections (of Jewish opponents according to Jeremias) and then answers them in what follows (so 3:1, 5, 7-8, 9; 6:1, 15; 7:7, 13; 8:31; 9:6a, 14, 19, 30; 11:1, 7). With regard to our verse Jeremias contends that everything (Rom 3:31b-4:25) which follows the protesting question (Rom 3:31a) serves to refute this difficult and constantly repeated objection by means of a Scripture proof.

Another argument focuses on the background of Paul's terminology in Rom 3:31. Thus Birger Gerhardsson, among others, thinks Paul's use of the words καταργεῖν and ἱστανεῖν in combination corresponds to the rabbinical use of בטל and קום. As Gerhardsson explains:

> To show, by means of a process of exegesis, that a certain doctrinal statement does not abolish (בישל) the Scriptures (or a passage of Scripture) is called by the Rabbis "to uphold," "to maintain" (קיים) the Scriptures (or a passage of Scripture).[34]

So it is a kind of reverse process, that is, one proves his doctrine from Scripture (in this case Gen 15:6 [Rom 4:3]), and then his doctrine in turn "upholds" Scripture.

However, the most crucial argument of those who regard Rom 3:31 as the introduction or transition to Rom 4 concerns the meaning of νόμος itself, especially in Rom 3:21, 27, 31. In contrast to those who define this word narrowly as referring to the demands of the law, these scholars usually understand νόμος (Rom 3:31) in a broader sense, that is, in terms of Scripture (the Pentateuch or the OT).[35] As a first step, they frequently point to Paul's statement that God's righteousness which has now been manifested is attested by the law (νόμος) and the prophets (Rom 3:21). Then, adopting Friedrich's argument[36] that the expressions, "law of works" and "law of faith" (Rom 3:27), actually refer to the OT law, they often define the "law of faith" in terms of the law's role as a witness to righteousness by faith (Rom 3:21), each giving a personal nuance to this definition. From this vantage point they explain Rom 3:31 in the light of Rom 3:21, 27 to mean that Paul upholds the law as Scripture by preaching faith, because, as Rom 4 shows, the law bears witness to faith.

As we have already intimated, in this approach the interpretation of Rom 3:31 is tied closely to Rom 4. In fact, Rom 4 is regarded as containing the proof of Paul's thesis that he upholds the law by faith. Quite typical is the interpretation of William Sanday and Arthur C. Headlam:

> The Jew looked at the O.T., and he saw there Law, Obedience to Law or Works, Circumcision, Descent from Abraham. St. Paul said, Look again and look deeper, and you will see--not Law but Promise, not works but Faith--of which Circumcision is only the seal, not literal descent from Abraham but spiritual descent. All these things are realized in Christianity.[37]

Allowing for their individual emphases, most scholars[38] who follow this approach would be in general agreement with Sanday and Headlam.

To sum up, we have traced by means of this survey the scholarly stalemate over the relationship of Rom 3:31 to its context and, consequently, over the interpretation of the verse itself. In the remainder of this chapter we will propose a solution to this deadlock. Then in the next chapter we will carry out an exegesis of Rom 3:21-4:25 to see whether the results will confirm our findings.

Paul's Use of Rhetorical Questions

Introduction

Above we observed that several scholars relied on stylistic or rhetorical considerations to support their understanding of the relationship between Rom 3:31 and its context. In view of the rhetorical question Paul employs in this verse, we propose that an examination of the apostle's style, particularly his use of such questions, will help to unlock this relationship.[39]

At the risk of oversimplification we note that, with regard to whether or not they receive an explicit answer, Paul's rhetorical questions are basically of two kinds. First, there are those whose answer is not normally stated but either implied by grammatical means (questions with οὐ or μή) or otherwise left open for the readers to decide on the basis of the context or their own attitude or knowledge, if indeed an answer is required.[40] These questions serve to introduce discussion (Rom 6:16; 1 Cor 15:12), to impart information or remind of something assumed to be known (Rom 6:3), to carry on an argument in an indirect manner (1 Cor 6:1-9), or to express emotions such as astonishment (Gal 3:1), indignation (1 Cor 6:1), elation (Rom 8:31-35).

While the vast majority of Paul's questions belong to this first category, there are, in the second place, other questions whose answer is explicitly stated whether or not it is implied in the question itself.[41] Within this group we find those questions negated by the formula of rejection, μὴ γένοιτο. Since we have such a question negated by μὴ γένοιτο in Rom 3:31, an investigation of its usage may shed light on the matter of the relationship of this verse to its context and thus on its proper interpretation.

Grammatically μὴ γένοιτο functions in two ways in the NT: dependently (only Gal 6:14)[42] and independently or absolutely (Lk 20:16; Rom 3:4, 6, 31; 6:2, 15; 7:7, 13; 9:14; 11:1, 11; 1 Cor 6:15; Gal 2:17; 3:21). Thus, except for Lk 20:16,[43] the absolute use of μὴ γένοιτο is confined to Paul in the NT. Outside the NT in the extant literature most contemporary to Paul, the absolute use of this expression occurs only in Arrian's *Discourses of Epictetus*.[44]

In each of the Pauline occurrences of absolute μὴ γένοιτο, it is preceded by a rhetorical question containing a false inference which could be drawn from his previous line of argument.[45] As an optative of wishing, μὴ γένοιτο expresses strong rejection in response to such questions.[46] While scholars have long recognized these facts, few have studied the relation of these questions to their context, except to note the manner in which they affect the immediately following discussion.[47]

In particular, we would ask whether the apostle uses these questions negated by μὴ γένοιτο to conclude discussion, to anticipate some topic to be treated much later in his epistles or to introduce a topic for immediate discussion. To answer this question it will be profitable first to examine Epictetus' use of questions negated by μὴ γένοιτο. Then, with the results of this examination in mind, we can analyze the Pauline uses in order to come to some conclusions about the effect that questions negated by μὴ γένοιτο have on Paul's train of thought.

Epictetus

In Epictetus[48] thirty-one occurrences of absolute μὴ γένοιτο can be documented.[49] In those instances where questions are negated by μὴ γένοιτο, we encounter two nuances of usage. First, the question may represent a false inference drawn from the previous discussion.[50] Second, the question may arise simply to highlight some absurdity which does not usually involve a false inference from the previous discussion.[51]

Moreover, in the first nuance μὴ γένοιτο is not usually the definitive answer to the question, for a clarification or grounding of the true nature of the case follows. By way of contrast, in the second nuance μὴ γένοιτο appears to be the definitive answer to the question with little or no further clarification or grounding being provided. In the following pages we will analyze examples of each nuance to confirm these assertions. To begin, we will consider all the examples of the first nuance in view of its close relationship to the Pauline occurrences to be discussed later.

First, in his discussion about how one may maintain one's proper role on every occasion, Epictetus asserts that few individuals are able to attain to greatness through discipline (*Discourses* 1.2.33-34). Since this statement seems to imply all others should abandon their efforts to excel, the question arises (1.2.35): "What then (τί οὖν;)? Because I have no natural gifts, shall I on that account give up my discipline? Far be it from me (μὴ γένοιτο)!" In opposition to this false consequence, Epictetus explains that we should not give up our discipline because we cannot attain the highest (1.2.36-37).

While lecturing on the reasoning faculties, Epictetus rejects the tendency to relegate to the profession of philosopher qualities which were evident in some philosophers but were not necessarily essential or even related to their profession, for example, Plato's handsomeness and strength (*Discourses* 1.8.11-14). This rejection might suggest Epictetus denigrates the need for such qualities as handsomeness and strength in a philosopher. Therefore, the question surfaces (1.8.15): "What then (τί οὖν;)? Am I depriving you of these faculties? Far be it from me (μὴ γένοιτο)!" Immediately Epictetus explains (γάρ) himself and counters (δέ) that the highest quality is to have moral purpose (1.8.16).

In his treatment of those who seek advancement at Rome, Epictetus inveighs against those who become too occupied in business or politics to enjoy life (*Discourses* 1.10.1-6). Such an attack might lead to the assumption that he recommends inactivity in relation to such matters. Thus the question arises (1.10.7): "What then (τί οὖν;)? Do I say that man is an animal made for inactivity? Far be it from me (μὴ γένοιτο)!" Epictetus answers by means of a counterquestion (ἀλλὰ διὰ τί) and then gives the example of his own life to disprove the false inference (1.10.7-13).

While discussing contentment, Epictetus inquires into the existence of the gods and their relation to people (*Discourses* 1.12.1-9). This inquiry revolves in particular around the issue of freedom (1.12.8). According to Epictetus a free person is one "for whom all things happen according to his moral purpose, and whom none can restrain (1.12.9)." To say that a free person is one whom none can restrain suggests the haphazard activity of a lunatic. So the question arises (1.12.10): "What then (τί οὖν;)? Is freedom insanity? Far from it (μὴ γένοιτο)." Epictetus then explains (γάρ) what he understands real freedom to be (1.12.10-16).

Commenting on the proper attitude toward tyrants, Epictetus argues people should pay no more attention to a tyrant than they do to their donkeys (*Discourses* 1.19.1-6). When an imaginary tyrant threatens him with beheading, he responds: "Well said! I had forgotten that I ought to pay attention to you as to fever or cholera, and set up an altar to you, just as in Rome there is an altar to God Fever (1. 19.6)." Since this statement might imply Epictetus has suddenly changed his mind about a tyrant's ability to control people's allegiance, the question emerges (1.19.7): "What is it, then (τί οὖν), that disturbs and bewilders the multitude? Is it the tyrant and his bodyguards? How is that possible? Nay, far from it (μὴ γένοιτο)!" Then Epictetus explains that that which is free by nature should not be disturbed or thwarted by anything but itself (1.19.7-10).

Epictetus also considers what are the important and unimportant things in life (*Discourses* 1.28.1-18). To show the ultimate insignificance of wars, factions, death and destruction of cities, he draws a similarity between people's houses and the nests of storks and between people's bodies and those of storks (1.28.14-18). On the surface it appears he makes little difference between people and storks. Thus the question arises (1.28.19): "Does a man, then (οὖν), differ in no wise from a stork? Far from it (μὴ γένοιτο)." Epictetus continues with a counter-assertion (ἀλλά), then a question (τίνι οὖν), and finally a rather detailed explanation (1.28.19-28).

In *Discourses* 1.29.1-8, Epictetus admonishes that one simply should not fear the things which are not under one's control, especially the threats of a tyrant. Such an assertion seems to imply that philosophers reject the authority of political leaders. Consequently, the question arises (1.29. 9): "Do you philosophers, then (οὖν) teach us to despise our kings? Far from it (μὴ γένοιτο)." To his rejection of this false inference Epictetus adds a counter-question followed by a lengthy clarification beginning with an imperative statement (1.29.9-15).

Again, in the course of evaluating the faculty of expression (*Discourses* 2.23), Epictetus lauds moral purpose as the greatest human faculty (2.23.9-22). Since this exaltation of moral purpose seems to denigrate other human faculties, the question arises (2.23.23): "Well, what then (τί οὖν;)? Does a man despise his other faculties? Far from it (μὴ γένοιτο)! Does a man say there is no use or advancement save in the faculty of moral purpose? Far from it (μὴ γένοιτο)!" Epictetus responds with a condemnatory statement and then a counter-assertion (ἀλλά), apparently continuing his clarification to the end of the chapter (2.23.23-47).

In addition, Epictetus assesses the value of personal adornment (*Discourses* 3.1). Once more he exalts moral purpose over human beauty (3.1.41-42). For confirmation of this matter he cites a statement of Socrates to Alcibiades and interprets it against possible misunderstanding: "No, he says, 'Make beautiful your moral purpose, eradicate your worthless opinions.' How treat your paltry body, then? As its nature is. This is the concern of Another; leave it to him (3.1.42-43)." But Epictetus' interpretation raises a false assumption, namely, that care for the body should be neglected (3.1.44): "What then (τί οὖν;)? Does the body have to be left unclean? God forbid (μὴ γένοιτο)!" Then Epictetus clarifies his meaning with a counter-command (ἀλλά) and further explanation (3.1.44-45).

In *Discourses* 3.23 Epictetus evaluates those who want to display their eloquence in reading or discussion. He denies that eloquence really fits into the category of that which philosophers call "the good." Since this denial seems to be a rejection of eloquence altogether, the question arises (3.23.25): "What then (τί οὖν;)? Ought one to take no pleasure in listening to such efforts? Far from it (μὴ γένοιτο)!" Then Epictetus explains (μέν) his true meaning and quotes Socrates by way of illustration (3.23.25-26).

Finally, lecturing on cleanliness, Epictetus strongly commends it by using examples from nature and from human custom, for example, the sacredness of temples (*Discourses* 4.11. 31-32). This emphasis on cleanliness might lead to the assumption that he is preoccupied with physical appearance. Thus the question surfaces (4.11.33): "Well, what then (τί οὖν;)? Is anyone demanding that you beautify yourself? Heaven forbid (μὴ γένοιτο)!" Immediately Epictetus clarifies his understanding of the matter: "Except (εἰ μή) you beautify that which is our true nature--the reason, its judgments, its activities; but (δέ) your body only so far as to keep it cleanly, only so far as to avoid giving offence (4.11.33)." He continues his elucidation to the end of the chapter (4.11.34-36).

An overall analysis of these occurrences of questions negated by μὴ γένοιτο yields the following results: First, these questions are introduced in one of two ways, that is, by either τί οὖν; or simply οὖν. Furthermore, as an answer, μὴ γένοιτο is sufficient only to a certain degree, for usually additional clarification or grounding is required, as can be seen in the examples above. Such clarification may be introduced in the form of a declarative sentence,[52] an explanatory sentence (γάρ),[53] a counter-statement (ἀλλά),[54] a counter-question (ἀλλά)[55] or a counter-command (ἀλλά).[56]

In addition, a basic pattern underlies this usage of questions negated by μὴ γένοιτο: assertion of varying length, question inferred from the previous assertion, negation by μὴ γένοιτο and clarification of the point at issue, usually consisting in only a few sentences or in an entire paragraph.[57] These questions serve to focus the reader's (hearer's) attention on some issue in the previous discussion which could be misunderstood. Once the writer (speaker) has brought attention to this false consequence and negated it, then the true nature of the matter can be explained. This clarification is not simply intended to prove but rather to elucidate the opposite of the propositional question negated by μὴ γένοιτο. Therefore, it is evident from the examples cited that questions negated by μὴ γένοιτο do not give an answer so definitive that further clarification of the writer's (speaker's) viewpoint becomes unnecessary.

Finally, in none of these cases can the question negated by μὴ γένοιτο be considered strictly as the end of a paragraph without first noting that sufficient clarification follows before the paragraph breaks off.[58] Rather the majority of questions negated by μὴ γένοιτο serve to introduce paragraphs or occur in the middle of them.[59]

As stated previously, the second nuance in the use of questions negated by μὴ γένοιτο is designed to put away some absurd thought which the writer (speaker) projects momentarily and which is not normally inferred from the preceding discussion. That is to say, these questions do not arise as a false inference from the writer's (speaker's) argument. A few examples should be sufficient to illustrate this point.

In *Discourses* 1.1.10-13 Zeus reminds Epictetus that the gods have given him a certain portion of themselves, that is, "the faculty which makes use of external impressions." Then Zeus asks Epictetus: "What then? Are these things small in thy sight?" Epictetus answers: "Far be it from me (μὴ γένοιτο)!" Zeus continues his questioning: "Art thou, then, content with them?" Epictetus replies: "I pray the Gods I may be."

In another instance (*Discourses* 1.26.5-7) Epictetus instructs his pupils how to defend themselves before parents who are angry because their children study philosophy. During this defense the child should say: "Really, what is your idea? That I intentionally fall into evil and miss the good? Far from it (μὴ γένοιτο)!" After this the child should continue to interrogate them: "What, then, is the cause of my going astray?" and so on.

Moreover, in *Discourses* 1.28.19-28, Epictetus declares that "no one comes to his fall because of another's deed." Then he gives an example: "When did Achilles come to his fall? When Patroclus died? Far from it (μὴ γένοιτο); but when Achilles himself was enraged, when he was crying about a paltry damsel, when he forgot that he was there, not to get sweethearts, but to make war." Epictetus continues by discussing the "falls" which come to humanity.

To introduce his treatment of the nature of God (*Discourses* 2.8.1-2), Epictetus asks: "What, then, is the true nature of God? Flesh? Far from it (μὴ γένοιτο)! Land? Far from it (μὴ γένοιτο)! Fame? Far from it (μὴ γένοιτο)! It is intelligence, knowledge, right reason." With this answer in mind he moves to a discussion of the true nature of God.

Furthermore, in *Discourses* 3.23.13-14, Epictetus scolds a hearer for lavishing praise on someone contrary to his honest opinion of that person. He then asks the man: "Did you want your children to be like that? Far from it (μὴ γένοιτο)!" With this Epictetus continues his questioning.

Finally, in *Discourses* 4.11.22-24, Epictetus asserts that people ought not to drive away the multitude from philosophy even by their bodily appearance: "See, O men, that I have nothing, and need nothing . . . . Yes, and you see that even my paltry body is not disfigured by my hard way of living." However, he adds: "But if I am told this by a person who has the bearing and face of a condemned man, what one of all the gods shall persuade me to approach philosophy, if she makes people like that? Far be it from me (μὴ γένοιτο)! I shouldn't be willing to do so, not even if it would make me a wise man." Epictetus continues this duscussion in the following paragraph (4.11.25-30).[60]

An overall analysis of these occurrences of questions negated by μὴ γένοιτο yields the following results: First, whenever these questions are formally introduced, it is done by means of τί οὖν; οὖν or τί δοκεῖτε;. Second, as an answer μὴ γένοιτο is usually sufficient, for little, if any, further clarification is given.[61] If an explanation is offered, it is often introduced in the form of a counter-statement (ἀλλά).[62] Most importantly, the basic pattern which underlies this usage of questions negated by μὴ γένοιτο is as follows: question (representing some absurd thought), negation by μὴ γένοιτο and sometimes a brief clarification, consisting in no more than a sentence or two but never approximating a paragraph.

Therefore, the basic difference between the first and the second nuance in the use of questions negated by μὴ γένοιτο is that in the first case the question involves a false inference from the preceding discussion, while in the second case it does not. Furthermore, in the first nuance the question negated by μὴ γένοιτο is always followed by an additional clarification of differing length, sometimes embracing a whole paragraph. Thus in the first nuance the question negated by μὴ γένοιτο leaves the reader (hearer) expecting additional explanation or grounding, but in the second the reader (hearer) senses that the matter is finished just as quickly as it began. As will become evident in what follows, these two nuances are present in Paul, but the former predominates.

Paul

With the preceding discussion in mind we now examine all the Pauline occurrences of questions negated by μὴ γένοιτο in order to compare Paul's use with that of Epictetus and, above all, to determine how an adequate understanding of the nature of such questions unlocks Paul's train of thought. As already suggested, Paul uses these questions with the same nuances as Epictetus. First, we will treat those questions which result from a false inference from Paul's previous argument. Then, we will consider those questions which do not arise from such a false inference. Hopefully, our findings will help to elucidate the relationship between Rom 3:31 and its context. In the course of the discussion we will involve ourselves in detailed exegesis only to the extent that it may be necessary for an adequate understanding of these questions.

Romans 3:4, 6. These two occurrences of questions negated by μὴ γένοιτο appear in the difficult paragraph, Rom 3:1-8. In the previous discussion (2:17-29) Paul lists the Jew's particular spiritual advantages (2:17-20) and then implies by a series of questions that even the Jew has broken the law and dishonored God (2:21-24). Next he proclaims the insignificance of such practices as circumcision without keeping the law and the corresponding significance of the uncircumcised state if one keeps the law (2:25-27). Real "Jewishness," according to Paul, is a matter of the inward person as opposed to the outward person (2:28-29).

If the true "Jew" cannot be recognized by the outward appearance, especially circumcision, and if the true "Jew" can be recognized only by the inner "circumcision of the heart in the Spirit," then the question inevitably arises: "What is the advantage of the Jew, or what is the value of circumcision (3:1)?"[63] Contrary to the expected negation, Paul answers affirmatively: "Much in every way. To begin with, the Jews are entrusted with the oracles of God (3:2)." The "oracles of God" probably refer to God's revelation of himself and his redemptive plan to Israel. Thus the advantage or profit of the Jews is simply that God spoke to them first.[64]

But a new question surfaces: "What (τί γάρ;) if some were unfaithful? Does their faithlessness nullify the faithfulness of God (3:3)?" The "some" to whom Paul refers are evidently the Jews whose sinfulness he has already depicted (2:17-29).[65] Viewing the fact that the Jews have been entrusted with God's oracles (3:2) against the background of their failure, one feels compelled to infer that God's plan has miscarried because of the infidelity of his people.[66] To such an inference Paul answers: "By no means (μὴ γένοιτο, 3:4a)!" Then he counters (δέ) with an imperatival statement[67] bolstered by Scripture (Ps 50:6b [LXX]): "Let God be true and [RSV, "though"] every man be false,[68] as it is written, 'That thou mayest be justified in thy words, and prevail when thou art judged' (3:4bc)."

With the statement "Let God be true and every man be false" and the accompanying confirmation from Scripture, we catch a glimpse of a court scene in which God and humanity are pitted against each other.[69] The outcome of this legal process is the vindication of God's faithfulness and the revelation of humanity's unfaithfulness. With the quotation of the words of Scripture Paul ends the discussion.

With regard to this first occurrence of a question negated by μὴ γένοιτο, one should note that the same pattern appears as in Epictetus: assertion (2:17-3:2), question inferred from this assertion (3:3), negation by μὴ γένοιτο (3:4a) and clarification (imperatival statement and scriptural citation, 3:4bc).[70] Also, μὴ γένοιτο alone is insufficient as an answer to the question (3:3). Rather it provides the opportunity for a more ample explanation of Paul's understanding of the issue (3:4bc) as opposed to that which might have been inferred from his argument to this point (2:17-3:3).[71]

Since the Scripture speaks the final authoritative word in this type of debate, this particular discussion ceases with the scriptural proof.[72] Though scholars observe that Paul takes up the question of God's faithfulness later in

Rom 9-11, especially 9:6-13,[73] it should be noted that there
the discussion assumes a different form and has a different
background, namely, the Jews' rejection of Christ, while here
it is a matter of the Jews' sinfulness (1:18-2:29, especially
2:21-24, 26-27).

As far as the second occurrence of a question negated
by μὴ γένοιτο is concerned, it is important to remember that
in the preceding Scripture proof Paul did not cite the first
part of the verse (Ps 50:6a [LXX]): "Against thee, thee only,
have I sinned, and done that which is evil in thy sight."
Coupled with the latter part of the verse (50:6b), the entire
text seems to say that the purpose of human sin is to manifest
God's righteousness. Even here Ps 50:6b (Rom 3:4c) preceded
by Rom 3:4b seems to lead to the same conclusion, that is,
that humanity's falsehood serves to reveal God's righteousness.
Based on this implication, another question arises (3:5):
"But if (εἰ δέ) our wickedness serves to show the justice of
God, what shall we say (τί ἐροῦμεν;)? That God is unjust to
inflict wrath on us? (I speak in a human way.)"[74] Thus in
his attempt to clarify (3:4bc) the previous misunderstanding
(3:3), Paul occasions another false inference from his argument.

Immediately Paul replies: "By no means (μὴ γένοιτο,
3:6a)!" Then he refutes this false inference by means of a
counter-question[75] designed to show the logical consequences
of such deductions: "For then (ἐπεί) how could God judge the
world (3:6b)?"[76] This elliptical question probably represents
the fuller thought: "For, if my rejection of the suggestion
that God is unjust is not right, how can it be true that God
shall judge the world?"[77]

Following this brief rebuttal the same question (as
in 3:5) returns in a more concrete, personal form (3:7): "But
if (εἰ δέ)[78] through my falsehood God's truthfulness abounds
to his glory, why am I still being condemned as a sinner?"
The relationship between 3:7 and the following verse (3:8) is
complicated by the problem of punctuating and construing the
latter.[79] Some consider 3:8 to be an answer to 3:7 in the
form of a counter-question which carries the logic of the
latter to the absurd.[80] Others regard 3:7 and 3:8 as two

unanswered questions (or objections) existing independently.[81] Still others view 3:7-8 as a compound question joined by καί (3:8a) and governed by τί (3:7b).[82] In this case the relative clause ὧν τὸ κρίμα ἔνδικόν ἐστιν (3:8b) is sometimes regarded as Paul's only answer to this double question or objection.[83]

To deal with this problem would take us far afield. What is certain is that 3:7 is not a question intended to be answered by μὴ γένοιτο.[84] With regard to 3:8, it could conceivably call for a μὴ γένοιτο, for the presence of μή (3:8a) implies the content of the question should be regarded as false. But this would be true only if this verse were considered in isolation from 3:7. However, the important thing is that Paul, for whatever reason, does not follow 3:8 with this form of negation.

Again, as in Rom 3:4, the basic pattern of usage appears: assertion (3:4), inferential question (3:5), negation (3:6a) and clarification (rebuttal, 3:6b). The brevity of Paul's response (3:6), as contrasted to other occurrences of questions negated by μὴ γένοιτο to be treated below, is apparently due to the categorical nature of the reply Paul gives. As Murray comments:

> Paul appeals to the fact of universal judgment and he does not proceed to prove it. He accepts it as an ultimate datum of revelation, and he confronts the objection of verse 5 with this fact. About the certainty of God's judgment there can be no dispute. Once the judgment is accepted as a certainty, then all such objection as is implied in verses 5, 7, 8 falls to the ground.[85]

Furthermore, while Paul takes up the issue of God's justice later in the epistle (see 9:14-18), it is important to note that there the discussion again assumes a different form and has a different background, that is, God's exercise of his prerogative of election. Here, on the other hand, the background is God's exercise of universal judgment on universal human sinfulness.

Romans 6:2. Postponing our treatment of Rom 3:31 till the end, we now move to the next occurrence of a question negated by μὴ γένοιτο. In the preceding section (5:12-21),

Paul asserts that wherever sin abounds, grace much more abounds (5:20). This statement could lead to a false inference: "What shall we say then (τί οὖν ἐροῦμεν;)? Are we to continue in sin that grace may abound (6:1)?"[86] Paul replies: "By no means (μὴ γένοιτο, 6:2a)!" Then he begins his clarification in the form of two counter-questions (6:2b-3): "How can we who died to sin still live in it? Do you not know that all of us who have been baptized into Christ Jesus were baptized into his death?" Next, Paul applies the concept of death with Christ to sin (6:4-11) in order to refute the false inference (6:1).[87] Concluding parenetically (6:12-14), the apostle shows what is to be the legitimate response of the Christian to God's grace as opposed to that suggested earlier (6:1).[88]

It is not possible in our investigation to enter into a detailed exegesis of this passage. Only the presence of the pattern already discovered should be noted: assertion (5:20), inferential question (6:1), negation (6:2a) and clarification (6:2b-14). The clarification is remarkably longer than that in Rom 3:4, 6. Of paramount importance here is the fact that the question negated by μὴ γένοιτο (6:1-2a) actually sets the theme for the following discussion (6:2b-14).

Romans 6:15. In the course of his preceding clarification (6:2-14) Paul makes an assertion that could be falsely interpreted: "For sin will have no dominion over you, since you are not under law but under grace (6:14)." The first part of this verse grounds (γάρ) the imperatives of 6:12-13 through the promise that sin (here a personified power) will no longer be lord of the Christians (6:14a).[89] The second part (6:14b) confirms this promise (6:14a) by explaining (γάρ) that Christians are not under law, that is, dominated by sin through the law, but under grace.[90]

However, as a consequence of Paul's previous statement (6:14b), the question arises: "What then (τί οὖν;)? Are we to sin because we are not under law but under grace (6:15ab)?" While Rom 6:15 seems superficially related to 6:1, the false conclusions under consideration are not the same, as Cranfield notes:

> Whereas in v.1 the false inference from the truth stated
> in 5.20 was that one should continue in sin so as to
> make grace abound still more, here the false inference
> from the truth stated in v.14b is that sinful acts do
> not matter any more as far as we are concerned.[91]

If the Christian is not under the law, then morality has gone with the wind. Therefore, life under grace allows the multiplication of sin.

Paul responds to this question: "By no means (μὴ γένοιτο, 6:15c)!" Immediately he begins his clarification with a counter-question, οὐκ οἴδατε ὅτι κ.τ.λ.; (6:16) and shows by the analogy of slavery (6:16-23) and of marriage (7:1-6) that Christians are still under obligation to God. As the first analogy (6:16-23), the second (7:1-6) is introduced by an interrogative formula, ἢ ἀγνοεῖτε, κ.τ.λ.; (7:1-6).[92] Once more the basic pattern is clearly evident: assertion (6:14b), inferential question (6:15ab), negation (6:15c) and clarification (6:16-23; 7:1-6). The initial question negated by μὴ γένοιτο marks the theme of the subsequent clarification which is noticeably longer than that of the previous section (6:1-14).

Romans 7:7. Several things that Paul expresses in the course of the preceding argument could give the impression the law is actually evil, to be identified with sin (5:20; 6:14; but especially 7:5-6). Consequently, the question surfaces: "What then shall we say (τί οὖν ἐροῦμεν;)? That the law is sin (7:7ab)?" Characteristically, the apostle replies: "By no means (μὴ γένοιτο, 7:7c)!" Then he proceeds to clarify the matter with a counter-statement (ἀλλά, 7:7d) and an exposition in which he argues that sin uses the law to deceive and kill the individual (7:8-12). As far as Paul is concerned, the law proves to be holy, and the commandment turns out holy, just and good (7:12).[93]

Again, the basic pattern for the usage of questions negated by μὴ γένοιτο reoccurs: assertion (7:5-6), inferential question (7:7ab), negation (7:7c) and clarification (7:7d-12). As in previous instances, the opening question (7:7ab) establishes the boundaries of the following discussion.

Romans 7:13. At the conclusion of his previous clarification (7:7d-12) Paul states that the law is holy, and the commandment is holy, righteous and good (7:12). However, viewed against the background of sin's employment of it as an instrument of death (7:9-11), it would seem logical to assume that this good thing, the law, has become the cause of human death. Thus the question arises: "Did that which is good, then (οὖν), bring death to me (7:13a)?" The apostle retorts: "By no means (μὴ γένοιτο, 7:13b)!" In an initial counter-statement (ἀλλά, 7:13c) he explains that sin exploited this good law and, in the process, actually fulfilled "two elements of the divine purpose in giving the law, namely, that sin might be shown to be sin and that by means of the commandment its sinfulness might be enhanced."[94]

Beginning with 7:14 Paul introduces evidence to confirm (γάρ) what was said in 7:13.[95] As these verses (7:14-25) clearly indicate, the real fault does not lie with the law but with the sin which dominates the individual ("I am carnal, sold under sin," 7:14).[96] At 7:24 he brings this problem of death through sin to an emotional peak: "Wretched man that I am! Who will deliver me from this body of death (θάνατος, repeated from 7:13)?" He answers that deliverance can be expected through Christ (7:25a). Paul concludes (ἄρα οὖν) the section by stating that the individual is torn between two opposing forces, that is, the law of God and the law of sin (7:25b).[97]

Following this statement, Rom 8 presents a picture strikingly opposed to that of 7:7-25. There is no condemnation for those who are in Christ (8:1). They no longer stand under the eschatological sentence of death so forcefully described in 7:7-25. Such freedom comes from the Spirit who brings life (8:2-11).[98]

As in those examples we have already studied, the usual pattern reappears: assertion (7:7-12), inferential question (7:13a), negation (7:13b) and clarification (7:13c-25). Again, it is interesting to observe how the question here sets the theme for the subsequent discussion.

Romans 9:14. In Rom 9 Paul takes up the problem of
Israel's present unbelief vis-à-vis the gospel. After expressing his concern for Israel and listing their spiritual
advantages (9:1-5), he probes the question of the unbelief of
the majority of his nation (9:6-13). Convinced that God's
word has not failed despite Israel's unbelief (9:6a), he
grounds (γάρ) this opinion by a redefinition of the meaning of
the term "Israel" (9:6b). Accordingly, not all those who come
from Israel really belong to "Israel." Further, not all the
children (of Abraham) are the "seed" of Abraham, but, as the
Scripture confirms, "Through Isaac shall your descendants be
named (9:7)."[99] The apostle explains (τοῦτ' ἔστιν) that the
children of the flesh are not the children of God, but the
children of the promise are reckoned as "seed" (9:8). "Seed"
is theologically equivalent to "children of God" as a comparison of the two clauses in this verse shows.

With a Scripture citation (9:9; see Gen 18:10, 14),
Paul proceeds to ground (γάρ) his statement about the children
of the promise (9:8). Isaac can be characterized a "child of
the promise" rather than a "child of the flesh" by virtue of
the miraculous nature of his birth. Yet, Paul has another
example by which he can explain his assertion about the children of promise (οὐ μόνον δέ, 9:10-13). This is the story of
Rebeccah and her two sons (9:10). Before the birth of Jacob
and Esau, God selected Jacob, the younger, to be the heir and
bearer of the promise and rejected Esau, the older, who should
have been rightfully the heir and bearer of the promise (9:11-13; see Gen 25:23; Mal 1:2-3). This selection occurred so
that God's elective purpose might be realized not on the basis
of works but on the basis of God's prerogative to call whomever he desires (9:11-12). Therefore, "the child of the
promise" (Jacob) is loved, while "the child of the flesh"
(Esau) is hated (9:13).

This choice of Jacob and rejection of Esau (9:13)
suggests that God acts unjustly in his redemptive work. Thus
the question arises: "What shall we say then (τί οὖν ἐροῦμεν;)?
Is there injustice on God's part (9:14ab)?" Paul promptly
replies: "By no means (μὴ γένοιτο, 9:14c)!" Then he reinforces (γάρ) his negation with a Scripture proof (9:15, see

Ex 33:19). From this Scripture the apostle concludes (ἄρα οὖν) that the execution of God's plan does not depend on human volition or exertion but on God who shows mercy (9:16). Moreover, Paul grounds (γάρ) this conclusion with an additional citation from Scripture (9:17, see Ex 9:16). From this second text he further concludes (ἄρα οὖν) that God shows mercy to whom he desires and hardens whom he desires (9:18). In all this Paul counters the inference that God is unjust by affirming God's exercise of mercy with that of his freedom.[100]

As before, the same pattern appears in this section (9:14-18): assertion (9:6-13), inferential question (9:14ab), negation (9:14c) and clarification (9:15-18). Again, the question (9:14ab) sets the theme for this brief digression in Paul's argument.

Romans 11:1. In the preceding section (10:14-21) the apostle describes the inexcusable nature of Israel's unbelief. Israel has heard the gospel but rejected it (10:16-18). As a result, God has turned to the Gentiles as the Scripture plainly predicts (10:19-20; see Deut 32:21; Is 65:1). But Israel has become a disobedient and obstinate people (10:21; see Is 65:2). Such assertions raise a very serious problem for Paul, for it could be inferred God has categorically finished with disobedient Israel. Thus the question surfaces: "I ask, then (οὖν), has God rejected his people (11:1a)?"[101]

Paul responds in the usual manner: "By no means (μὴ γένοιτο, 11:1b)!" Immediately he proceeds to show (γάρ) why this assumption cannot be true, first by using himself as an example (11:1c). Next, he states explicitly that "God has not rejected his people whom he foreknew (11:2a)." He follows this statement with a confirmatory question (ἢ οὐκ οἴδατε) about Elijah (11:2bc) which gives him the opportunity to quote Scripture (11:3-4; see 1 Kgs 19:10, 14, 18). From this passage the apostle concludes (οὖν) that now as then there is a remnant of Israel chosen by grace (11:5). Parenthetically he asserts that if this election comes by grace, then works are excluded (11:6).[102] He returns (τί οὖν;) to the original question of Israel's unbelief by stating that the elect obtained what they sought,[103] but the rest of Israel did not because they were hardened (11:7). Finally, he documents this hardening from Scripture (11:8-10; see Deut 29:4; Is 29:10; Ps 69:22-23; 35:8).

The now familiar pattern is also present in this occurrence of a question negated by μὴ γένοιτο: assertion (10:14-21, especially 10:21), inferential question (11:1a), negation (11:1b) and clarification (11:1c-10). The question (11:1a) prescribes the topic for the discussion (11:1c-10).

Romans 11:11. As the Scripture proof (10:21) leads to the question of God's rejection of Israel (11:1a), so here the Scripture proof (11:8-10) reinstates this question but now with an eye on the majority of Israel who were hardened (11:11a):[104] "So (οὖν) I ask, have they stumbled so as to fall?" Once more Paul answers: "By no means (μὴ γένοιτο, 11:11b)!" Thereupon he begins to explain the true nature of the case (ἀλλά, 11:11c). In summary, he argues that the defection of the Jews is only temporary and serves an important purpose, namely, the salvation of the Gentiles. When this purpose has been accomplished, the Jews will return to God bringing in eschatological blessedness (11:11c-32).

To recapitulate his argument in Rom 1-11, Paul states that God in his plan has shut up the entire world to disobedience so that he might have mercy on all (11:32). Thus God has caused his gracious plan to triumph in spite of human failure. In the final verses (11:33-36) he concludes by praising God for his riches, wisdom and knowledge in the arena of human history.

Again, we find the basic pattern: assertion (11:1-10, especially 11:8-10), inferential question (11:11a), negation (11:11b) and clarification (11:11c-32). As in other cases, the question (11:11a) raises the topic for the subsequent discussion (11:11c-32).

Galatians 2:17. Concluding the narrative section of Galatians (1:11-2:14), Paul describes his confrontation with Cephas at Antioch, Syria (2:11-14). On this occasion he had rebuked Cephas before everyone (2:14b): "If you, though a Jew, live like a Gentile and not like a Jew, how can you compel the Gentiles to live like Jews?" Without lingering to decide whether 2:15-21 are a continuation of this rebuke (2:14b), we begin the analysis of these difficult verses.

First, within the larger sentence (2:15-16) the clause, ἡμεῖς φύσει 'Ιουδαῖοι καὶ οὐκ ἐξ ἐθνῶν ἁμαρτωλοί (2:15), may be regarded as concessive in relation to the main clause, καὶ ἡμεῖς εἰς Χριστὸν 'Ιησοῦν ἐπιστεύσαμεν (2:16b): "We though Jews by nature and not sinners[105] of Gentile origin, . . . , even we have believed in Christ Jesus."[106] The subsequent participial clause, εἰδότες [δὲ] ὅτι οὐ δικαιοῦται ἄνθρωπος ἐξ ἔργων νόμου ἐὰν μὴ διὰ πίστεως 'Ιησοῦ Χριστοῦ (2:16a), which interrupts the connection between 2:15 and 2:16b-d, describes the theological outlook of the "we" (2:15): "yet who know that a man is not justified by works of the law but through faith in Jesus Christ."

Moreover, the main clause (2:16b) complemented by the final clause, ἵνα δικαιωθῶμεν ἐκ πίστεως Χριστοῦ καὶ οὐκ ἐξ ἔργων νόμου (2:16c), conveys the central fact Paul wishes to express: "even we have believed in Christ Jesus, in order to be justified by faith in Christ, not by works of the law." In addition, the following causal clause, ὅτι ἐξ ἔργων νόμου οὐ δικαιωθήσεται πᾶσα σάρξ (2:16d), which reiterates what has already been said twice in this verse, confirms the main clause through Scripture (Ps 143:2): "because by works of the law shall no one be justified."

While 2:15-16 form the background for the question raised in 2:17ab, the import of this question is not readily discerned. It occurs within a conditional sentence in which the dependent clause, εἰ δὲ (ζητοῦντες δικαιωθῆναι ἐν Χριστῷ) εὑρέθημεν καὶ αὐτοὶ ἁμαρτωλοί (2:17a), forms the protasis, and the independent clause, ἆρα Χριστὸς ἁμαρτίας διάκονος (2:17b), forms the apodosis. The protasis (2:17a) refers to the Jewish Christians' act of faith in Christ (cf. ζητοῦντες δικαιωθῆναι ἐν Χριστῷ with 2:16). It implies that in this act they were actually proven to be sinners as the Gentiles who neither possess the law nor perform its works (cf. εὑρέθημεν καὶ αὐτοὶ ἁμαρτωλοί with 2:15).[107]

Furthermore, the interrogative apodosis (2:17b) infers (ἆρα)[108] from the statement of the protasis (2:17a) that

Christ is a minister of sin. In other words, does this reduction of the Jewish Christians (by virtue of their justification in Christ) to the spiritual rank of Gentile "sinners" somehow implicate Christ as a promoter of sin?

What this "ministry of sin" actually signifies continues to be a subject of debate. The argument that it revolves around the issue of immorality in the church and the necessary safeguards against it has much to commend it, since this practical problem appears to have been at the heart of the difficulties in Galatia and to have paved the way for the "other gospel" which Paul combats.[109] Thus Paul would be inquiring whether the denial of the saving role of the works of the law through justification by faith in Christ, a denial which reduces the Jews to the same sinful condition as the Gentiles, leads to a sinful life.

At any rate, the apostle rejects this inference in the usual manner: "Certainly not (μὴ γένοιτο, 2:17c)!" Evidently he does not deny the premises (2:17a) but rather the conclusion (2:17b).[110] Paul immediately proceeds to ground his rejection in two ways (2:18-19).[111] In the first place, he explains (γάρ) that, if he[112] builds again the things that he previously destroyed, he shows himself to be a transgressor (2:18). A contrast between "Is Christ then a minister of sin (2:17)?" and "I show myself a transgressor (2:18b)" may be intended. The implication seems to be that if Jewish Christians attempt to reassert their prior spiritual claims (see 2:15),[113] they demonstrate they are transgressors.

Precisely what one transgresses Paul does not say. Most exegetes argue the apostle envisions the transgression of the law (cf. Rom 2:23; 4:15; 5:14; Gal 3:19). Therefore, in this statement he disavows that Christ is a promoter of sin when the Jews' sinfulness comes to light in the event of justification. Rather Jewish Christians who attempt to restore their past spiritual claims constitute themselves transgressors of the law in this very act. Because they can no longer return to their "privileged" status *ante Christum* (see 2:15), they must invariably land in the only other condition available outside of Christ, namely, that of a transgressor. Hence, by again regarding the works of the law as a means of salvation, they fall under the guilty verdict of the law whose saving validity they once denied (see 2:16-17). In this manner Paul grounds negatively his rejection of the false inference (2:17b).

In the second place, Paul grounds (γάρ, 2:19) his statement in 2:18 while also pointing back to 2:17b.[114] As contrasted to 2:18, his argument here is more positive in nature.[115] Through the law he died to the law so that he might live for God (2:19a). By the phrase "through the law" Paul apparently refers to the death sentence which the law passes on the sinner.[116] Believers undergo this sentence through their association with the death of Christ: "I have been crucified with Christ (2:19b)."[117] Therefore, they are no longer dominated by the law. This death to the law, however, is followed by a new life to God (ἵνα θεῷ ζήσω, 2:19a). Contrary to being a minister of sin (2:17b) Christ has overcome the dominance of the law so that (Jewish) Christians may now devote their lives to God. A new allegiance has been formed.

In the next verse (2:20) the apostle describes the nature of this new life for God which forms a bulwark against sin. Dying with Christ has as its consequence Christ's coming to live in the believer (2:20a; cf. 2:19b). In turn the believer is sustained in this new life by faith in Christ (2:20b).

By way of conclusion Paul declares he does not set aside God's grace (2:21a). As the next sentence (2:21b) explains, "setting aside God's grace" means seeking justification through the law (cf. 2:18). Those who do this render Christ's death useless. At this juncture Paul stops, for he has now prepared the way for the argumentative section of the epistle (Gal 3-4) by focusing on the current problem in these few verses (2:15-21).

Whatever the merit of our interpretation of these difficult verses, the analysis of the thought of the passage is not wholly dependent on it. As most interpreters agree, 2:18-21 are in some way a grounding and explanation of Paul's μὴ γένοιτο (2:17c). Thus we again find the customary pattern for questions negated in this manner: assertion (2:15-16), inferential question (2:17ab), negation (2:17c) and grounding or clarification (2:18-21).

Galatians 3:21. In the argumentative section of Galatians (chaps. 3-4), Paul takes up the relationship between the law and the promise (3:15-20). He builds his argument on the ordinary human experience that once a will (διαθήκη) has been ratified it is not to be changed subsequently by a third party (3:15). Applying this principle to God's covenant with Abraham, Paul contends that the law which came centuries afterward cannot modify the prior covenant and, thus, the promise it contained (3:16-17).[118] Therefore, he concludes that the law and the promise are mutually exclusive with regard to the inheritance, since God freely gave it to Abraham through the promise (3:18).

At this point the apostle logically inquires as to the true purpose of the law (3:19-20). According to his reasoning, the law was added on account of transgressions (3:19ab). Evidently Paul means the law came in order to produce transgressions, that is, violations of explicit laws.[119] This function of the law is apparently restricted to the period before the coming of the "seed" to whom the promise had been made, that is, Christ (3:19c; cf. 3:16). He further adds that this law was enacted through the agency of angels by the hand of a mediator (3:19d).

The next verse expands on 3:19d by focusing on the idea of a mediator mentioned there. But now it is not a specific mediator (Moses) but the general concept of "mediator" which concerns Paul:[120] "Now an intermediary implies more than one; but God is one (3:20)." Some interpret this statement to mean that the duality of persons between whom a mediator acts and the notion that God is one imply that the law came indirectly from God and is, thus, inferior to the promise which was given directly (3:16, 18)[121] or that the law is conditional because it was a contract between God and the Jewish people.[122] Others, however, understand Paul's assertion to mean that, since a mediator represents a plurality but God, on the other hand, is one, then the law does not stem at least directly from God but from the multitude of the angels.[123]

In view of the preceding discussion where the law and the promise are mutually exclusive as far as salvation is concerned (3:15-20), one could infer that the law is really antagonistic to the promise. For if the law produces transgressions and thus brings death, it works contrary to the promise which brings righteousness and life (cf. 3:10-11, 13, 19 with 3:14, 18).[124] Consequently, the question arises: "Is the law then (οὖν) against the promises of God (3:21a)?" To this illegitimate inference Paul replies: "Certainly not (μὴ γένοιτο, 3:21b)." He promptly clarifies his negation with a conditional sentence (3:21cd) and then with a counter-assertion (3:22).

First, the apostle explains (γάρ) that the law is not in conflict with the promise because its function is not to give life after all (3:21cd).[125] If such were the case, then justification would come through the law (3:21d) and a real conflict would arise between the law and the promise. Second, Paul asserts (ἀλλά) that Scripture itself has locked up all things under sin (3:22a).[126] To be "under sin" is probably equivalent to being under condemnation (cf. 3:10).[127] The purpose of this confinement is that "what was promised to faith in Jesus Christ might be given to those who believe (3:22b)." Therefore, no conflict exists between the law and the promise because the Scripture, by its universal condemnation of humanity, has excluded the law as a way of salvation. Indeed, the law has an entirely different function, as Paul will show.

In the subsequent verses (3:23-29) he describes the function of the law by applying the analogy of "custodianship."[128] Although the argument introduced in 3:23 is concluded in 3:29 by returning to the thought of the "seed" (3:19c), Paul takes up again (λέγω δέ, 4:1) the condition under the law by using the analogy of "guardianship" (4:1-7).[129] For the son such a condition is tantamount to slavery (4:1-3), but God has terminated it by sending Jesus Christ (4:4-7). It is important to observe that 4:7 is substantially a repetition of 3:29.

As in previous instances, the accustomed pattern is present: assertion (3:15-20), inferential question (3:21a), negation (3:21b) and clarification (3:21c-4:7). Moreover, the question negated by μὴ γένοιτο (3:21a) fixes the theme for the subsequent discussion about the relationship of the law and the promise and about the function of the law (3:21c-4:7).

1 Corinthians 6:15. In the preceding chapter (1 Cor 5) Paul passes judgment on a Corinthian man who is apparently living with his step-mother. In the following discussion (6:1-11) he deals with the problem of lawsuits among Christians. At the end of this discussion the apostle lists those sins which exclude one from the kingdom of God (6:9-10). Yet, he does not expect such conduct from the Corinthians, for they have been washed, sanctified and justified in the name of the Lord Jesus Christ and in the Spirit of God (6:11). These concluding verses (6:9-11) enable Paul to work his way back to the theme of sexual license (6:12-20) that he left at the end of chapter 5.[130]

He renews this theme not by reference to immoral conduct but by citing twice a principle which may come from the Corinthians themselves: "All things are lawful for me (6:12ac)."[131] In both instances Paul apparently qualifies this principle with a counter-assertion (ἀλλά, 6:12bd). In the following verses (6:13-20) he applies this notion of unrestrained freedom in two areas: food/stomach (6:13ab) and fornication (6:13c-20).

In the first case, he may again quote a slogan current at Corinth: "Food is meant for the stomach and the stomach for food, and God will destroy both one and the other (6:13ab)."[132] This statement seems to imply that the transience of food and of the stomach makes them morally irrelevant things.[133]

But Paul rejects the Corinthian viewpoint especially its implications for fornication. The body is not meant for fornication but for the Lord, and the Lord for the body (6:13cd). Moral neutrality does not exist because the body (ἡμᾶς = σῶμα) will actually continue its existence by means of the resurrection (6:14).¹³⁴ Paul promptly repeats and reinforces his argument with a question embodying a fact assumed to be common knowledge: "Do you not know that your bodies are members of Christ (6:15a)?" In view of this union with Christ and of the immoral tendencies of some of the Corinthians, the apostle asks the unthinkable question: "Shall I therefore (οὖν) take the members of Christ and make them members of a prostitute (6:15b)?" As several scholars have noted,¹³⁵ this question does not surface as a false inference which could be drawn from Paul's previous argument.

To this absurd proposition he replies: "Never (μὴ γένοιτο, 6:15c)!" The next verses (6:16-17) appear to give reasons for this rejection of fornication.¹³⁶ Paul bases his rejection on an obvious fact (6:16a, 17) which is confirmed by Scripture (Gen 2:24; 6:16b): those who engage in illegitimate intercourse tear themselves away from Christ.

Next he gives a negative exhortation: "Shun immorality (6:18a)," which he follows with what may represent another Corinthian slogan: "Every sin which a man commits is outside the body (6:18b)."¹³⁷ As in the case of 6:13, Paul counters the suggestion that the body has nothing to do with sin by the statement, "But the immoral man sins against his own body (6:18c)."

Then the apostle reminds the Corinthians of a fact which they should know, namely, that their body is the temple of the Spirit (cf. 6:17) and that they belong to another, a fact which he bases on God's redemptive act (6:19-20a). By way of conclusion he indicates the positive behavior they should pursue: "So glorify God in your body (6:20b; cf. 6:18a)."

Unlike the previous occurrences of the questions negated by μὴ γένοιτο, the usual pattern is not entirely present here. The rhetorical question (6:15b) is not based on a false inference from Paul's preceding argument but on the fact of the unity of the believer with Christ (6:15a) and the potential for immoral action on the part of some Corinthians (see 1 Cor 5). However, as in the other occurrences in Paul, the rejection is amplified to some extent in the subsequent argumentation (6:16-20). Thus in this instance Paul's use of a question negated by μὴ γένοιτο corresponds to the second nuance evinced in the usage of Epictetus.[138]

Conclusion

With our brief survey of the Pauline occurrences of questions negated by μὴ γένοιτο thus concluded, we may now give an overall summary of his usage.[139] First, the questions negated in this manner are introduced by τί οὖν; (so Epictetus), οὖν (so Epictetus), τί γάρ;, τί ἐροῦμεν;, τί οὖν ἐροῦμεν;, λέγω οὖν or ἄρα/ἆρα.

Furthermore, as an answer to these questions, μὴ γένοιτο is not sufficient, for normally additional clarification or grounding is provided, as the above examples have shown. This may be introduced in the form of an explanatory sentence with γάρ (Rom 9:15; 11:1; Gal 2:18; 3:21), in the form of a counter-assertion with ἀλλά (Rom 7:7, 13; 11:11), in the form of a counter-question (Rom 3:6; 6:2-3; 6:16; 7:1) or in the form of an imperatival sentence with δέ (Rom 3:4).[140] In addition, this clarification or grounding may include the citation or exposition of Scripture (Rom 3:4; 7:7; 9:15-18; 11:1-10; 11:26-27).

Moreover, as we discovered in examining the first nuance of Epictetus' use of these questions, a basic pattern underlies Paul's use of questions negated by μὴ γένοιτο: assertion (of varying length), question based on a false inference from the previous assertion, negation and immediate clarification or grounding, consisting in a sentence or two (Rom 3:4, 6) or in a whole paragraph or even paragraphs (Rom 6:2b-14; 6:16-7:6; 7:7d-12; 7:13c-25; 9:15-18; 11:1c-10; 11:11c-32; Gal 2:18-21; 3:21c-4:7).[141]

Why more lengthy clarification or grounding is lacking in two instances (Rom 3:3-4, 5-6) we have already tried to explain.[142] Although the topics of these two questions seem to anticipate similar topics to be treated later in the epistle (cf. 3:3-4 with 9:6-13 and 3:5-6 with 9:14-33), it is important to note that in the succeeding passages the discussion takes on a different form and has a different background.

Also, the initial questions receive satisfactory clarification or grounding in relation to the circumstances from which they emerge.

Further, in no instance did we find that a question negated by μὴ γένοιτο concluded a paragraph or topic in the course of Paul's discussion. Rather, the use of such questions seems deliberately designed to focus the reader's (hearer's) attention on some issue in the previous discussion which could be misunderstood. Once Paul has brought this false inference to light and negated it, he can then explain the true nature of the case or ground his rejection of the false conclusion. Thus, these questions set the theme for the subsequent discussion functioning as a caption for what follows, for example, sin and grace (Rom 6:1-14); sin, grace and law (Rom 6:15-7:6); sin and law (Rom 7:7-12); death and law (Rom 7:13-25); God's justice (Rom 9:14-18); God's rejection of Israel (Rom 11:1-10); Israel's ultimate failure (Rom 11:11-32); Christ and sin (Gal 2:17-21) and law and promise (Gal 3:21-4:7).[143]

Finally, as one can sense from the discussion above, questions negated by μὴ γένοιτο are not of such a nature that they can be readily dismissed without some kind of strong clarification or grounding. The issues they raise are not of such a kind that they can be ignored or postponed until later.

Conclusion

With this analysis of Paul's use of questions negated by μὴ γένοιτο in mind, we can now return to the question in Rom 3:31 which is the focal point of our investigation. As most scholars recognize, this question arises as a false inference from Paul's previous discussion (3:21-30). In this discussion the apostle has constantly contrasted righteousness by faith with righteousness by the law or the works of the law (3:21-22, 27-28). Because of this rejection of the law as a means of salvation one could infer Paul is invalidating the law altogether: "Do we then (οὖν) overthrow the law by this faith (3:31a)?" Paul answers: "By no means (μὴ γένοιτο,

3:31b)!" To this negation he adds a counter-assertion: "On the contrary (ἀλλά), we uphold the law (3:31c)." Again, we must ask whether 3:31c is Paul's only clarification or grounding of his rejection of this false conclusion. For several reasons we are inclined to think it is not.

First, while Rom 3:31 issues logically from Paul's preceding discussion (3:21-30), this does not obligate us to consider it as simply a conclusion to this discussion. Indeed, all the Pauline occurrences of questions negated by μὴ γένοιτο (except 1 Cor 6:15) stand in an intimate relation to what precedes. Such is their nature. However, in no other occurrence do they form the conclusion to a paragraph or topic. Rather in the majority of cases they determine the topic for the discussion which immediately follows.

Second, the argument that Paul can dismiss an objection (see Rom 3:8) abruptly without further ado would be substantial if we were not dealing with questions negated by μὴ γένοιτο which do not usually behave in this manner. Rather, as we have already indicated, they focus the attention on some issue in the discussion which could be misunderstood in order to allow the writer (speaker) to elaborate on this problem.

Third, attempts to view Rom 3:31 as an interjection which anticipates some future discussion in Romans (apart from Rom 4) must face two difficulties. On the one hand, the other Pauline occurrences of questions negated by μὴ γένοιτο do not appear to function in this manner. On the other hand, the examples frequently cited (Rom 5; 6; 7; 8:4; 9-11; 12-15) do not seem to deal specifically with the relationship between faith and law as Rom 3:31 would require (see 3:21-30). Rather they treat the relation of sin, grace and law (6:15-7:6), sin and law (7:7-12) or death and law (7:13-25), to give a few examples. In these passages Paul does not take up directly the relationship between faith and law as he posed it in Rom 3:31. If this is true, then we are compelled to inquire where Paul discusses this issue.

Fourth, on the basis of the other Pauline instances of such questions, we suggest Rom 4 should be regarded as the logical clarification of Rom 3:31, especially of the counter-assertion: "On the contrary, we uphold the law (3:31c)."

This question follows the usual pattern: assertion (3:21-30), inferential question (3:31a), negation (3:31b) and clarification (3:31c). As in other occurrences where Paul begins his clarification with a counter-statement (ἀλλά) and then enlarges it through discussion (see Rom 7:7d + 7:8-12; 7:13c + 7:14-25; 11:11c + 11:12-32), so also here Rom 4:1-25 may be regarded as the expansion of 3:31c. Moreover, as in other cases, Paul cites and expounds Scripture (Rom 4:3). Therefore, as is generally true with questions negated by μὴ γένοιτο, this question (Rom 3:31a) sets the theme for what follows (Rom 4).

Finally, we can say on the basis of our study of these questions that those scholars are right who sense that Paul would not dismiss such an important issue as the relationship between faith and the law with a simple, "On the contrary, we uphold the law." These questions are not of such a nature that they can be readily dismissed without a satisfactory explanation or grounding. Consequently, we are inclined to concur with those who want to put Rom 3:31 at the head of Rom 4 rather than simply at the end of Rom 3, provided the intimate relation between this verse and the preceding argument (3:21-30) is not overlooked.[144]

Of course, we must test these conclusions by means of an exegesis of the entire passage, Rom 3:21-4:25, in order to determine if and how it speaks to the issue of faith as the upholding of the law. In the course of this exegesis we shall deal with other objections lodged against the proposed connection between Rom 3:31 and 4:1-25.

CHAPTER III

THE EXEGESIS OF ROMANS 3:21-4:25

Introduction

In this chapter we want to assess the validity of our conclusion in Chapter II that the question negated by μὴ γένοιτο (Rom 3:31ab) introduces the topic of Paul's subsequent discussion in Rom 4, namely, that faith is the establishment of the law (3:31c), a theme which he would then develop in Rom 4. Thus an exegesis of Rom 3:31-4:25 becomes necessary in order to show that a connection exists between Rom 3:31 and Rom 4:1-25 and, above all, to uncover the meaning of Paul's important statement that he upholds the law by faith.

However, in order to deal adequately with Rom 3:31-4:25, we must first examine briefly Paul's preceding discussion (3:21-30), which forms the theological center of this epistle and, more importantly, the background for Rom 3:31. Only then can we achieve a proper understanding of the import of Paul's question (3:31a) and of his reply (3:31b-4:25). Once this has been accomplished, we can conduct an exegesis of Rom 3:31 and then Rom 4:1-25 so as to ascertain the meaning of Rom 3:31 and the way in which Rom 4 expands upon it. Finally, by way of conclusion, we shall review Paul's argument in Rom 3:21-4:25 and state succinctly the results of our inquiry to that point.

The Exegesis of Romans 3:21-30

It is generally affirmed that Rom 3:21ff. represents an important turning point in the Epistle to the Romans, resuming positively Paul's theme of the righteousness of God from faith to faith (1:16-17). After the statement of this theme he had posed and subsequently substantiated the guilt of all humankind before God (1:18-2:29). Next he had silenced

some objections which might be raised against his indictment
of the Jews (3:1-8). Finally, the apostle had adduced a catena
of OT passages to show that both Jew and Gentile are under sin
(3:9-20), thereby confirming his previous allegations (1:18-
2:29). He concludes this catena by stating that whatever the
νόμος says, it speaks to those who are in the νόμος so that
every mouth may be stopped and the whole world may become
guilty before God (3:19). Paul justifies this statement by
declaring that on the basis of the works of the νόμος no one
will be justified in God's sight (see Ps 143:2b), for through
the νόμος comes the knowledge of sin (3:20).

From the outset one should pause to note how Paul uses
the word νόμος in the concluding verses of this passage
(3:19-20). With regard to 3:19 one observes that in the first
occurrence νόμος clearly refers to the entire OT (see 3:10-18;
cf. 1 Cor 14:21). In the second occurrence it may again
designate the OT (cf. 3:2)[1] or less likely the Mosaic legislation (cf. 3:20).[2] Thus in this verse Paul asserts that what
the OT says about human unrighteousness, it addresses first to
those who are within its sphere of authority (i.e., the Jews,
2:12, 20, 23) so that with the indictment of God's chosen
people the whole world must silently admit its guilt before
God.[3]

In the following verse (3:20) νόμος appears to denote
more narrowly the Mosaic legislation by whose works (so 3:20a)
the Jews hoped to establish their own righteousness before
God. Again, the unqualified use of νόμος (3:20b) could imply
the "law" in this narrower sense. At any rate, this verse
identifies the reason for the universal guilt of humanity,
especially of the Jews, as the inability of the works of the
law to justify the individual before God (3:20a). This is so
because the law has another function: to bring knowledge of
sin (3:20b).

This brief digression on the word νόμος can alert us
to some of the various ways in which Paul can use this term
and thus anticipate similar phenomena in what follows. At the
same time, it should help us to recognize, as scholars often
have, that our translation "law" for the Greek νόμος (= Torah)
is at best inadequate. For Paul, as for contemporary Judaism,

νόμος was apparently more than a comprehensive term for a collection of laws. Rather it approximated the concept of divine revelation or instruction.[4] This fact should warn us against a too narrow restriction of its meaning. In the final analysis, the meaning of νόμος must be determined by its use in each individual context.

Returning to the passage under consideration, we notice that Paul, in what represents a definite turning point in the letter, declares that now (νυνὶ δέ) God's righteousness has been manifested apart from the law (χωρὶς νόμου, 3:21a). While the phrase χωρὶς νόμου may be shorthand for χωρὶς ἔργων νόμου (3:28; cf. 3:20; 4:6),[5] the contrasting occurrence of νόμος that directly follows (ὑπὸ τοῦ νόμου, 3:21b) makes it likely that one and the same νόμος (the Pentateuch) is meant, though viewed from different perspectives.[6] At least the apostle wants to point out in this initial statement that the law played no part in effecting the manifestation of God's righteousness.[7]

Though the law had no role in the manifestation of God's righteousness, still the law and the prophets bear witness to this righteousness (3:21b). Since Paul uses the expression ὁ νόμος καὶ οἱ προφῆται for the OT only here in his letters, it may reflect a conscious attempt to set in relief the law's (the Pentateuch's) role as a witness alongside that of the prophets (cf. 1:2). In this way, as we shall see, the apostle prepares the readers for his subsequent statements about the law (3:27, 31) and makes a connection between 3:21 and these verses.[8]

Moreover, it is significant that only here in the Pauline corpus do we find the function of the law as a witness described in this specific manner. In the NT μαρτυρεῖν denotes "the declaration or confirmation, on the basis of first-hand knowledge, of individual acts or general facts of experience."[9] As a witness, the law, together with the prophets, confirms Paul's gospel about the righteousness of God.

In view of the dual presence of νόμος in this verse, scholars[10] have noted that Paul sets up a dialectical tension over the law here. On the one hand, the manifestation of God's righteousness occurs apart from the law; on the other hand, this righteousness is witnessed by the law. Though he proceeds to describe the manifiestation of God's righteousness (3:24-26), Paul does not immediately explain the content of this witness.[11] Hence he still owes an explanation of this assertion (3:21b).[12] However, at this point it is sufficient to notice Paul's certainty that this witness of the law and the prophets to God's righteousness prevents the misunderstanding that this righteousness, though revealed apart from the law, is in opposition to the OT and thus a baseless innovation in salvation history.[13]

In continuation (δέ) Paul defines more precisely this righteousness of God to which the law and the prophets bear witness. It is the righteousness of God given through faith in Jesus Christ[14] to everyone who believes (3:22a). This restriction of the awarding of God's righteousness to faith finds its basis (γάρ) in the fact that God does not allow distinctions in his plan of salvation (3:22b). With the addition of this verse the apostle gives a keener edge to the tension he has created over the law (3:21). Though it is ineffectual in the manifestation of God's righteousness, nevertheless, along with the prophets, the law bears witness to this righteousness as a righteousness by faith. This positive association of the law with righteousness by faith will reappear explicitly in Rom 3:27, 31 and implicitly in Rom 4.

The next verse (3:23) bases (γάρ) the absence of distinctions in God's plan of salvation (3:22b) on the fact that all people have sinned and lack the glory of God. It is this universal sinfulness and degradation of humanity that excludes the law and necessitates faith as the way of attaining righteousness. With this statement Paul sums up all that was said in the first major section of the epistle (1:18-3:20).

Beginning with the participial clause (3:24),[15] Paul states the antithesis of 3:23 by describing the manner in which God's righteousness has been revealed (cf. 3:21-22). That is, justification takes place freely by God's grace through the redemption which comes in Christ Jesus. In this way he grounds his doctrine of justification christologically.[16]

In the extended relative clause that follows (3:25-26), Paul apparently adapts a traditional formula to explain the nature and purpose of this redemption in Christ. God set forth Jesus as a ἱλαστήριον[17] in his blood, that is, in his cross (3:25a). The apostle's apparent addition of the phrase διὰ πίστεως stresses that one appropriates this ἱλαστήριον through faith not through the works of the law (cf. 3:20-22, 24).

This work of God in Christ is designed to show God's righteousness because he has forgiven past sins in his tolerance (3:25b-26a).[18] However, according to Paul, God's activity in Jesus also demonstrates his righteousness in the present eschatological moment (cf. 3:21) in order that he may be righteous even when he justifies the person who believes in Jesus (3:26bc).[19] Thus Paul concludes by emphasizing the role of faith in the appropriation of God's righteousness without respect to the performance of the works of the law.

In the following section (3:27-30) the apostle sharpens his emphasis on justification by faith by focusing on the Jew's boast in the possession of the law and the performance of its works. With the question, "Then what becomes of our boasting (3:27a)?" Paul appears to glance back at previous statements (cf. 2:17, 23; 3:9, 19-20). Such boasting implies the assertion of a claim on God based on one's works.[20] In view of the sinfulness of humanity (1:18-3:20, 23) and of God's redeeming work in Christ (3:22, 24-26), Paul's answer is unavoidable: "It is excluded (3:27b)."

Yet Paul still asks διὰ ποίου νόμου such boasting is excluded (3:27c). The interrogative pronoun ποῖος probably means "what kind of," thus inquiring about the nature of the νόμος which has excluded boasting.[21] Is it [διὰ νόμου] τῶν ἔργων (3:27d)? No, he replies, rather it is διὰ νόμου πίστεως (3:27e). The uniqueness and interpretative difficulties represented by these two expressions have caused wide divergences in the exegesis of this verse.

While some consider [νόμος] τῶν ἔργων to be the Mosaic law, they understand νόμος πίστεως to designate a special law valid only for Christians (cf. "law of the Spirit," Rom 8:2; "law of Christ," Gal 6:2 and "in the law of Christ," 1 Cor 9:21).[22] The problems with this approach are evident. On the one hand, it is difficult to relate the statements in Rom 3:27

materially to the texts just mentioned. On the other hand, to speak of the "law of faith" in terms of a special law for Christians forces these exegetes to soften the legalistic sense they would normally assign to νόμος. Otherwise, this "law of faith" would become another legalism, and the difference between the "law of faith" and the "law of works" (as they understand it) would disappear.[23]

Others view the "law of works" as a reference to the Mosaic law but consider the "law of faith" a paradoxical expression due more to rhetoric than to theological reflection. In this case it means something like the saving order of faith.[24] However, as Friedrich[25] points out, when Paul asks by what kind of νόμος boasting is excluded, then the answer must contain an expression about one and the same νόμος. Thus, if the "law of works" refers to the Mosaic law, it would seem that the "law of faith" must also. Otherwise, this difference would involve an unwarranted change in the meaning of νόμος.

Finally, most scholars interpret νόμος here in a general sense as principle, norm, system, rule, order and so forth, appealing for support to the use of the word in Rom 7:21-25; 8:2. For example, Kuss interprets the verse in this manner:

> Durch was fur eine Ordnung wurde das Sichrühmen ausgeschlossen? Durch eine Ordnung, die das Heil auf die Werke stellt? Nein, sondern durch eine Ordnung, die das Heil allein auf Glauben stellt" (. . .).[26]

But, as Friedrich[27] again argues, it would be unusual for Paul suddenly to give to νόμος a meaning which it does not have in either the immediately preceding (3:19-26) or the immediately following context (3:28-30), where it clearly refers to the OT law under one aspect or another. Furthermore, that the occurrence of νόμος (Rom 7:21-25; 8:2) furnishes evidence that Paul employs the word in such a general sense is at present the subject of debate.[28]

In view of the difficulties with the previous approaches, Friedrich[29] contends that νόμος in this verse denotes the OT law in both occurrences. If νόμος does mean the OT law, this raises the problem of how to understand the

Exegesis of Rom 3:21-4:25   69

following genitives, ἔργων and πίστεως. Scholars have offered
a variety of answers to this question. Pointing to 3:21b (cf.
3:31-4:25), Friedrich[30] understands [νόμος] τῶν ἔργων as the
law which demands works but νόμος πίστεως as the law which
bears witness to faith.

Modifying Friedrich's interpretation to some extent,
Cranfield[31] considers the "law of works" as "a law which
directs men to seek justification as a reward for their works"
and the "law of faith" as a law "summoning men to faith."
For Klaus Berger[32] the "law of works" is the law to the extent
that it could be fulfilled in works, while the "law of faith"
is the law fulfilled in faith as far as its goal of righteousness is concerned. According to Peter von der Osten-Sacken,[33]
the "law of works" is the law which people make their own in
order to present themselves to God as givers, thus, in order
to offer him works. On the other hand, the "law of faith" is
the law to the extent that it is met by faith. It is the
Torah brought to validity by faith.

Moreover, Hahn[34] views the "law of works" as the law
through whose works people must produce their own salvation
and the "law of faith" as the law which is recognized in its
character as a witness and in its task of pointing beyond
itself by reason of the promise to faith. Finally, Ulrich
Wilckens[35] speaks of the "law of works" as the Torah to the
extent that it demands works of righteousness and measures
justification by them alone but of the "law of faith" as the
law allied with faith now that God has revealed his righteousness in Christ and thus through faith.

These interpretations have much in common and each
contains elements of truth. However, on the assumption that
Paul's meaning would begin to be evident to anyone who has
read the epistle to this point, we should first return to
the preceding context in order to understand what the expressions, "law of works" and "law of faith," suggest.[36] On the
one hand, the law was denied a role in the realization of
God's righteousness (cf. 3:21a with 3:27de). If such were
not the case, the law and its works would incite boasting.
On the other hand, the law is a witness to righteousness by
πίστις (cf. 3:21b-22 with 3:27e). As such the law excludes
boasting.[37]

Thus, by taking the genitives as qualitative,[38] we have a law characterized by works and a law characterized by faith. Having in mind the definitions already suggested, it seems safe to say that the "law of works" is the OT law viewed primarily from the perspective of the works that it prescribes and that have falsely become a means of salvation. Perceived in this way the law can lead to boasting (cf. 2:17, 23; 3:9, 19-20). The "law of faith" is the same law viewed primarily from the perspective of the faith to which it bears witness, a faith that truly mediates righteousness (cf. 3:21b-22). Perceived in this way the law excludes boasting on the basis of one's works.[39]

However, this is not to suggest that Paul holds a double concept of the law but only that he intimates a difference in the way in which one perceives it (cf. Rom 9:31-32).[40] For him this difference in perception is due to the Christ event which he has just described (3:24-26). Above all, it is important to recognize that, as in 3:21-22, Paul retains the tension he has created with respect to the law.

Without explaining in more detail the meaning of the phrases, "law of works" and "law of faith," Paul proceeds to support (γάρ)[41] what he has just said (3:27): "For we hold that a man is justified by faith apart from the works of law (3:28)." This judgment grounds both Paul's statement that boasting has been excluded and his contention that it is the "law of faith" which has excluded it. At the same time this verse sums up the essence of 3:21-22 (cf. δικαιοῦσθαι πίστει ἄνθρωπον with 3:21b-22 and χωρὶς ἔργων νόμου with 3:21a).[42]

The next two verses (3:29-30) are really an argument for Paul's thesis that one (whether Jew or Gentile) is justified by faith apart from the works of the law (3:28) based on the oneness of God. As Cranfield[43] notes, the question, "Or is God the God of Jews only (3:29a)?" indicates the logical consequences if one should regard Paul's thesis (3:28) as false. If this thesis is not true, salvation by the works of the law would effectively deny God's saving lordship over the Gentiles and consequently his oneness.

The following question (3:29b) complements the first: "Is he not the God of Gentiles also?" His answer (3:29c) is

one which every Jew could accept without, perhaps, drawing the
same consequences as Paul: "Yes, of Gentiles also." In support of this answer Paul appeals to the basic fact of God's
oneness as confessed in the Shema of Israel: "Since God is
one (3:30a; cf. Deut 6:4)." The attached relative clause
(3:30b) describes God's oneness as demonstrated in his uniform
saving act toward all humankind: "who justifies the circumcised on the basis of faith and the uncircumcised through
faith."[44] This solemn statement marks the conclusion of the
discussion.

In reflecting on this section we observe that Paul
sets up, as it were, a dialectic over the OT law (see 3:21-22,
27). To this point, however, he has not shown from the law
the basis for this dialectic nor for his claim that the law
attests righteousness by faith and can thus be labelled a "law
of faith" as opposed to a "law of works." It is with the new
question (3:31) that Paul will direct our attention to this
matter.

The Exegesis of Romans 3:31

After Paul's blunt rejection of the law's role in salvation in favor of faith (3:21-30), the question arises
(3:31a): νόμον οὖν καταργοῦμεν διὰ τῆς πίστεως; To this he
replies (3:31bc): μὴ γένοιτο, ἀλλὰ νόμον ἱστάνομεν. Before
attempting to explicate the meaning of this question and the
apostle's reply, we must investigate briefly the meaning of
the principle concepts Paul uses here.

First, scholars have understood the word νόμος in a
variety of ways in this context, for example, the Mosaic law
or legislation,[45] all moral law,[46] the Pentateuch,[47] the
entire OT,[48] a divine order or system of salvation,[49] or a
specifically Christian law.[50] Of these approaches those which
understand νόμος as the Mosaic law, the Pentateuch or the
entire OT offer the most viable alternatives and are most
widely entertained among scholars.

In the light of the context it seems likely that Paul
means at least the Pentateuch when he employs νόμος in this
verse (cf. 3:21, 27; 4:3). The objection that one cannot

relate 3:31 to 3:21b because there Paul talks of "the law and
the prophets" but here of "the law" only might be cogent if
it were not for the intervention of 3:27. Unless we are to
assume that νόμος there refers to the entire OT, in that verse
Paul apparently abandons the reference to "the prophets."
Rather he is concerned with indicating the two perspectives
from which one can view the law (the Pentateuch), namely, as
a law which prescribes works or as a law which bears witness
to righteousness by faith. Furthermore, in the next chapter
Paul takes up this witness of the law to righteousness by
faith by a direct appeal to the Pentateuch (4:3). His return
to the theme of boasting in the preceding verse (4:2) shows
that he is not finished with his treatment of the question
about the "law of faith" as opposed to the "law of works"
(3:27).

Other objections to taking νόμος as the Pentateuch also
lose their force when one looks closely at the context. The
objection that, if νόμος means the law primarily in its scriptural
witness rather than in its demand, the continuity of
Paul's argument from 3:28 (χωρὶς ἔργων νόμου) onward is
destroyed proves unconvincing in view of the tension that the
apostle sets up over the νόμος (3:21-22, 27-28) and the unparallelled
mention of νόμος as a component of the OT Scripture
(3:21b). It is at 3:31 that Paul again takes up the positive
aspect of this tension, for here faith (πίστις) and the law
(νόμος) are complementary to each other (cf. 3:21b and "the
law of faith," 3:27e).[51]

Moreover, the argument that it would be pointless for
Paul to speak of the abiding validity of the OT after his
earlier use of it to substantiate humanity's sinfulness
(3:10-18) overlooks the nature of Paul's question and its
background (3:21-30). The apostle is not simply concerned
with defending the validity of the OT, a validity which he
already assumes. Rather he is concerned with preserving the
validity of the law in view of his blatant rejection of its
presumed role in salvation (3:20, 21a, 27de, 28).

Finally, the objection that νόμος always has the
article when it refers to Scripture is not tenable. If
adopted, it would lead, on the one hand, to the assumption

that anarthrous νόμος could never mean Scripture (whether the
Pentateuch or the OT) with regard to its content and, on the
other hand, to the assumption that articular νόμος would
always entail Scripture to some degree. Yet, as Peter Bläser[52]
has shown, the article or the lack of it cannot be regarded as
a criterion for determining the meaning of νόμος.

In conclusion, it appears that Paul means the Pentateuch when he speaks of overthrowing the law in this verse.
While it is conceivable he means the entire OT,[53] the context,
especially 3:21, 27, 4:3, seems to argue in favor of the former.
Again, we must bear in mind the fluidity with which Paul uses
νόμος. That νόμος would mean the Mosaic law or legislation in
the narrower sense is unlikely given our analysis of the preceding context and the positive way in which it is associated
with faith here.

In addition to this discussion of the meaning of νόμος,
we should also consider Paul's use of the verbs, καταργεῖν and
ἱστάνειν. The widely accepted notion that the rabbinical use
of בטל and קום underlies the apostle's application of these
verbs would support our proposal of a relationship between Rom
3:31 and 4:1-25 if it could be substantiated.[54] In this case
Paul would be establishing the law by demonstrating from the
law itself (Rom 4) his doctrine of justification by faith.

Yet, in spite of the purported parallels,[55] there is
little, if any, evidence that בטל and קום were employed jointly
as exegetical terms to describe annulling or, conversely,
upholding the law (the Torah) by means of one's teaching and
interpretation of Scripture.[56] While קום may refer to the
exegetical process by which one establishes a scriptural text
that seems to conflict with one's opinion (e.g., Mekilta on
Ex 14:29),[57] בטל simply is not used as an exegetical term much
less connected with קום in exegetical parlance.

Moreover, Paul uses καταργεῖν and ἱστάνειν frequently
enough in other contexts to render unnecessary and even dubious
an appeal to a possible rabbinic background for understanding
these terms. As in the case of the law, we find καταργεῖν used
with other important theological concepts, for example, God's
faithfulness (Rom 3:3), the promise (Rom 4:14; Gal 3:17), death
(1 Cor 15:26), glory (2 Cor 3:7) and the cross (Gal 5:11).

Likewise, the apostle employs ἱστάνειν with the central theological concept of righteousness (Rom 10:3). Thus, on the basis of Pauline usage, καταργεῖν would mean "to make ineffective, powerless, idle,"[58] while ἱστάνειν would mean "to establish, confirm, make or consider valid."[59]

Having examined these pivotal concepts, we are ready to explain the significance of Rom 3:31. Paul's question (3:31a) presupposes the previous discussion (3:21-30) where he vigorously claims that all are justified by faith and not by the works of the law. This assertion of the universal character of justification by faith and, conversely, this denial of the saving role of the law provoke the question whether Paul invalidates the law, God's revelation, by his teaching about justification by faith (3:31a): "Do we then (οὖν) overthrow the law by this faith."

Because Paul understands the law as a "law of faith" (3:27e), a law that bears witness to righteousness by faith (3:21b-22), it is unthinkable to accuse him of invalidating the law, even though he denies the validity of its works for salvation. Thus he responds: "By no means (μὴ γένοιτο, 3:31b)!" To this the apostle adds: "On the contrary (ἀλλά), we uphold the law (3:31c)." Thus his categorical rejection of the saving role of the law (3:28-30) elicits the question (3:31a) that permits Paul to resume the as yet undeveloped notion of the law's positive association with righteousness by faith (3:21b-22, 27e). For, as in those texts, so also here the law is allied positively with faith. Indeed, the law is established, not abolished, by faith (3:31c).

Where the apostle justifies or explains how faith establishes the law is the crucial issue we are seeking to address. Concluding our analysis of Paul's use of questions negated by μὴ γένοιτο,[60] we suggested that his statement that faith upholds the law sets the theme for Rom 4 and, therefore, best accounts for the introduction of his midrash on Abraham at this point in the letter. Hence, we must turn at last to the exegesis of this passage in order to ascertain if, in fact, it develops this theme and explains his other positive assertions about the law (3:21b-22, 27e).

The Exegesis of Romans 4:1-25

Before embarking on the exegesis of this passage, several preliminary remarks are in order. First, regardless of their stance on the relationship between Rom 3:31 and Rom 4, scholars have generally understood Rom 4 as a Scripture proof for Paul's doctrine of justification by faith (3:21-30). Although it may indeed provide such proof, the preceding question and reply (3:31) indicate that something else is at stake. As we have already argued,[61] the apostle uses questions negated by μὴ γένοιτο to pinpoint and then overcome certain false conclusions which could be drawn from what he has said. This process often involves him in a lengthy explanation or grounding of a counter-thesis (cf. Rom 7:7-12, 13-25; 11:11-32). Accordingly, Rom 4 can be seen as Paul's attempt to overthrow the false inference that faith abolishes the law (3:31a) but especially to expand his counter-assertion that faith actually establishes the law (3:31c). For this purpose he turns to the law itself, the principal authority in Judaism, and to its witness concerning Abraham.

When we inquire why Paul moves back to the case of Abraham, several answers merit consideration. Besides the fact that Gen 15:6 is perhaps the clearest expression of the Pauline conception of justification by faith in the OT and may also have formed the center of the Jewish position in opposition to Paul, another reason suggests itself. As Joseph Huby[62] recognizes, the question the apostle raises (3:31a) is basically one of continuity. Can the continuity between the Christian message of justification by faith and the Torah, the cornerstone of the religion of Judaism, be maintained? Actually, the only way in which this continuity can be upheld is to carry the matter of the proper understanding of salvation back to its origin, that is, to Abraham, the fountain head of God's chosen people. If Paul can show from the law's statements about Abraham that justification is truly by faith, then he maintains the continuity between the Christian message and the law and, consequently, upholds the law (3:31c).

In order to show from the case of Abraham that the law witnesses to righteousness by faith, Paul does two things:

first, he gives the law's testimony; second, he separates
Abraham's justification from works and circumcision and, thus,
from the mediacy of the law. Using selected texts from the
Abraham stories (primarily Gen 15:6), he focuses particularly
on the witness of the law to the exclusion of boasting on the
grounds of the performance of its works (Rom 4:1-8; see 3:27)
and to the universal character of justification by faith not
by the works of the law (4:9-22; see 3:28-30). Once the
apostle has finished his explanation, he will have established
the validity of the law in its role as a witness (3:21, 27)
and, consequently, its validity in the church where one
believes in order to be justified (4:23-25; see 3:31).[63]

As we have already intimated in so many words, the new
question about Abraham (4:1) is apparently the apostle's way
of introducing a needed explanation or grounding of his brief
counter-assertion (3:31c) by giving a midrash on the Pentateuchal account of the patriarch: τί οὖν ἐροῦμεν εὑρηκέναι
'Αβραὰμ τὸν προπάτορα ἡμῶν κατὰ σάρκα; The objection that the
conjunction οὖν (4:1, often used inferentially) is not the
natural one to introduce the proof of an immediately preceding
statement cannot repudiate this connection between Rom 3:31c
and 4:1.[64] For one thing, it is possible, as happens with
other questions negated by μὴ γένοιτο,[65] to regard Rom 4:1ff.
as not strictly bringing proof but rather clarification of Paul's
counter-thesis (3:31c).

Moreover, this objection isolates the conjunction οὖν
from its use in the idiomatic expression, τί οὖν ἐροῦμεν.
Though this expression at times introduces inferences drawn
from Paul's argument (see 6:1; 7:7; 8:31; 9:14; cf. 3:5), it
functions first of all as a deliberative question.[66] When one
looks at the entire sweep of the question, it becomes evident
there is a difference between its use here and in those
instances cited above. In the latter it can be translated
separately; in the former it forms part of the sentence as a
whole: "What then shall we say was gained by Abraham, our
forefather according to the flesh (RSV margin)?"[67] In addition, the conjunction οὖν is not always inferential but may
function in other ways, for example, transitionally (cf. Rom
9:30).[68]

Finally, the parallel in Epictetus[69] shows that it is possible to introduce the explanation of a counter-thesis (ἀλλά) after a question negated by μὴ γένοιτο by means of the conjunction οὖν. Therefore, we conclude that this question (4:1) calls on Paul's readers to join him in contemplating the case of Abraham as a way of illustrating his claim that he upholds the law by his message about faith.

Beyond the difficulty occasioned by the transition from Rom 3:31c to 4:1, the textual variation and the application of the phrase κατὰ σάρκα have hampered the understanding of Paul's question in this verse. The textual variation involves the addition or omission of a word (εὑρηκέναι), the transposition of a word (εὑρηκέναι) and the substitution of words (προπάτορα/πατέρα). While some[70] view the shorter reading as original, taking εὑρηκέναι to be an explanatory addition as its different positions in the text would seem to indicate, Hans Lietzmann's inclination[71] to adopt the longer reading with it seems more plausible.

Therefore, we are adopting the reading, εὑρηκέναι Ἀβραὰμ τὸν προπάτορα ἡμῶν. In this reading εὑρηκέναι appears before Ἀβραάμ in the sentence, separated from κατὰ σάρκα. Though some[72] want to connect κατὰ σάρκα with this verb rather than with τὸν προπάτορα ἡμῶν, others[73] rightly relate it to the latter. Hence, the question is basically the following: What then shall we say Abraham, our (the Jews') human forefather, has found? By his introduction of προπάτωρ Paul sets the stage antithetically for his subsequent discussion of Abraham's spiritual fatherhood (see vv. 11-16).[74] Moreover, as Michel[75] suggests, Paul's use of εὑρίσκειν may be prompted by the common septuagintal expression, εὑρίσκειν χάριν (see, e.g., Gen 18:3). With this question Paul asks his readers to deliberate with him about what Abraham experienced in relation to God in the pre-Christian era. As Wilckens[76] points out, the only answer can be that he experienced grace (So Rom 4:4).

In the next two verses Paul indicates what he considers to be the wrong (4:2) and the right answer (4:3) to his question about Abraham's relation to God (4:1). First, he explains (γάρ) that if Abraham was justified by works (of the law),[77] he has a ground for boasting (4:2ab). This conditional sentence is most likely real, for Paul can hypothetically take up an opposing view in order to reject its premises (as he does in 4:2c).[78] It is not necessary to introduce a πρὸς ἄνθρωπον at the end of this sentence (4:2b) as though Abraham might have a ground for boasting "before men" but not before God.[79] The apostle's subsequent rejection (4:2c) may apply to the entire sentence if not more specifically to the protasis (4:2a; cf. Rom 3:20, 27-28).

That Abraham achieved righteousness by the works of the law was the subject of Jewish speculation prior to Paul. Thus Sirach praises the patriarch: "He kept the law of the Most High, and was taken into covenant with him; he established the covenant in his flesh, and when he was tested he was found faithful (44:20)." In the Book of Jubilees, Abraham's perfection is lauded: "For Abraham was perfect in all his deeds with the Lord, and well-pleasing in righteousness all the days of his life (23:10a)." In these cases it is apparently assumed that Abraham had the law in some form and obeyed it faithfully.[80]

By taking up the concept of boasting (4:2ab) Paul returns to his previous discussion, where he states that the "law of faith" not the "law of works" has excluded boasting (3:27).[81] Now he will finally reveal the content of this "law of faith" which excludes boasting. To the suggestion that Abraham was justified by works and thus has a ground for boasting (4:2ab; cf. 3:27a), the apostle answers: ἀλλ' οὐ πρὸς θεόν, that is, not in God's sight (4:2c; cf. 3:27b). God's viewpoint is represented in the Scripture, here a synonym for the law in a broader sense (Rom 4:3; Gen 15:6; cf. Gal 3:6):[82] "For what does the scripture say? 'Abraham believed God, and it was reckoned to him as righteousness.'" While the "law of faith" (3:27e), apparently the law in its role as witness (3:21b), excludes boasting generally, here the law (the Scripture) in its role as witness provides the basis for the exclusion of boasting in the particular case of Abraham.

In other words, if the law taught that Abraham was justified by works, then he would have a ground for boasting (4:2ab). This ground would eliminate Paul's thesis of justification by faith alone and his claim to validate the law by

his message of faith. If Abraham was justified by works (of
the law), Paul would be invalidating the law by proclaiming
faith, because the law as a "law of works" would be more correctly appreciated as prescribing works than as attesting
faith (cf. 3:27d).

But, if the law declares that Abraham was justified by
faith not by works (of the law), then he has no ground for
boasting (4:2c). The absence of such a ground would support
Paul's thesis of justification by faith alone and his claim
to validate the law by his message of faith. If Abraham was
justified by faith, Paul would be validating the law by proclaiming faith, because the law as a "law of faith" actually
bears witness to righteousness by faith rather than by works
(4:3; cf. 3:21b, 27e).[83]

In his recourse to the Scripture (the law) Paul appeals
to a text (Gen 15:6; Rom 4:3) that was understood in some Jewish circles as a reference to Abraham's justification by works.
Perhaps the clearest example is the statement found in 1 Maccabees 2:52: "Was not Abraham found faithful when tested, and
it was reckoned to him as righteousness." The testing mentioned in this text evidently refers to Abraham's "sacrifice"
of Isaac (Gen 22; cf. Jas 2:21-23). As can be seen from the
Maccabean passage, πίστις and its cognates are understood in
the sense of "faithfulness."[84]

That Paul is not working here with such an understanding of πίστις becomes evident in the following verses, where
he defines more precisely what it means (4:4-5). First, he
maintains (4:4) that if one works, his wages are not counted
as a gift (κατὰ χάριν) but as a debt (κατὰ ὀφείλημα). But the
Genesis passage says nothing about Abraham's working.[85] Thus
Paul can conclude that if one does not work but believes on
the one who justifies the ungodly, his faith is reckoned to
him as righteousness (4:5; cf. 3:20-22, 27-28; 4:6).[86] Understood in the light of the OT context (Gen 15:1-5) it becomes
clear that for Paul faith is trust in God and his promise and,
therefore, the opposite of works.

Significantly, this faith is directed toward the One
who justifies the ungodly (ἀσεβής, cf. 4:6-8). To assert that
Abraham's faith was reckoned to him as righteousness and thus

he had no ground for boasting on the basis of his works (4:5a) apparently means he must be aligned with the ungodly (cf. 1:18; 5:6).[87] This conclusion seems to run counter to the OT idea that God does not justify the ungodly[88] and to the Jewish notion that God justifies only the godly, those who keep the law (see Rom 9:32; 10:5).[89] For Paul, however, it is essential to his teaching of justification by faith alone, because it is predicated on the universal sinfulness of humanity and, consequently, on the universal need of forgiving grace (see 1:18-3:20; 3:22-23, 28). This justification of the ungodly can take place only because God has revealed his righteousness in forgiving sins and in justifying the believer through the Christ event (3:24-26).

In the following verses (4:6-8) Paul supports (καθάπερ) from Scripture his assertion that the ungodly is justified by faith not by works, citing the words of David about the blessing of having one's sins forgiven (Ps 32:1-2). It is widely postulated that the apostle is using here the rabbinic exegetical principle of *gezerah shawah* (inference by analogy).[90] This principle assumes that the similarity of expression of two biblical texts or laws implies an analogy of interpretation between them. Such analogy could be used for solving lexicographical problems or contradictions within Scripture and for expanding or applying the law.

While the presence of the verb λογίζεσθαι in the Psalm text could have prompted Paul to associate this passage with Gen 15:6,[91] it is not readily evident that the analogy (Ps 32:1-2) actually serves to clarify the meaning of this term in the Genesis passage.[92] In fact, the apostle betrays no concern over the meaning of λογίζεσθαι. Rather he seems to use the Psalm passage in an ad hoc fashion to furnish additional scriptural proof for his argument about Abraham, especially the fact of his ungodliness (cf. 4:5). Moreover, as W. Sibley Towner[93] argues, it is difficult to detect here any formal, stereotyped structure in the text like that which is present in the rabbinic application of the *gezerah shawah*.

Accordingly, we can affirm with Hans Wolfgang Heidland that the Genesis text is not to be equated with the one from the Psalms, as though the imputation of faith as righteousness and the non-imputation of sin are identical. But, as Heidland says, Ps 32:1-2 "provides the negative basis of the antithesis δικαιοσύνη χωρὶς ἔργων (v. 6) as Gn. 15:6 had previously provided the positive basis."[94] The Psalm text shows that justification is not a reckoning of good works but a non-reckoning of sin (cf. 2 Cor 5:19). If the reckoning of faith as righteousness includes the non-reckoning of sin, then Abraham could really be called "ungodly," for his faith was reckoned to him as righteousness. Moreover, if the reckoning of faith as righteousness is not a reckoning of good works, then the efficacy of works would be excluded in Abraham's reception of God's gift of righteousness.

In this manner Paul has overturned the Jewish position that Abraham's relation to God was based on his works (so 4:2a) and is well on his way to illustrating his thesis that he establishes the law by faith (3:31c), for the law bears witness to righteousness by faith as the case of Abraham shows (Gen 15:6).

With his new question (4:9) Paul focuses again on his main text, Gen 15:6 (see 4:9b), describing what is reported about Abraham there as a "blessing" (cf. 4:6-8): "Is this blessing pronounced only on the circumcised, or also upon the uncircumcised? We say that faith was reckoned to Abraham as righteousness."[95] This question and the subsequent one (4:10) inquire about the circumstances which surrounded Abraham's justification. The apostle intends to remove any possible dependence of Abraham's justification on his circumcision. This rite, which initiated all male Israelites into the covenant community (so Gen 17), had become in the Jewish mind a guarantee of the saving relationship with God (so Rom 2:25-29). According to Paul, it obligated one to keep the whole law (so Gal 5:3). Thus, as Christian Dieztzfelbinger[96] argues, circumcision functions here as a type of the law.

Paul's answer (4:10) that justification is not tied causally to circumcision is based on the chronological priority of Abraham's justification (Gen 15:6) to his circumcision (Gen 17:1-14, 22-27). Since Abraham's circumcision occurred some thirty years[97] after his justification, Paul is confident that the reckoning of his faith as righteousness took place while he was uncircumcised. Thus Abraham was justified as a Gentile (ἐν ἀκροβυστίᾳ) not as a Jew (ἐν περιτομῇ) and that by faith. In this way Scripture excludes the role of works, even that of circumcision, in Abraham's justification.

Though circumcision had no role in Abraham's salvation, this sign[98] still functioned as a seal of the righteousness by faith which he received while still uncircumcised (4:11ab). As a seal, Abraham's circumcision simply ratified the righteousness by faith that he had received before being circumcised (cf. 1 Cor 9:2).[99] Circumcision, therefore, played no effectual part in Abraham's justification.

What happened to Abraham, both his justification by faith and, above all, his later circumcision (4:11ab), had a divine purpose. First, it occurred in order that he might be the father of all those who believe as uncircumcised, that is, the Gentile Christians,[100] so that righteousness might be reckoned to them (4:11cd). At this juncture Paul abandons the physical use of "father" in reference to Abraham (4:1) and takes up a purely spiritual application of the term, which he seems to employ uniformly in what follows (4:12, 16-18; cf. Gal 3:7). By this redefinition of the term "father" as it applies to the patriarch, Paul is able to include Gentiles within its scope.

The Jews attached great spiritual advantages to this physical descent from Abraham.[101] Only Jews and perhaps proselytes[102] to Judaism could lay claim to these advantages. Now the apostle calls Abraham the "father" of all the uncircumcised who believe, thereby refuting purely physical claims to this spiritual kinship. This kinship consists in the fact that all the Gentile Christians have received the same divine verdict as Abraham whose faith was reckoned to him as righteousness while he was a "Gentile" (cf. 4:23-24).[103] In this manner Paul eliminates the relevance of circumcision and thus of becoming a proselyte in order to attain the benefits of Abrahamic sonship.[104]

Second, Abraham's experience (Gen 15, 17) also came about in order that he might be πατέρα περιτομῆς τοῖς οὐκ ἐκ περιτομῆς μόνον ἀλλὰ καὶ τοῖς στοιχοῦσιν τοῖς ἴχνεσιν τῆς ἐν ἀκροβυστίᾳ πίστεως τοῦ πατρὸς ἡμῶν Ἀβραάμ (4:12). The

presence of the article τοῖς before στοιχοῦσιν represents a
major difficulty for the interpretation of this verse. This
second article leaves the impression that Paul is speaking
of two distinct groups when he refers to Abraham as πατέρα
περιτομῆς (cf. 4:16). There has been a common tendency among
scholars to strike out this article, regarding it as a stylistic or scribal error, or to emend the text in some way as, for
example, changing τοῖς to αὐτοῖς, and thus to understand this
verse as a reference to Jewish Christians who not only share
Abraham's circumcision but also the faith which he had before
being circumcised.[105]

Objecting that this approach places circumcision on
the same footing as faith as far as claiming Abrahamic sonship
is concerned and pointing to what he regards as analogous texts
(see Rom 2:26, 28-29; Phil 3:3; Col 2:11-12), Lucien Cerfaux
argues that the first occurrence of περιτομή in this verse
denotes "spiritual circumcision" and thus embraces all Christians. According to Cerfaux, the first group (4:12a) are Jewish Christians, the second (4:12b) Gentile Christians. Hence
he paraphrases:

> Et il est père en circoncision (de tous les chrétiens),
> de ceux de la circoncision, et non seulement de ceux-ci,
> mais encore de tous ceux que marchent sur les traces de
> la foi, reçue dans l'incirconcision, de notre père
> Abraham (v. 12).[106]

While Cerfaux's interpretation has some merit, his positioning
of οὐ μόνον ("non seulement") in the translation is indefen-
sible despite the evidence he produces.[107]

Thus, none of these solutions is able to deal to complete satisfaction with the presence of the second τοῖς without
resorting to elision, emendation or uncharacteristic interpretation of the terminology of the text. However, it is clear
that Abraham, by virtue of his own circumcision after his justification by faith (4:11a), can be the "father of circumcision" to those Jews who, though already circumcised, believe
like him for their justification. Only after they believe can
their circumcision be properly related to kinship with Abraham.[108] Even though faith is now subsequent to circumcision,
it still retains its unique efficacy for the individual's justification.

With the explanatory sentence (γάρ, 4:13) Paul grounds his rejection of the works (of the law) and of circumcision as means to righteousness (so 4:1-12):[109] "The promise to Abraham and his descendants, that they should inherit the world, did not come through the law but through the righteousness of faith." For the first time since Rom 3:31 Paul uses the specific term νόμος. The reappearance of this term should not surprise us for it shows that Paul has not strayed from the thesis with which he introduced the discussion of Abraham (3:31c). Moreover, as we have argued, Paul evidently uses the concepts of works (4:2-8) and circumcision (4:9-12) as synonyms for the law viewed as a "law of works," as a law that prescribes works and, thus, can become an impulse to spiritual boasting (cf. 3:27d).

As in Gal 3, the apostle takes up the concept of promise (ἐπαγγελία) in his discussion of justification by faith. Scholars have noted that Paul distinguishes within the law (understood in a broader sense) between the promise and the law or rather the works of the law. Therefore, Friedrich[110] suggests that ἐπαγγελία here is practically synonymous with νόμος πίστεως (3:27e), because the promise is found in the law itself. Given to Abraham and his seed (σπέρμα), this promise entailed the inheritance of the world. The inheritance of Canaan promised to Abraham and his descendants (Gen 15:7, 18-21) had subsequently taken on universal dimensions (so Sirach 44:21).[111] For Paul it has also assumed an eschatological reference (1 Cor 6:2). With his use of σπέρμα he apparently envisions believers rather than the physical progeny of Abraham.[112]

In rejecting the law's role in communicating this promised inheritance, Paul seemingly introduces into the Genesis account of Abraham a conflict not explicitly stated there. In fact, Gen 26:1-5 flatly contradicts his viewpoint. But, as Dietzfelbinger[113] explains, Paul's interpretation of the Abraham stories is not based solely on the contents of the text but on his understanding of the Christ event.

By νόμος, then, the apostle apparently has in mind the works of the law both here and in the following verses (cf. 3:20-21, 27-28; 4:2, 4-6).[114] The law does not mediate the

Exegesis of Rom 3:21-4:25

promise; on the contrary, the promise comes διὰ δικαιοσύνης πίστεως, that is, through the righteousness which believers have acquired by their faith.[115] So Paul argues that Abraham and his spiritual offspring obtain the divine promise only because they have been justified by faith.

However, the apostle feels it necessary to ground (γάρ, 4:14) this rejection of the law and corresponding affirmation of righteousness by faith (4:13). His elimination of the law as a means of obtaining the inheritance is based on his conviction that one way of salvation excludes the other. Therefore, if those whose claim to the inheritance is their possession and performance of the law should turn out to be heirs, then faith as the way of attaining righteousness would be vain and the promise which comes through this righteousness of faith would be invalidated (cf. 4:4-5, 16; Gal 3:18). Stated in terms of human experience, it would mean that those who have exercised faith have done so vainly and that, consequently, they will not inherit the promise.

That the law is not a way of salvation and thus is not in competition with faith as Rom 4:14 proposes can be seen from the role it actually plays (4:15). The apostle explains (γάρ, 4:15a) that the law produces wrath which is really the opposite of the promise (see 1:18; 3:19; 7:7-12). To this Paul adds (δέ, 4:15b) that in the absence of the law there is no transgression. This is so because for him transgression is the willful disobedience of a divine command made known in the law.[116] Moreover, in Paul's way of thinking, the law not only makes transgressions known but also promotes them (see 3:20; 5:20; 7:7-12; Gal 3:19). Thus, where the law is present transgressions occur and the transgressor incurs God's wrath not his salvation.

In view of (διὰ τοῦτο)[117] this damning function of the law, Paul can confidently assert that the inheritance[118] is based on faith so that it may be a gift (4:16ab; cf. 4:4-5). The purpose of this grace character of the inheritance is that the promise might be confirmed to all the spiritual descendants of Abraham, not to those who possess and perform the law alone, but also to those who have believed as Abraham (4:16cd). If

the inheritance is based on faith and is a gift, then all of
Abraham's spiritual descendants, whether Jews or Gentiles, can
receive it.[119]

Consisting of two extended relative clauses (4:16e-17
and 18-21), the next five verses describe Abraham and his
faith. The first clause begins with the statement, ὅς ἐστιν
πατὴρ πάντων ἡμῶν, which recapitulates what has just been said
(4:16cd) and elicits its own Scripture proof (4:17a): "As
(καθώς) it is written, 'I have made you the father of many
nations.'" This short text (Gen 17:5) is apparently designed
to bolster Paul's claim that Abraham is the "father" of all
believers, but especially of Gentile Christians, οἱ ἐκ πίστεως
Ἀβραάμ. Thus he understands πολλὰ ἔθνη as referring to the
"Gentiles" who have embraced a faith like that of Abraham (cf.
Gal 3:8).[120]

The attached clause (4:17b) indicates Abraham's
response to the divine promise recorded in Scripture (4:17a)
and moves the discussion toward a comparison of the faith of
Abraham to that of Christians. The awkward connection of
κατέναντι οὗ ἐπίστευσεν θεοῦ with what precedes may be due to
the attraction of the relative, the complete thought being
κατέναντι τοῦ θεοῦ ᾧ ἐπίστευσεν.[121] Though it is customary to
relate 4:17b to the previous relative clause (4:16e) as
explaining that Abraham is "father" of us all in God's
sight,[122] Käsemann's contention[123] that it should be connected
with the subject (God) of τέθεικα (4:17a) may be closer to
Paul's intention, for it discloses Abraham's response over
against God's promise and opens the way for the apostle's
treatment of Abraham's faith in the matter of the miraculous
birth of Isaac (4:17b-21; Gen 17-18, 21).

Abraham's faith in the God who promised that he would
be the "father" of many nations is depicted here as faith in
the God who brings the dead back to life and calls the non-
existent into existence. Using these prevalent Jewish epi-
thets for the God of Israel,[124] Paul envisions the quickening
of the body of Abraham and of the womb of Sarah (cf. 4:19)
but, more importantly, sets the stage for a comparison between
Abraham's faith and that of Christians (cf. 4:24). By connect-
ing Abraham's faith (Gen 15:6) to the promise that he would be

Exegesis of Rom 3:21-4:25

the "father" of many nations (Gen 17:5) and then of the miracle child Isaac (Gen 17:15-21; 18:9-15; 21:1-7), Paul seemingly goes beyond the OT text.[125] Nevertheless, this hermeneutical maneuver is not entirely arbitrary, for Gen 15 links the patriarch's faith to the promise of an innumerable posterity (cf. Gen 15:6 with 15:5 [Rom 4:18b] and Gen 15:5 with 17:5 [Rom 4:18a, 17a], 6, 17).

In the second extended relative clause Paul continues his description of Abraham's faith (4:18a). He believed against hope in hope. When human hope was exhausted (cf. 4:19), God-given hope came into operation (cf. 4:20-21).[126] The result of Abraham's faith was that he became the "father of many nations" (Gen 17:5; cf. Rom 4:17a).[127] This fatherhood came about in accordance with the divine promise: "So shall your descendants be (4:18b; see Gen 15:5)." Thus, as we have already indicated, by linking this promise to the similar one (Gen 17:5; Rom 4:17a, 18a), Paul connects Gen 17:5 to Abraham's righteousness by faith (Gen 15:6) and thereby to the principal text treated in Rom 4 (cf. also 4:22).

While the preceding verse stated that Abraham believed against hope in hope, the following verses spell out more clearly the radical nature of this belief (4:19-21). Without weakening in his fatih, Abraham considered[128] his own body as good as dead, since he was about a hundred years old, and the deadness of Sarah's womb (4:19). As Cranfield suggests, Paul may be reflecting on Abraham's statement in Gen 17:17 "as the expression not of unbelief but of an honest and clear-sighted recognition of the facts of the situation."[129]

In the next two verses (4:20-21) Paul concludes his description of Abraham's faith. The patriarch did not waver in unbelief with respect to God's promise (Gen 15:5; 17:5) but became strong in his faith (4:20a). This comparison between wavering in unbelief and being empowered in faith reveals "the true nature of faith by showing it in its opposition to, and victory over, unbelief."[130] At the same time Abraham gave glory to God (4:20b). His faith permitted him to do what sinful humanity was apparently unwilling to do (cf. Rom 1:21-23).[131] Moreover, he was fully persuaded that God was also able to do what he had promised (4:21).

At 4:22 the apostle expresses the outcome (διό) of Abraham's undaunted faith: "That is why his faith was 'reckoned to him as righteousness.'" Because Abraham's faith in God and his promise was like that which Paul has just described (4:17-21), God reckoned it to him as righteousness.[132] Abraham's reception of the promised child by faith was, in retrospect, the reason for his faith's being reckoned to him as righteousness (Gen 15:6).

In returning to Gen 15:6 by way of conclusion (4:22), Paul brings us back to Rom 4:1-3, where he first raised the matter of Abraham's justification and introduced this crucial text. The significance of this fact should not be underestimated. As we have argued, in this text the law (the Pentateuch) speaks in favor of justification by faith and substantiates Paul's claim that he does not annul the law by preaching faith (3:31c). Therefore, it is not surprising that at this juncture Paul raises the issue of the validity of this particular text of Scripture for the present. He asserts that the statement, "it was reckoned to him" (short for Gen 15:6), was not written down only for Abraham's sake (as a memorial of him)[133] but also for us to whom it (faith) would be reckoned (as righteousness), who believe on the One who raised Jesus our Lord from the dead (4:23-24).

The apostle discerns a divine intention (ἐγράφη διά) in the recording of Abraham's story, first in relation to Abraham himself but, more importantly, in relation to contemporary Christians (4:23-24a; cf. Rom 15:4; 1 Cor 9:9-10; 10:11). The scriptural report about Abraham serves as a witness[134] of righteousness by faith (3:21b-22) to us, to whom faith would be reckoned as righteousness.[135] These decisive verses show that Paul's interest in this chapter has not been simply to prove the doctrine of justification by faith but rather to meet head on the question of the law's validity in the preaching of the apostle.

On the basis of the correspondence between Abraham's faith and ours, Paul can assert the validity of the scriptural witness for our time. Consequently, he describes our faith as lodged in One who raised Jesus our Lord from the dead (4:24b; cf. 4:18-19). With Leonard Goppelt[136] we may view this correspondence as essentially typological. The righteousness of faith of Christians is the intensified correspondence to that of Abraham. He believed with respect to his and Sarah's barrenness that God would raise up for him a posterity; Christians believe with respect to the cross in the God who raised Jesus.

By means of the attached relative clause (4:25), which probably represents a pre-Pauline formula,[137] the apostle binds the faith of the Christians (4:24b) to the person of Jesus and to the salvation given in his death and resurrection.[138] Jesus' death and resurrection bring in the ultimate salvation, that is, forgiveness of transgressions and justification (cf. 3:24-26). With this verse his treatment of Abraham is concluded and the way is prepared for his discussion of the results of justification (Rom 5:1-11).

Conclusion

With our exegesis concluded we can now recapitulate Paul's argument in Rom 3:21-4:25 while glancing back at our original question about the status of the law as one of the basic elements of continuity between Judaism and Christianity. At the first crucial turning point in the epistle the apostle reports the manifestation of God's righteousness apart from the law (3:21a). Though God does not take the law into account in the manifestation of this righteousness, a righteousness given impartially to all through faith in Jesus Christ, it is witnessed by the law and the prophets (3:21b-22). For the moment, Paul does not particularize about the content of this witness. It is the universal sinfulness and degradation of humanity, he explains, that excludes the law and necessitates faith as the way of obtaining righteousness (3:23). Adapting a traditional formula, Paul describes God's activity in the person of Jesus Christ in providing this righteousness (3:24-26).

In what follows (3:27-30) he sharpens his emphasis on righteousness by faith, first by focusing on the Jew's boast in the possession of the law and the performance of its works (3:27-28). To the question about the possibility of

boasting (3:27a) in view of the redeeming work of Christ and
of the sinfulness of humanity, Paul answers that it is
excluded (3:27b). Yet he still asks by what kind of "law"
such boasting is excluded (3:27c), thus intentionally inquiring about the nature of that "law" which has excluded boasting.
Boasting is eliminated not by the "law of works" but by the
"law of faith" (3:27de). On the one hand, the "law of works"
is the OT law viewed primarily from the perspective of the
works it calls for and thus as an impulse to boasting. On the
other hand, the "law of faith" is the same law viewed primarily
from the perspective of the faith to which it bears witness
and thus as an inhibition to boasting (cf. 3:21b). Again,
Paul does not enter into detail about the content of this
"law of faith," but supports his assertion (3:27de) by expressing the judgment that one is justified by faith not by the
works of the law (3:28).

Second, Paul argues from the unity of God for this
thesis of justification by faith apart from the works of the
law (3:29-30). Since God is God of both the Jews and the
Gentiles, this unity of lordship requires also that he act
uniformly with humanity. Thus the apostle can confidently
insist that God justifies both the circumcision (the Jews) and
the uncircumcision (the Gentiles) by faith.

In view of Paul's disassociation of the works of the
law from righteousness by faith (3:28-30) the question arises
whether Paul overthrows the law by preaching faith (3:31a).
He replies that, to the contrary, he establishes the law through
faith (3:31bc). Previous statements of Paul have already
hinted at his meaning here. His preaching of faith as the
means to righteousness establishes the law because the law
witnesses to righteousness by faith (3:21b-22) and can itself
be called a "law of faith" (3:27e). Now he is ready to reveal
the content of this witness of the law to justification by
faith. As our analysis of the apostle's use of questions
negated by μὴ γένοιτο has credibly shown, it is to clarify
his counter-thesis that faith establishes the law (3:31c) that
Paul turns to the law's account of the patriarch Abraham
(4:1-25).

Exegesis of Rom 3:21-4:25   91

     Beginning with a rhetorical question (4:1), Paul moves
to the case of Abraham to explain from the law itself that
faith has always been the basis of justification (4:2-3). If
justification is by works, then God becomes indebted to the
one who works and the factor of grace is eliminated (4:4).
But when a person does not rely on works for justification but
believes on the One who justifies the ungodly, his faith is
reckoned to him as righteousness (4:5). That God indeed justifies the ungodly through faith apart from works can be seen in
David's words about the blessing of forgiveness (4:6-8).
     Returning to the story of Abraham, Paul argues from
the chronological priority of Abraham's justification that
faith has always been the basis of justification since it
occurred before the administration of circumcision, that rite
which inducts one into the community of the law (4:9-10).
Therefore, his circumcision was only a seal, a ratification of
the righteousness which Abraham already possessed (4:11a).
The fact that Abraham's justification preceded his circumcision enables him to be the spiritual "father" of Gentile as
well as Jewish Christians (4:11b-12).
     If works (4:2-8) and circumcision (4:9-12) played no
effective role in Abraham's justification, then we can rule
out the works of the law, for the promise to Abraham and his
descendants that they would be heirs of the world was not
actuated through the law but through the righteousness of
faith (4:13). In reality, faith and the works of the law are
mutually exclusive as ways of salvation, because the law produces wrath, which is the opposite of the promise (4:14-15).
Thus, the inheritance is received graciously through faith so
that the promise may be assured to all of Abraham's posterity,
not only to the Jewish but also to the Gentile Christians
(4:16a-d).
     This Abraham is father of us all as God affirms in
Scripture (4:16e-17a). Faced with this divine promise, Abraham believed God as One who brings the dead back to life and
calls the non-existent into existence (4:17b). In spite of
the futility of human hope this same Abraham believed in hope
with the result that he became the father of many nations
according to God's promise recorded in Scripture (4:18). Even

when he considered the deadness of his body and of Sarah's womb, his faith did not weaken (4:19). In fact, he did not waver in unbelief as he contemplated God's promise but became strong in faith (4:20a). At the same time he gave glory to God and was fully convinced of God's ability to keep his promise (4:20b-21). As a result, Abraham's faith (4:17-21) was reckoned to him as righteousness (4:22).

In conclusion, Paul argues that the correspondence between Abraham's faith and that of Christians links Abraham with the first century, enabling the law's word to retain its validity for the present time (4:23-25). Thus the scriptural report about Abraham's faith serves as a witness to righteousness by faith (3:21b-22) for contemporary Christians and shows that Paul's preaching of faith upholds the law (3:31c).

Within Rom 4 we see the same dialectic over the law that we found earlier. In Rom 3:21a the law is severed from righteousness by faith, but then reassociated with it (3:21b-22). In Rom 3:27 the law is detached from righteousness by faith (3:27d) and at the same time associated with it (3:27e). Moreover, the law is disassociated from righteousness by faith in Rom 3:28-30 only to be reassociated with it in 3:31.

As in these instances, so also in Rom 4 the law is disassociated from righteousness by faith (4:2, 4-6, 9-10, 13-16). In this case the law is viewed from the perspective of the works which it prescribes and which can become a ground for boasting (cf. 3:27 with 4:2). On the other hand, the law is also associated with righteousness by faith (4:3, 9, 22-24). In this case the law is viewed from the perspective of its witness to righteousness by faith (cf. 3:21b-22, 27e, 31 with 4:3, 9, 22-24).

In view of these circumstances, Rom 4 leads us to conclude that, falsely conceived as a way of salvation, the law, particularly its works, is discontinuous with faith (so also 3:20-21a, 27-28). To this extent Judaism, as Paul confronted it (Rom 9:32; 10:5), is not continuous with Christianity. However, rightly understood as a witness to righteousness by faith, the law is continuous with faith (so also 3:21b-22, 27e, 31). To this extent Judaism, as Paul came to understand it *post Christum*, is not discontinuous with Christianity. Thus, with regard to the apostle's assertion that faith upholds the law (Rom 3:31c), we conclude that *it is the law in its role as witness that is established in the apostolic preaching of justification by faith as Rom 4 illustrates.*[139]

CHAPTER IV

ROMANS 10:4 ONCE MORE

Introduction

Because the central concepts of law, faith and righteousness reappear in Rom 9:30-10:21, it is important to consider this text, especially Rom 10:4, in connection with Rom 3:21-4:25. As we have already indicated, the interpretation of Rom 10:4, particularly of the word τέλος, is much disputed.[1] Nonetheless, in the discussion of this verse, scholars are in general agreement over certain points. For example, all admit the Greek word τέλος can have a wide range of meanings, depending, of course, on the context in which it is used.[2] Moreover, that the word νόμος refers to the OT law in some sense is widely held.[3] In addition, the subject of this elliptical sentence is Χριστός, τέλος νόμου being brought forward for emphasis. Finally, the conjunction γάρ shows that Rom 10:4 grounds or clarifies the preceding verses (10:2-3).

But, aside from this agreement, some[4] understand τέλος as "end" in the sense of termination and interpret the verse to mean Christ has ended the law as a way of salvation. They view this "end" of the law in either historical or existential categories.[5] Moreover, many insist this "termination" of the law occurs only in the realm of faith.[6]

On the contrary, taking τέλος as "goal" or "fulfilment," others[7] interpret Rom 10:4 to mean that in Christ the law has reached its goal or fulfilment. They regard this attainment of the goal of the law or fulfilment of the law through Christ in terms of its requirement or promise of righteousness.

Further, numerous scholars[8] attempt to mediate between these two extremes or to tone down the extremeness of their own positions by accepting both of the aforementioned approaches as proper interpretations of Rom 10:4. Thus we often hear, on the one hand, that what has reached its end has also reached its goal or been fulfilled and, on the other hand, that what has reached its goal or fulfilment, has also reached its end.[9]

In favor of the interpretation of Rom 10:4 which asserts that Christ has ended the law as a way of salvation, scholars have adduced several arguments. First, on the basis of Pauline usage, some[10] contend τέλος can only mean "end" in the sense of termination in this verse. Furthermore, the preceding context where Paul presumably opposes righteousness from the law to righteousness from faith (9:30-10:3) demands a negative understanding of the relationship between law and faith in Rom 10:4.[11] In addition, the following context where righteousness from the law is contrasted with righteousness from faith (cf. 10:5 with 10:6-8) supports this negative interpretation of the law in our text.[12] Finally, other passages in this epistle (3:21; 5:20; 7:1-6; 8:2-3) and Paul's theology in general (Galatians; 2 Cor 3; Phil 3) confirm the view that τέλος refers to the cessation of the law's role in salvation.[13]

Nevertheless, other scholars have raised several objections against this interpretation of τέλος in Rom 10:4. First, that Paul can use τέλος in the sense of "goal" or "fulfilment" even in Romans itself is clear (see 6:21-22).[14] Moreover, in the preceding section (9:30-10:3) the apostle does not actually oppose righteousness from the law to righteousness from faith but righteousness from works to righteousness from faith.[15] Furthermore, some[16] argue that Rom 10:5 and 10:6-8 do not stand in antithesis to one another and, therefore, do not imply a contrast between righteousness from the law and righteousness from faith. Also, it is difficult to perceive how a statement to the effect that Christ has ended the law can explain (γάρ, 10:4) the fact that Israel, ignoring God's righteousness and seeking to establish their own, did not submit to God's righteousness (10:2-3).[17] In addition, this interpretation weakens the connection between τέλος γάρ νόμου Χριστός and εἰς δικαιοσύνην παντί τῷ πιστεύοντι because it makes little sense to speak of an "end to or for righteousness."[18] Finally, such an understanding of Rom 10:4 suggests that prior to Christ the achievement of righteousness by the works of the law was a valid principle.[19]

In favor of the interpretation of Rom 10:4 which declares that Christ is the goal or fulfilment of the law, scholars have produced several arguments. First, this interpretation flows naturally from the preceding context (9:30-10:3) which is concerned with Israel's striving yet failing to attain to the "law of righteousness" (9:31-32) because they falsely understood works and rejected Christ who brings the righteousness which the law demands or promises.[20] Moreover, the interpretation of τέλος as "goal" or "fulfilment" explains more satisfactorily the connection between Rom 10:5 and 10:6-8, especially when one understands this connection as complementary rather than antithetical.[21] Also, when Paul understands Christ to stand in the place of the law by applying statements about the law from Deut 30:12-14 (Rom 10:6-8) to him, he can do this only if he regards Christ as the goal or fulfilment of the law.[22] Finally, this interpretation agrees with other Pauline statements concerning the law (cf. Rom 3:21, 31; 7:12; 8:4; 13:8-10; Gal 3:24).[23]

However, opponents have taken exception to this approach to Rom 10:4. For one thing, it stresses the connection of Rom 10:4 with the image of the race (9:30-31) at the risk of overlooking Paul's subsequent statements about the antithesis between works and faith (9:32-33).[24] For another, to interpret τέλος as "goal" or "fulfilment" does not do justice to the importance that the apocalyptic notion of the turn of the aeons plays in Paul.[25] Finally, this interpretation of Rom 10:4 in the sense that Christ is the "goal" or "fulfilment" of the law often grows out of the modern inquiry about the relationship between the OT and the NT.[26]

In view of this disagreement over the interpretation of Rom 10:4 and its context, it becomes necessary to examine the entire complex (Rom 9:30-10:21) in order to discover the significance that Rom 10:4 has for Paul's understanding of the law. At the same time we can bring to bear on this exegesis the results of our study of Rom 3:21-4:25, where the law receives a positive as well as a negative evaluation. The comparison of these two passages may reveal the unity, if any, in the apostle's view of the law.

The Exegesis of Romans 9:30-10:21

By dividing our exegesis of this passage in two sections, Rom 9:30-33 and 10:1-21, we hope to accomplish two things. First, we intend to point out the new turn that Paul's discussion takes at 10:1 but at the same time to underscore that this new twist does not indicate a change in theme. Second, in conjunction with the first objective, we want above all to stress the thematic importance that the first section, Rom 9:30-33, has for a proper understanding of Paul's subsequent discussion (10:1-21) and particularly of his much debated statement (Rom 10:4).

The Exegesis of Romans 9:30-33

This section of the epistle (along with 10:1-21) falls within chaps. 9-11, a passage usually treated as a unit. These chapters are concerned in particular with the wholesale unbelief of Israel vis-à-vis the gospel of justification by faith in Christ apart from the works of the law (Rom 1-8). They offer an explanation for this unbelief (chaps. 9-10) and a hopeful outlook for its subsequent reversal (chap. 11).

Having expressed his personal concern over the salvation of much advantaged Israel (9:1-5), Paul strongly asserts that God's word has not failed despite their unbelief (9:6-13). For it is God's sovereign election, not works, that determines who is called to salvation. In the ensuing discussion the apostle faces two possible misunderstandings of his notion of election, namely, that it compromises God's justice (9:14-18) and that it eliminates human accountability (9:19-29). He concludes his treatment of the second misunderstanding by contrasting and verifying scripturally the relative success of the gospel among the Gentiles with its relative failure among the Jews (9:24-29).

With the introductory question, "What shall we say, then (9:30a)?" Paul invites his readers to ponder the nature of the Gentiles' obedience (9:30) but primarily of the Jews' disobedience (9:31-10:21) in relation to the gospel.[27]

On the one hand, although they were not pursuing (διώκειν) righteousness (δικαιοσύνη), some Gentiles (i.e., Gentile Christians) obtained (καταλαμβάνειν) righteousness, that is, righteousness by faith (πίστις, 9:30bc). These Gentiles were not seeking after righteousness in terms of a right relationship with God as taught in the law (cf. 10:19-20).[28] Yet under the preaching of the gospel they had obtained righteousness by faith in spite of not having the law (cf. 10:6).

On the other hand, though Israel was pursuing νόμος δικαιοσύνης, they did not attain (φθάνειν) to this νόμος (9:31). By means of antithetical parallelism Paul contrasts the Gentiles who did not pursue righteousness but obtained it without knowing the law (9:30) with the Jews who pursued the "law of righteousness" but did not attain to it (9:31). However, the appearance of νόμος (9:31) disturbs this parallelism and overshadows the concept of δικαιοσύνη. He introduces νόμος because, in contrast to that of the Gentiles, Jewish piety is inextricably tied to the law, the Torah.[29]

The interpretation of this verse and, for that matter, of what follows (9:32-10:21) depends to a large degree on the meaning of the phrase νόμος δικαιοσύνης.[30] Despite the reluctance of a few scholars,[31] most exegetes understand νόμος as referring to the OT law in one sense or another. Disagreement results when scholars try to define νόμος in the light of the qualifying genitive, δικαιοσύνης.[32] For example, scholars interpret this phrase as denoting the law which demands righteousness (cf. 8:3-4),[33] the law which promises righteousness,[34] or the law falsely understood as a way of righteousness.[35] Of course, with these three basic approaches the possibilities are not exhausted.

Before examining the immediate context for clues to a proper interpretation, it is instructive to glance back at Paul's previous discussion of the law (3:21-4:25). There he evaluates the law in relation to righteousness by faith in positive as well as negative terms (cf. 3:21b-22, 27e, 31; 4:3, 9, 22-24 with 3:21a, 27d, 28; 4:2, 4-6, 9-10, 13-16). Moreover,

the apostle uses νόμος with qualifying genitives as here (see
3:27de). As we argued in our exegesis of that passage, νόμος
ἔργων (3:27d) signifies the OT law viewed from the perspective
of the works which it prescribes; νόμος πίστεως (3:27e) is the
same law viewed from the perspective of the faith to which it
bears witness, a faith which mediates righteousness (cf.
3:21b-22). Thus the "law of faith" is the OT law in its
witness to righteousness by faith (cf. Rom 4). In view of
this precedent (νόμος πίστεως), it seems unlikely one should
view νόμος δικαιοσύνης in a negative sense here as, for
example, the law which is falsely understood as a way of righteousness. Indeed, the context gives no other indication but
that Paul evaluates the law in a positive manner here, for the
Jews are not faulted with pursuing the "law of righteousness"
but with the way in which they pursue it (see 9:32 and the discussion below).

Also, because of the imagery of the race that the context depicts (διώκειν/καταλαμβάνειν; διώκειν/φθάνειν, 9:30-31),
it is preferable to understand νόμος δικαιοσύνης as the OT law
viewed from the perspective of the righteousness which it
promises rather than demands.[36] As the example of the Gentiles
shows (9:30) and as the following verses reiterate, it is righteousness by faith that the law promises. Though the apostle
does not specify precisely how the law promises this righteousness, it is not improper to reflect on its witness to righteousness by faith (3:21-4:25; 10:6-8).[37]

Significantly, Paul does not indicate that the Jews'
pursuit of this law which promises righteousness is somehow
misguided.[38] As a matter of fact, his subsequent statements
show that the real problem lies elsewhere, that is, in pursuing
the law from a false perspective (9:32). Rather it is this
positive concept of the "law of righteousness" that the apostle
introduces here to condition the discussion of νόμος in what
follows.

Despite their pursuit of the "law of righteousness"
the Jews did not attain to this law.[39] This attainment of the
law corresponds to the attainment of righteousness by faith in
the case of the Gentiles (9:30). Thus to attain to the law
and to receive righteousness by faith are practically

identical.⁴⁰ Israel failed to attain to the law because they did not pursue it ἐκ πίστεως but ὡς ἐξ ἔργων (9:32ab).⁴¹ They falsely imagined (ὡς)⁴² that they could attain to the law by performing its works (cf. 10:5)⁴³ rather than by faith (cf. 10:6-8). They overlooked the gracious character of the righteousness that God gives (see 3:24; 4:4).

As previously (3:27), Paul designates two perspectives from which one may approach the law (cf. διώκειν νόμον δικαιοσύνης . . . ἐκ πίστεως with νόμος πίστεως, 3:27e and διώκειν νόμον δικαιοσύνης . . . ὡς ἐξ ἔργων with νόμος τῶν ἔργων, 3:27d). If the Jews had accepted righteousness by faith, they would have attained to the law in its promise of righteousness.⁴⁴ But, because of their mistaken preoccupation with its works, they missed the law and the righteousness it promised.

In all this Paul does not disparage the law. To the contrary, it stands on the side of righteousness by faith (cf. 3:21b-22, 27e; 3:31-4:25). Foreign to this context, also, is the idea that the Jews did not attain to the law because they were unable to comply with its demands.⁴⁵ On the contrary, their ability to perform its works apparently stood in the way of their attainment of the law by faith. They failed to reach the law because they misunderstood it and transformed it into a tool of personal achievement (cf. 10:2-3, 5; see also 2:17, 23; 3:27d; 4:2; Phil 3:6, 9).⁴⁶ Moreover, Paul's rejection of the works of the law as a means of attaining to the "law of righteousness" should not be construed as a rejection of the law's demands altogether. He does not fault Israel with pursuing the law per se but with pursuing it as though it could be reached by works.⁴⁷

The Jews' failure to attain to the "law of righteousness" because of their insistence on works rather than faith is epitomized in their rejection of Christ: "They have stumbled over the stumbling stone, as it is written, 'Behold, I am laying in Zion a stone that will make men stumble, a rock that will make them fall; and he who believes in him will not be put to shame (9:32c-33).'"⁴⁸ By his conflation⁴⁹ of a negative and a positive prophetic word about a stone (Is 8:14; 28:16) Paul imparts to the second word a negative tone in addition to its otherwise positive one.⁵⁰ Thus for the Jews who have failed to reach the law because of their rejection of faith, Christ is, in God's saving plan, the cause of their perdition,[51] that is, a "stone of stumbling" and a "rock of offense" (9:32c-33a). But for those who trust in this same stone,[52] he is their guarantee of confidence in the divine judgment (9:33b; cf. 10:11).[53]

One should note very carefully the connection of the law with Christ. By faith the Jews should have attained to the law which promises righteousness. As the Scripture proof clearly shows (9:33b), this faith is faith in Christ, the stone. Therefore, faith in Christ permits one to attain to this "law of righteousness"![54] It would have allowed the Jews to reach successfully the goal they were pursuing. From this vantage point one begins to suspect that Paul's subsequent evaluation of the law vis-à-vis Christ (10:4) may be positive rather than negative.[55]

The Exegesis of Romans 10:1-21

In spite of the personal address and the obvious reference to 9:1-5 (10:1), this section does not introduce a new theme but explains in more detail the reason for Israel's failure (9:31-33).[56] One must continually bear in mind that this failure is due to the Jews' pursuit of the "law of righteousness" not by faith (in Christ) but by works (of the law).

Paul prefaces the discussion by indicating to the Roman Christians that his sincere desire and prayer to God for Israel is that they might be saved (10:1; cf. 9:1-3). His concern for Israel is based (γάρ) on the fact that they have a "zeal for God" but not "according to knowledge" (κατ' ἐπίγνωσιν, 10:2). This zeal for God characterized Jewish piety in Paul's day (cf. Gal 1:14; Phil 3:6). Such zeal is not reprehensible. But in the case of Israel it was not κατ' ἐπίγνωσιν, that is, it was not an "obedient recognition and insight into the will of God" (cf. 10:3).[57]

In the following verse (10:3) the apostle explains (γάρ) to what extent Israel's zeal was not according to knowledge: "For, being ignorant of the righteousness that comes from God, and seeking to establish their own, they did not submit to God's righteousness." This undiscerning zeal consists basically in the fact that the Jews did not submit (ὑποτάσσειν) to God's righteousness (10:3c).[58] Now we also learn that the righteousness promised to the Jews in their pursuit of the law (9:31) is not man's but God's righteousness.[59]

Moreover, Israel's ignorance (ἀγνοεῖν) of God's righteousness and their endeavor to establish (ἱστάνειν) their own (19:3ab) caused this insubordination. Because of their willful ignorance of God's righteousness, the Jews tried to establish their own by the works of the law (cf. 9:32; 10:5; Phil 3:9).[60] This ignorance and attempt to establish their own righteousness led them to refuse God's righteousness. This refusal is to be equated with the Jews' rejection of faith in Christ and insistence upon the saving efficacy of the works of the law (9:32-33).[61] It is, in fact, disobedience against the law which witnesses to righteousness by faith (3:21b-22).[62]

With his next statement (10:4) Paul grounds his preceding assertions (10:2-3): τέλος γὰρ νόμου Χριστὸς εἰς δικαιοσύνην παντὶ τῷ πιστεύοντι. Not surprisingly the word νόμος reappears. Actually, it has been at the center of Paul's discussion of Israel's failure since 9:31, where it was described as νόμος δικαιοσύνης, as the law which holds forth the promise of righteousness (cf. εἰς δικαιοσύνην here). Nor should the association of νόμος with Χριστός astonish us. The apostle has already indicated that faith in Christ, the stone, enables one to attain to the law which promises righteousness (9:32-33). Undoubtedly the term Χριστός stands for the death and resurrection of Jesus through which God's righteousness becomes available to all (3:24-26; 4:25; cf. 1 Cor 1:30; 2 Cor 5:21). Correspondingly, faith (πᾶς ὁ πιστεύων) is belief in this crucified and resurrected Lord (9:32-33).[63]

Nothing in the preceding statements of Paul suggests a negative relationship between Christ and the law as would be the case if the crucial term τέλος were understood as "end" in the sense of termination. Rather, it is only the Jewish notion that the works of the law are a means of attaining to the law and thus to righteousness that is faulted (9:32; cf. 10:5). While the apostle would certainly agree that Christ ends this false conception of the law for believers, such is not his point here. Paul's point so far has been that the Jews would

have attained to the "law of righteousness" if they had
believed on Christ (9:31-33). It would be pointless if he now
suddenly speaks of Christ as being the "end" rather than the
"goal" of the law.[64]

Thus, in light of these facts and of the positive
relationship which Paul finds between righteousness by faith
in Christ and the law (3:21-4:25), it is preferable to interpret τέλος as "goal" in this verse.[65] Incited by their willful ignorance of God's righteousness and their attempt to
establish their own, the Jews' undiscerning zeal for God had
led them to reject his righteousness in Christ (10:2-3),
because they did not recognize that *in Christ the law in its
promise of righteousness*[66] *reaches its goal, so that*[67] *God's
righteousness may be available to everyone who believes*
(10:4).[68] The Jews pursued but did not attain to the "law of
righteousness" (9:31) because they spurned faith in Christ in
whom the law realizes its goal in its promise of God's righteousness (cf. 9:32-33). Instead, they continued in their
misguided attempt to establish their own righteousness by the
works of the law (9:32; 10:2-3). However, every one who
believes in Christ receives God's righteousness in him and
thus achieves the goal of the law with respect to righteousness.[69]

By the introduction of scriptural proof (10:5-8) Paul
grounds (γάρ) his thesis that Christ is the goal of the law so
that righteousness may be available to everyone who believes
(10:4). The initial textual variation (10:5) does not seem to
cause exegetes serious interpretative conflicts. In its most
significant aspects this variation involves the transposition
of a word (ὅτι), the addition or omission of a word (αὐτά) and
the substitution of words (αὐτοῖς/αὐτῇ). By all appearances
scribal assimilation to Gal 3:12 lies at the root of the variation. While the reading in which ὅτι follows νόμου might be
original,[70] it seems more likely that it actually came immediately after γράφει. Assuming scribal assimilation, the insertion of αὐτά after ποιήσας demanded the transposition of ὅτι
to a new place after νόμου. Otherwise ποιήσας would have two
direct objects.[71] In addition, the substitution of αὐτοῖς
for αὐτῇ belonged to this assimilation. Thus, the original

text is probably Μωϋσῆς γὰρ γράφει ὅτι τὴν δικαιοσύνην τὴν ἐκ νόμου ὁ ποιήσας ἄνθρωπος ζήσεται ἐν αὐτῇ and translates: "[For] Moses writes that the man who practices the righteousness which is based on the law shall live by it."

Significant interpretative differences arise with regard to the relationship between 10:5 and 10:6-8 and, consequently, over the interpretation of 10:5. On the one hand, those who interpret τέλος (10:4) as "end" usually find a sharp antithesis between 10:5 and 10:6-8.[72] On the other hand, those who interpret τέλος as "goal" or "fulfilment" sometimes contend for a harmonious relationship between these two texts. Of these some resort to a christological interpretation of 10:5.[73] Though avoiding this particular interpretation, others give this verse a specifically Christian application.[74]

However, for several reasons it is paramount to maintain the antithesis between 10:5 and 10:6-8.[75] First, τὴν δικαιοσύνην τὴν ἐκ νόμου ποιεῖν (10:5)[76] corresponds to διώκειν νόμον δικαιοσύνης . . . ὡς ἐξ ἔργων (9:32) and τὴν ἰδίαν (δικαιοσύνην) ζητεῖν στῆσαι (10:3), while ἡ ἐκ πίστεως δικαιοσύνη (10:6) corresponds to διώκειν νόμον δικαιοσύνης . . . ἐκ πίστεως (9:30, 32) and (πᾶς) ὁ πιστεύων (9:33; 10:4). Moreover, Paul's negative use of Lev 18:5 elsewhere (Gal 3:12; cf. Rom 2:13) supports this antithetical understanding of 10:5 (= Lev 18:5) and 10:6-8, 10:5 forming the negative pole of the antithesis.[77] Finally, the concept of ἡ δικαιοσύνη ἡ ἐκ νόμου appears in opposition to ἡ ἐκ πίστεως δικαιοσύνη in the apostle's description of his own Christian experience (Phil 3:6, 9).[78]

Thus these verses (10:5-8; cf. Phil 3:9) contrast (δέ)[79] Moses' notation that he who does the righteousness based on the law will obtain life (10:5) and the assertion of "the righteousness based on faith" that access to Christ and righteousness becomes a reality through "the word of faith" which Paul preaches (10:6-8). To retain this antithesis is not necessarily damaging to the interpretation of τέλος (10:4) as "goal." In fact, as we intend to show, this contrast is essential if 10:5-8 are designed to ground Paul's assertion (10:4). However, we must postpone our answer until we have finished the exegesis of 10:5-21.

To begin with, Paul cites Lev 18:5 as the words of Moses (10:5). Actually, they are God's words through Moses to the people of Israel (Lev 18:1-2). But he has modified this text by substituting τὴν δικαιοσύνην τὴν ἐκ νόμου for ἅ which refers to πάντα τὰ προστάγματά μου καὶ πάντα τὰ κρίματά μου (Lev 18:5a) and αὐτῇ for αὐτοῖς (Lev 18:5b) to agree with the new object of ποιήσας. In this manner the apostle ties this citation more closely to the Jewish conception of δικαιοσύνη in the previous verses (9:32; 10:3) and sets up a contrast with the righteousness based on faith (10:6-8; cf. 9:30-33; 10:4). As a result, Paul depicts a way of salvation dependent on the individual's doing the righteousness based on the law, that is, on the works of the law (cf. 9:32; 10:3). How Paul evaluates this way of salvation becomes clear in what follows (10:6-8).

In contrast to Lev 18:5 he now cites Deut 9:4 and 30:12-14 as the words of ἡ ἐκ πίστεως δικαιοσύνη (10:6-8). In reality, the OT represents these statements as the words of Moses (see Deut 5:1; 29:1-2). That Paul ascribes them to "the righteousness based on faith" reveals that he finds another way of salvation delineated in the law, the way of faith, and also prepares the readers for his "unusual" exegesis of Deut 30:12-14 which follows.[80] Thus Moses, representing[81] the Jewish conception of righteousness by the works of the law, is overruled by the motif of "righteousness by faith" which speaks in the law.[82]

Through Paul's interpretation of the OT text this personified righteousness can express itself clearly. Consequently, the apostle[83] modifies and interprets his text so that it acquires a meaning radically opposite to its original one. Unlike Lev 18:5, it no longer applies to the commandment, the law, but to Christ and faith. Working with Deut 30:12-14 as a basis, he first prefaces this text with a phrase from Deut 9:4: μὴ εἴπῃς ἐν τῇ καρδίᾳ σου (10:6b). Next, omitting all references to the central motifs of the commandment and its performance (ποιεῖν), he interprets three selected clauses of this passage with reference to Christ and faith (10:6c-8). Only the second clause appears significantly changed, for instead of τίς διαπεράσει εἰς τὸ πέραν τῆς θαλάσσης; (Deut 30:13) Paul has τίς καταβήσεται εἰς τὴν ἄβυσσον; (10:7).[84]

To each of these clauses Paul attaches his own interpretative comment by means of the explanatory "that is" (τοῦτ' ἔστιν):[85] "But the righteousness based on faith says, Do not say in your heart, 'Who will ascend into heaven?' (that is, to bring Christ down) or 'Who will descend into the abyss?' (that is, to bring Christ up from the dead). But what does it say? The word is near you, on your lips and in your heart (that is, the word of faith which we preach)." Though they originally described the dispensability of superhuman efforts in the performance of the commandment (the law), the inquiries about ascending into heaven and descending into the abyss are now understood in terms of bringing Christ down from heaven and up from the dead.[86] On the one hand, it is a matter of fetching the exalted Christ back to earth (10:6cd),[87] but, on the other hand, of bringing Christ back from the dead (10:7).[88] Behind these queries lies a desire to have access to Christ in whom salvation becomes available (see 10:9-13).

As such superhuman efforts were not necessary to attain to the commandment (Deut 30:14), so also such efforts are not required for gaining access to Christ. Rather (ἀλλά), speaking out of the law, "the righteousness based on faith" teaches that accessibility to Christ becomes a reality solely through τὸ ῥῆμα τῆς πίστεως (10:8): "But what does it say? The word is near you, on your lips and in your heart (that is, the word of faith which we preach)." Therefore, it is not necessary to fetch back the exalted Christ nor to resurrect the dead Christ, for the resurrected, exalted Christ is already present in the word of faith Paul preaches (cf. 10:9-10).

While this ῥῆμα originally referred to the commandment and the facility of its performance (Deut 30:14), it now applies to the ῥῆμα τῆς πίστεως. As the subsequent mention of the confession of the gospel shows (10:9), this "word of faith" is the word in which faith expresses itself, the faith which proclaims.[89] At the same time, the expression, "in your mouth and in your heart," which once indicated total preparedness to perform the commandment, now refers to the Christian confession of faith.[90] In addition, the apostle's complete removal of references to performance (ποιεῖν) in the Deuteronomy passage, especially in Deut 30:14, serves to contrast sharply the performance demanded by Moses as a means of salvation (Lev 18:5) with the readily accessible word of faith. Those who follow Moses at this point are committed to this way of salvation. But "the righteousness based on faith" points to the way of faith. Thus the focus of the entire section (10:5-21) falls on this verse.

By his juxtaposition (ὅτι *recitativum*) of a pre-Pauline formula (10:9)[91] to his mention of "the word of faith" (10:8), Paul gives content to this "word": "If you confess with your lips that Jesus is Lord and believe in your heart that God raised him from the dead, you will be saved." This word entails both confession of Jesus' lordship (cf. 10:6) and belief in the divine origin of his resurrection (cf. 10:7), acts occurring in Christian worship. That this confession and belief are assigned to the mouth and heart respectively corresponds to the presence of "the word of faith" in one's mouth and in one's heart (cf. 10:8).

This confession and faith mediate salvation as the apostle explains (γάρ) in chiastic fashion (10:10): "For man believes with his heart and so is justified, and he confesses with his lips and so is saved." Notably, Paul defines this salvation in terms of his teaching of justification by faith.[92]

Scripture (Is 28:16) supports (γάρ) Paul at this juncture (10:11; cf. 9:33b): "No one who believes in him will be put to shame." As his interpolation of πᾶς into the Isaiah text shows, he wishes to stress the universal validity of faith as the means of salvation (cf. 10:4).

Moreover, in his explanatory remarks (γάρ, 10:12), he makes this point explicit: "For there is no distinction between Jew and Greek; the same Lord is Lord of all and bestows his riches upon all who call upon him (cf. 9:24)."[93] Christ's universal lordship is the basis (γάρ, 10:12b) for justification by faith rather than by the works of the law (cf. 3:29-30).[94] The image of calling upon the Lord pictures Christians at worship (cf. 1 Cor 1:2). It is such who will share the riches of salvation which he brings, as the OT (Joel 3:5[LXX]) clearly confirms (γάρ, 10:13): "For, 'every one who calls upon the name of the Lord will be saved.'"

In his concluding section (10:14-21) Paul lays bare the guilt of Israel in its rejection of "the word of faith" (cf. 9:32-33). Taking up the motif of "calling upon the Lord" in worship (10:13), he moves backward by means of a chain of rhetorical questions through Christian experience to the moment of saving faith (10:14a),[95] with its antecedents of hearing (10:14b), preaching (10:14c) and being commissioned to preach the gospel (10:15a): "But how are men to call upon him in whom they have not believed? And how are they to believe in him of whom they have never heard? And how are they to hear without a preacher? And how can men preach unless they are sent?" Scripture (Is 52:7) shows (καθάπερ γέγραπται) that the commissioning and, thus, the preaching of the gospel have happened and are happening (10:15b): "How beautiful are the feet of those who preach good news!"[96] The reality of this happening means that all the conditions for hearing and believing are now fulfilled.

Despite (ἀλλ') the presence of these conditions, the majority of the Jews have not obeyed the gospel (10:16a; cf. 9:32-33; 10:3). Such obedience should have been manifested in faith (Rom 1:5; 9:32-33). In his lament the prophet Isaiah (53:1) confirms (γάρ) Israel's unbelief: "Lord, who has believed what he has heard from us (10:16b)?" On the basis of this passage and with conscious allusion to 10:14-15a, Paul concludes (ἄρα): "So faith comes from what is heard, and what is heard comes by the preaching of Christ (10:17)." The ῥῆμα Χριστοῦ probably refers to Jesus' word mediated through the apostolic preaching in which Christ manifests himself.[97]

But (ἀλλά), if Israel has not heard, then they have an excuse for their unbelief, for a vital link in the chain would be missing (10:18a). On the contrary (μενοῦνγε), the OT (Ps 18:5[LXX]) discloses that they have truly heard the gospel: "Their voice has gone out to all the earth, and their words to the ends of the world (10:18b)."[98] Thus Paul envisions the whole world already filled with the Christian message. Israel cannot object that they have not heard.

Even though the Jews have heard, it is, nevertheless (ἀλλά), conceivable they have not understood the meaning of the message and, therefore, can excuse themselves (10:19a).[99] Again, the testimony of Scripture is unanimously against such an assumption (10:19b-21). First Moses (10:19b; Deut 32:21), then the prophets (10:20; Is 65:1) predict the conversion of the Gentiles so that Israel should have recognized in the fulfilment of their prophecy the beginning of the end-time:[100] "First Moses says, 'I will make you jealous of those who are not a nation; with a foolish nation I will make you angry.'"[101] Then Isaiah is so bold as to say, "I have been found by those who did not seek me; I have shown myself to those who did not ask for me.'"[102]

Moreover, the same OT (Is 65:2) prophesies Israel's disobedience with respect to the gospel: "All day long I have held out my hands to a disobedient and contrary people (10:21)"[103] With this statement one's thoughts return to Paul's earlier indictment of the Jews for their unbelief and their attempts to establish their own righteousness by the works of the law (9:31-33; 10:3). Finally, he is prepared to take up the ultimate fate of the majority of Israel who have refused the gospel of justification by faith (Rom 11).

Returning at last to the question of the relation between Rom 10:4 and 10:5-8, it is important to note that the latter are designed to confirm the former in its three principal propositions. First, *Christ* brings the law in its promise of righteousness to its goal. This fact is clearly affirmed in Paul's elaboration of "the word of faith" (cf. 10:6-8 and 10:9-13). By virtue of Christ's resurrection and exaltation, those who confess his lordship and believe that God raised him from the dead receive salvation, that is righteousness (εἰς δικαιοσύνην, 10:10; cf. 10:4). Thus the righteousness promised by the law becomes available in Christ.

Second, Christ brings *the law in its promise of righteousness* to its goal. Paul demonstrates this point by his application and interpretation of the law itself. Taking a text from the law that originally referred to the commandment (Deut 30:12-14), he interprets it with reference to Christ and faith (10:6-8). Thus the law becomes a witness to

righteousness by faith in Christ, because the apostle hears
the motif of "righteousness by faith" speaking out of the law
(cf. 3:21b-22).[104] Such a hermeneutical maneuver can only
result if Paul finds a positive relationship between Christ
and the law, as is the case when one interprets Rom 10:4 in
the sense that Christ is the "goal" of the law.

Third and most important, Christ brings the law in its
promise of righteousness to its goal *so that (God's) righteousness may be available to everyone who believes*. It is essential to observe that the heart of Israel's failure lies in
their refusal to believe (9:32-33; 10:16). Thus, in his
grounding of Rom 10:4, Paul stresses faith (10:8) over works
(10:5). In fact, as the strong adversative ἀλλά (10:8) indicates, the accent of the whole section (10:5-13) rests on 10:8
and its expansion in the following verses (10:9-13).[105] Therefore, one must view the total impact of 10:5-8 as a grounding
for 10:4 rather than interpret 10:5 in such a way that it is
in harmony with 10:4, 6-8.[106]

Simply stated, faith as a way of salvation excludes the
works of the law as a way of salvation (10:5-8; cf. Gal 3:12).
The basis for this exclusion does not lie in the inability of
the individual to do the righteousness based on the law.[107]
Rather it lies in the fact that Paul hears in the law the motif
of "righteousness by faith" forbidding evasive excuses for not
attaining salvation, that is, Christ, and pointing to the
readily accessible "word of faith" (10:6-8).[108] Thus the real
emphasis in 10:5-8 lies on 10:6-8 (see δέ, 10:6) and especially
on 10:8.

When considering Rom 10:4 in relation to 10:6-8, one
should not overlook the fact that the former ends with the
words, εἰς δικαιοσύνην παντὶ τῷ πιστεύοντι. In his grounding
of Rom 10:4 through 10:5-8, Paul is not only concerned with the
partial statement that Christ is the goal of the law but also
with the complete statement that Christ is the goal of the law
so that righteousness may be available to everyone who
believes.[109] The universal tone of this assertion is unmistakable. It is no less unmistakable in what follows. Thus in his
subsequent confirmation (10:5-8), Paul shows from the law the
incompatibility of the Jewish notion of salvation by the works

of the law (10:5) and the Christian message of righteousness
by faith to all (10:6-8).[110]

Though he offers it only as an alternative interpretation, Cranfield's explanation of the function of Rom 10:5-8 in relation to 10:4 clearly expresses our point:

> The fact that Christ is the goal of the law means that a righteous status is available for all who believe in Him; for, while justification by works is as Moses indicates (v.5), justification by faith is in accordance with the passages quoted in vv.6-8 and interpreted in v.9f.[111]

Conclusion

In the interpretation of Rom 9:30-10:21 much scholarly discussion has focused on the meaning of Rom 10:4. However, the central thrust of this section concerns the nature of Israel's disobedience vis-à-vis the gospel. From the beginning Paul views this disobedience with reference to the law (9:31). Thus he discusses the law, the mainstay of the Jewish religion, at the same time. After summarizing this discussion, we can compare our earlier findings (Rom 3:21-4:25) with those from Rom 9:30-10:21.

The apostle begins by pointing out that, despite its pursuit of the "law of righteousness," the law which promises righteousness, Israel did not attain to this "law" (9:31). This happened because they did not pursue the "law of righteousness" on the basis of faith but mistakenly on the basis of works (9:32ab). Though a proper goal, the Jews had pursued this "law" improperly because of their preoccupation with works and their rejection of faith. This rejection is epitomized in their rejection of Christ, the stone, prophesied by Isaiah (9:32c-33). Faith in him would have caused them to attain to the law in its promise of righteousness and, thus, brought them confidence in judgment. But their rejection of Christ had resulted in their perdition.

Turning to address the Roman Christians directly, Paul explains in more detail the reason for Israel's failure to attain to the "law of righteousness" (10:1-21). He sincerely desires and prays for Israel that they might be saved (10:1). His concern is grounded in the fact that Israel has a zeal for

God but not according to knowledge (10:2). This undiscerning zeal consists basically in the fact that the Jews have not submitted to God's righteousness due to their ignorance of it and their attempt to establish their own (10:3).

With his next statement (10:4) the apostle grounds his preceding assertions (10:2-3). Rooted in their ignorance of God's righteousness and their endeavor to establish their own, the Jews' undiscerning zeal had led them to reject his righteousness in their pursuit of the "law of righteousness." This in turn was due to their failure to recognize that *in Christ the law in its promise of righteousness reaches its goal so that (God's) righteousness may be available to everyone who believes*. The Jews pursued but did not attain to the "law of righteousness" because they spurned faith, faith in Christ in whom the law reaches its goal with respect to its promise of righteousness, God's righteousness. Instead, they misguidedly attempted to establish their own righteousness by doing the works of the law (9:32; 10:2-3). However, when a person believes in Christ, that person receives God's righteousness in him and, consequently, attains to the law in its promise of righteousness, for Christ is the goal of the law.

By the introduction of scriptural proof (10:5-8) Paul grounds his thesis that Christ is the goal of the law so that righteousness may be available to everyone who believes. Here the apostle contrasts Moses' notation that the person who does the righteousness based on the law shall live in it (10:5) with the assertion of the personified "righteousness by faith" that access to Christ and to righteousness becomes a reality through "the word of faith" (10:6-8). These verses along with their amplification (10:9-13) are designed to confirm Rom 10:4 in its three principal propositions about Christ, the law and righteousness by faith.

First, *Christ* brings the law in its promise of righteousness to its goal. Paul demonstrates this fact by his elaboration of "the word of faith" (cf. 10:6-8 and 10:9-13). He points to the resurrection and exaltation of Christ in which God's righteousness, the righteousness promised by the law, becomes available to all through faith.

Second, Christ brings *the law in its promise of righteousness* to its goal. He supports this claim by his application and interpretation of the law itself. Taking a text from the law, which originally referred to the commandment (Deut 30:12-14), he interprets it with reference to Christ and faith (10:6-8). Thus the law becomes a witness to righteousness by faith in Christ, because Paul hears the motif of "righteousness by faith" speaking out of the law.

Finally, Christ brings the law in its promise of righteousness to its goal *so that righteousness may be available to everyone who believes*. Paul confirms this point by contrasting works (10:5) with faith (10:6-8) as a way of salvation. Faith excludes the particularistic and mistaken notion that works bring salvation because the motif of "righteousness by faith," speaking from the law, overrules what Moses has written in this regard. Thus through faith, righteousness becomes universally accessible, no longer falsely connected with the practice of the Jewish Torah.

When comparing Rom 9:30-10:21 with 3:21-4:25, one detects a theological cohesion between the principal thoughts expressed in these two passages, a cohesion that suggests Rom 3:21-4:25 is to some extent a presupposition for 9:30-10:21. In the former Paul associates the law in its role as a witness with righteousness by faith (3:21b-22). In the latter he views the law as the "law of righteousness," the law which promises righteousness by faith, and thus as a witness to faith (9:31; 10:6-8). This notion of the "law of righteousness" is the corollary to that of the "law of faith," the law viewed from the perspective of its witness to righteousness by faith (3:27e).

Moreover, in both instances Paul, by his interpretation and application of the law itself, allows this witness to be clearly expressed. Thus, in the former, Gen 15:6 becomes the primary witness of the law to righteousness by faith (4:3, 9, 22-24); in the latter, Deut 30:12-14 stands at the head of Paul's argument for righteousness by faith (10:6-8). In both cases the apostle's use of supportive texts from the law follows a crucial and, in fact, positive statement about the law in its relation to righteousness by faith in Christ (3:31; 10:4).

Furthermore, in both passages Paul describes two opposing perspectives from which one may regard the law. On the one hand, he contrasts the "law of works," the law viewed solely from the perspective of the works that it prescribes, with the "law of faith," the law viewed from the perspective of the faith to which it witnesses (3:27de). On the other hand, he faults his own people, the Jews, with not attaining to the "law of righteousness," the law in its promise of righteousness, because they pursued it falsely from the perspective of works rather than from the perspective of faith (9:32).

In addition, that the righteousness witnessed to and promised by the law as righteousness by faith becomes a reality in Christ is clearly indicated in both texts. In the former the righteousness to which the law witnesses (3:21b-22) finds its realization in Christ (3:24-26; 4:25). In the latter the righteousness promised by the law (9:31) becomes effective in Christ (10:4, 6-13).

Also, in the former Paul argues that his message about justification by faith in Christ establishes the law because the law itself witnesses to justification by faith (3:31-4:25). In the latter to establish one's own righteousness by the works of the law (10:3) is the antithesis to submitting to God's righteousness through faith. Therefore, any attempt to establish one's own righteousness by the works of the law is against the law itself, for the law witnesses to and promises righteousness by faith (3:21b-22, 27; 3:31-4:25; 9:31-33; 10:6-8). One can attain to the law (9:31-32; 10:4) and establish the law (3:31) only by faith.

Finally, in both passages Paul makes equally bold statements about the law in positive as well as negative tones. No doubt, his negative statements are sparked by what he considers a false view of the law (3:27; 4:2; 9:32; 10:5) which he cannot accept because of his insistence upon righteousness by faith. Though akin to the statement that faith establishes the law (3:31), his subsequent assertion that Christ is the goal of the law so that righteousness may be available to everyone who believes (10:4) carries the association of faith, righteousness and the law one step further. Thus, while faith may be said to establish the law in its witness to righteousness by faith, it is also true that Christ brings the law in its promise of righteousness to its goal, namely, that righteousness may be available to everyone who believes. Yet the faith which establishes the law is also faith in Christ in whom God's righteousness becomes available (Rom 3:22, 24-26; 4:25).

Nowhere in the Pauline correspondence do we find two more positive statements about the relationship between faith, righteousness, the law and Christ.[112] Though Paul can also regard this relationship negatively, in these two instances he takes a positive viewpoint. Faith establishes the law (3:31). Christ is the goal of the law (10:4). We must ponder the bearing of these statements on Paul's understanding of the continuity between Judaism and Christianity in our Conclusion.

CONCLUSION

In this study we have been concerned with the question of the continuity between Judaism and Christianity as it relates to Paul's understanding of the law. In Chapter I we outlined the three main scholarly approaches to this issue, namely, discontinuity, continuity and mediating positions. What we discovered was a large measure of disagreement or even contradiction about the continuing validity of the law in the church. At this point we suggested that Paul's remark that faith establishes the law (Rom 3:31) should probably serve as the starting point for any assessment of the apostle's attitude toward the law and, therefore, for his view of its status in Christianity.

With these particulars in mind, we proceeded in Chapter II to describe the two opposing ways in which scholars construe Rom 3:31 in the context of the epistle along with the resultant interpretations of this verse. To overcome this stalemate we examined Paul's use of rhetorical questions, especially those negated by μὴ γένοιτο, as a means of unravelling the relationship of this important verse to its context. As a result of our investigation we concluded that, when the apostle uses such questions as the one in Rom 3:31, he does so in order to focus the reader's attention on some issue in the previous discussion which could have been misunderstood and which he now intends to explain. Thus Rom 3:31c and the whole of Rom 4 should be regarded as Paul's clarification of the possible misconception that he abolishes the law through faith.

Subsequently, in Chapter III we both tested these conclusions and examined the significance of Rom 3:31 for Paul's conception of the status of the law in the church by an exegesis of the entire passage, Rom 3:21-4:25. The outcome of this exegesis was that, when Paul declares he establishes the law by faith (Rom 3:31c), he means that *the law in its role as witness to righteousness by faith is established in the apostolic preaching of justification by faith as Rom 4 (Gen 15:6) clearly shows.*

Finally, in Chapter IV we brought the results of our analysis of Rom 3:31 to bear on Paul's further statement that Christ is the τέλος of the law (Rom 10:4). After a brief survey of the two principal interpretations of this text, we conducted an exegesis of its immediate context (Rom 9:30-10:21). As a result of this exegesis, we came to understand Rom 10:4 in the sense that *in Christ the law in its promise of righteousness reaches its goal so that God's righteousness may be available to everyone who believes.*

On this basis we continued in the same chapter with a comparison between Rom 3:31 and 10:4, finding, as a result, evidence of theological cohesion between these two texts. For example, in both instances the law is viewed as a witness to righteousness by faith (Rom 3:21b-22; 9:31; 10:6-8). Moreover, in both cases it is Paul's interpretation and application of the law itself which allows this witness to be clearly expressed (Gen 15:6 = Rom 4; Deut 30:12-14 = Rom 10:6-8). In addition, in both passages Paul describes two opposing perspectives from which one may regard the law, that is, from the perspective of works or of faith (Rom 3:27; 9:32). Furthermore, that the righteousness witnessed to and promised by the law as righteousness by faith becomes a reality in Christ is plainly indicated in both texts (Rom 3:24-26; 4:25; 10:4, 6-13).

Also, while Paul argues, on the one hand, that faith establishes the law (Rom 3:31), he declares, on the other, that to establish one's own righteousness by the works of the law is the antithesis to receiving God's righteousness by faith (Rom 10:3). Thus, to attempt to establish one's own righteousness by works is against the law, for the law witnesses to and promises righteousness by faith (Rom 3:21b-22; 9:31). Last, Paul's statement that Christ is the goal of the law (10:4) carries his assertion that faith establishes the law (3:31) one step further by stressing the fact that Christ himself brings the law in its promise of righteousness to its goal, namely, that righteousness may be available to everyone who

Conclusion

who believes. Yet, as is evident, this faith (which establishes the law) is faith in Christ in whom God's righteousness is received (Rom 3:22, 24-26; 4:25). Hence the two statements cohere admirably.

To return to the original question which spawned this study, we must ask: What bearing do these pronouncements (Rom 3:31; 10:4) have on Paul's conception of the continuity between Judaism and Christianity in the matter of the law? Is the phrase "faith establishes the law" a more adequate way in which to label Paul's understanding of this continuity?

First, it is generally recognized that the Christian Paul does not consider the works of the law to be a way of salvation (see Rom 3:20-21, 28; Rom 4; but cf. Rom 2:12-13). Moreover, one must doubt that in his theological reflection the apostle betrays the view that the works of the law were ever a way of salvation (see Rom 4). Thus to speak of an abolition of the law as a way of salvation without additional clarification could lead to a misunderstanding of Pauline theology, the misunderstanding that God has now substituted faith as a way of salvation for the law which failed in this role.

What Paul attacks is not simply the law as a way of salvation but rather the *notion* that the law is a way of salvation. Quite apart from the conflict over the Judaization of Gentile Christians, he makes it very clear that it is a false perception of the law and its works that he rejects (Rom 3:27; 9:32). Consequently, *as far as the Jewish notion of the works of the law as a way of salvation is concerned, the relationship between Judaism and Pauline Christianity is discontinuous*.

Furthermore, in regard to Paul's statement that he establishes the law by faith (Rom 3:31), it is now evident that in terms of its witness to justification by faith the law possesses continuing validity in the church (Rom 3:21b-22; 4:23-24). It is the eschatological appearance of the faith attested in the law that actually establishes the law in this role. From his perspective *post Christum* Paul finds righteousness by faith confirmed in the law (Rom 4; cf. 10:6-8). Therefore, *in its witness to righteousness by faith, the law as the object of the synagogue's religious pursuits is upheld in the preaching and acceptance of the gospel in the church.* Though Pauline Christianity may not be continuous with the Judaism in which Paul had earlier so excelled, it is certainly continuous with Judaism to the degree that it finds its raison d' être in the law which witnesses to (and also promises) righteousness by faith (Rom 3:21-4:25; cf. 9:30-10:21).

Next, in terms of the law's promise (or possibly demand) of righteousness (Rom 9:31), the apostle's assertion that Christ is the goal of the law for righteousness to everyone who believes (Rom 10:4) shows that the very essence of Christ's work is to supply the righteousness which the law promises. *Whenever someone receives righteousness by faith in Christ, the law's goal of righteousness is realized in this act of faith in the work of the resurrected and exalted Christ. Thus, the equation, Christ is the goal of the law for righteousness, represents the apex of Paul's understanding of the continuity between Judaism and Christianity.*

For this reason, we cannot agree with Mussner and van Dülmen[1] when they declare that anyone who understands Rom 10:4 in the sense that Christ is the goal of the law has either totally misunderstood Paul's theology or is completely at odds with his conception of Heilsgeschichte. Rather, to understand Paul's theology properly, one must recognize, as our exegesis of Rom 9:30-10:21 demonstrates and as Rom 3:21-4:25 confirm, that *the object of Christ's work was to provide the righteousness which the law both promised (9:31) and attested (3:21). If Christ's work had had any other outcome, it would have meant a break in the continuity of God's plan of salvation as it is revealed in the law.*

In conclusion, even if our study has not exhausted all of the Pauline statements about the law, it may, for several reasons, be regarded as paradigmatic for Paul's understanding of the law and especially for his understanding of the continuity between Judaism and Christianity as it relates to the law. First, as noted earlier with respect to Rom 3:31, Paul himself raises and answers this question about the validity of the law (3:31-4:25) at the climax of a statement (3:21-30)

Conclusion

that has come to be regarded as the theological center of the Letter to the Romans. Therefore, *the assertion that he establishes the law by faith is the apostle's own way of spotlighting and then explaining the validity of the law in the Christian community.*

In view of what we have just said, it no longer seems appropriate, in the second place, to stress such notions as "the abolition of the law" when referring to Paul's understanding of the law's status and especially as captions for Pauline theology. Rather, as our discussion of Rom 3:31 and its context has shown, *a more proper starting point and a more adequate caption would be Paul's notion of "the establishment of the law."*

Third and finally, in the light of our exegesis of Rom 3:31 and 10:4, *it is time to reopen the question of Paul's view of the law's status and to take a fresh look at his statements about the law, particularly from the standpoint of the two possible perspectives that the apostle delineates in the passages discussed above (see Rom 3:27; 9:32).* Such a reexamination of Paul's statements will, in our opinion, give a more balanced picture of Paul's understanding of the validity of the law in the church than we have been able to obtain heretofore. Thus, we suggest that Rom 3:31 should be the logical starting point for addressing the issue of the law's continuing role in the church.

INTRODUCTION

[1]*Paul and Palestinian Judaism: A Comparison of Patterns of Religion* (Philadelphia: Fortress Press, 1977), p. 552. Italics his.

[2]In this study we are limiting ourselves to the relatively undisputed Pauline letters, i.e., Romans, 1 & 2 Corinthians, Galatians, Philippians, 1 Thessalonians and Philemon.

[3]Unless otherwise indicated scriptural quotations are taken from *The New Oxford Annotated Bible with the Apocrypha: Revised Standard Version*, ed. Herbert G. May and Bruce M. Metzger (New York: Oxford University Press, 1977). Quotations in the Pseudepigrapha are taken from *The Apocrypha and Pseudepigrapha of the Old Testament*, ed. R. H. Charles; 2 vols. (Oxford: Clarendon Press, 1913).

CHAPTER I

THE STATUS OF THE LAW *POST CHRISTUM*

[1]"Religion in Everyday Life," in *The Jewish People in the First Century: Historical Geography, Political History, Social, Cultural and Religious Life and Institutions*, ed. S. Safrai and M. Stern, Compendia Rerum Iudaicarum ad Novum Testamentum, 1, 2 vols. (Assen: Van Gorcum & Co., B.V., 1974-76), 2:793.

[2]See Sanders' recent treatment of the subject and the literature cited there. *Paul and Palestinian Judaism*, pp. 33-428. We cannot agree entirely with the viewpoint mentioned and later endorsed by Sanders that "the description of Judaism implicit in Paul's attack on 'works of law' is wrong." Ibid., pp. 7, 426-28. While this may be true with regard to rabbinic Judaism as Sanders depicts it, it is not wholly adequate when speaking of Judaism contemporary to Paul. For one thing, Paul's portrayal of Judaism (Rom 9:30-10:21) is not influenced only by polemics but also by sincere concern for his kindred (Rom 9:1-3; 10:1). For another, if Paul misunderstood the Judaism of his day, as some claim, then he apparently spent much of his time boxing shadows. Finally, whether Paul is right or wrong in his understanding of Judaism, it is over against Judaism as he understands it that we must initially interpret his position.

[3]"Moses und das Gesetz bei Paulus," in *Moses in Schrift und Überlieferung*, ed. Fridolin Stier and Eleonore Beck, Kommentare und Beiträge zum Alten Testament und Neuen Testament (Düsseldorf: Patmos Verlag, 1963), p. 256. Italics his.

[4]For surveys of recent literature dealing with Paul and the law including literature from the nineteenth century, see Francis Irving Fesperman, "Freedom from the Law: Paul's Doctrine and Its Role in the Early Church," (Ph.D. dissertation, Vanderbilt University, 1969), pp. 2-36; Reimer Gronemeyer, *Zur Frage nach dem paulinischen Antinomismus: Exegetisch-systematische Überlegungen mit besonderer Berücksichtigung der Forschungsgeschichte im 19. Jahrhundert* (Hamburg: By the author, 1970), pp. 143-246; Otto Kuss, "Nomos bei Paulus," *MüTZ* 17 (1966) 177-210 and Joseph Shou-Jen Wang, "Pauline Doctrine of Law," (Ph.D. dissertation, Emory University, 1970), pp. 11-61.

The scholars cited in what follows may at times work with different conceptions of the law. We will not attempt in most cases to sort out the differences. However, they usually have in mind the Mosaic legislation, especially that contained in the Pentateuch. For discussions of the range of meaning the word "law" (νόμος) can have in Paul's letters, see Peter Bläser, *Das Gesetz bei Paulus*, NTA, Bd. 19, Hfte. 1-2 (Münster: Aschendorffsche Verlagsbuchhandlung, 1941), pp. 31-38 and *TDNT*, s.v. "νόμος," by Walter Gutbrod, 4:1069-71.

[5]A notable exception is Reimer Gronemeyer whose investigation of Paul's "antinomianism" becomes an exposition of Pauline antinomianism. Gronemeyer even interprets in a negative sense several Pauline texts which most scholars regard as expressing a positive relationship between the law and the Christian faith, e.g. Gal 5:13-14 and Rom 13:8-10. Ibid., pp. 75, 135-40. His assessment of Paul's theology of the law (understood narrowly as the Mosaic legislation) is epitomized in the astonishing statement: "Das Gesetz wird as nicht ewig, als nicht göttlich entlarvt." Ibid., p. 88, n. 1. See further the entire section, Ibid., pp. 78-95. As is evident from his references, Gronemeyer is simply building on the exegetical foundation of other NT scholars.

[6]So Paul Althaus, *Der Brief an die Römer*, Das Neue Testament Deutsch, Bd. 6, Aufl. 11 (Göttingen: Vandenhoeck & Ruprecht, 1970), p. 108; Günther Bornkamm, "Wandlungen im alt- und neutestamentlichen Gesetzesverständnis," in *Geschichte und Glaube*, Gesammelte Aufsätze, Bd. 4, T. 2, BEvT, Bd. 53 (Munich: Chr. Kaiser Verlag, 1971), pp. 105-6; F. F. Bruce, "Paul and the Law of Moses," *BJRL* 57 (1975) 262; Rudolf Bultmann, "Christ and the End of the Law," in *Essays, Philosophical and Theological*, trans. James C. G. Greig, with an Introduction by R. Gregor Smith, The Library of Philosophy and Theology (London: SCM Press, 1955), p. 54; Hans Conzelmann, *An Outline of the Theology of the New Testament*, trans. John Bowden (New York: Harper & Row, 1969), pp. 223-24; Andrea van Dülmen, *Die Theologie des Gesetzes bei Paulus*, Stuttgarter biblische Monographien, Bd. 5 (Stuttgart: Verlag Katholisches Bibelwerk, 1968), pp. 126-27; Paul Johannes Du Plessis, ΤΕΛΕΙΟΣ: *The Idea of Perfection in the New Testament*, Theologische Academie uitgaande van de Johannes Calvijn stichting te Kampen (Kampen: J. H. Kok, [1959]), p. 142; Gerhard Ebeling, "Reflections on the Doctrine of the Law," in *Word and Faith*, trans. James W. Leitch (Philadelphia: Fortress Press, 1963), pp. 270-71; Georg Eichholz, *Die Theologie des Paulus im Umriss* (Neukirchen-Vluyn: Neukirchener Verlag, 1972), p. 246; Joseph A. Fitzmyer, "Paul and the Law," in *A Companion to Paul: Readings in Pauline Theology* ed. Michael J. Taylor (New York: Alba House, 1975), p. 75; Ernst Gaugler, *Der Römerbrief*, Prophezei Schweizerisches Bibelwerk für die Gemeinde, 2 Teile (Zurich: Zwingli-Verlag, 1945-52), 2:94-118; Leonhard Goppelt, *Theologie des Neuen Testaments* ed. Jürgen Roloff, Göttinger theologische Lehrbücher, 2 T.: *Vielfalt und Einheit des apostolischen Christuszeugnisses* (Göttingen: Vandenhoeck & Ruprecht, 1975-76), 2. T.: *Vielfalt und Einheit des apostolischen Christuszeugnisses* (1976):282; Eduard Grafe, *Die paulinische Lehre vom Gesetz nach den vier Hauptbriefen*, Aufl. 2 (Leipzig: J. C. B. Mohr, 1893), p. 17; Gronemeyer, Ibid., pp. 124-26; Ferdinand Hahn, "Das Gesetzesverständnis im Römer- und Galaterbrief," *ZNW* 67 (1976) 49-51; Eberhard Jüngel, *Paulus und Jesus: Eine Untersuchung zur Präzierung der Frage nach dem Ursprung der Christologie*, HUT, Bd. 2 (Tübingen: J. C. B. Mohr, 1962), pp. 50-55; Ernst Käsemann, *An die Römer*, HNT, Bd. 8a (Tübingen: J. C. B. Mohr, 1973), p. 270; H. A. A. Kennedy, "St. Paul and the Law," *The*

Expositor, 8th Series, 13 (1917):353; Karl Kertelge, *"Recht-fertigung" bei Paulus: Studien zur Struktur und zum Bedeutungs-gehalt des paulinischen Rechtfertigungsbegriffs*, NTA, n. F., Bd. 3 (Münster: Verlag Aschendorff, 1967), p. 97; Kuss, "Nomos bei Paulus," p. 212; George Eldon Ladd, "Paul and the Law," in *Soli Deo Gloria: New Testament Studies in Honor of William Childs Robinson*, ed. J. McDowell Richards (Richmond: John Knox Press, 1968), pp. 57-58; Marie Joseph Lagrange, *Saint Paul Épître aux Romains*, ÉtBib (Paris: J. Gabalda, 1950), pp. 253-54; Richard N. Longenecker, *Paul, Apostle of Liberty* (New York: Harper & Row, 1964), pp. 144-53; Ulrich Luz, *Das Geschichtsverständnis des Paulus*, BEvT, Bd. 49 (Munich: Chr. Kaiser Verlag, 1968), pp. 139-41; Christian Mauer, *Die Gesetzeslehre des Paulus nach ihrem Ursprung und in ihrer Entfaltung dargelegt* (Zollikon-Zurich: Evangelischer Verlag, 1941), pp. 53, 64, 66; Otto Michel, *Der Brief an die Römer*, KExKNT, Abt. 4, Aufl. 10 (Göttingen: Vandenhoeck & Ruprecht, 1955), pp. 223-24; John Murray, *The Epistle to the Romans*, NICNT, 2 vols. (Grand Rapids: Wm. B. Eerdmans Publishing Co., 1959-65), 2:49-51; Johannes Munck, *Christ and Israel: An Interpretation of Romans 9-11*, trans. Ingeborg Nixon, Foreword by Krister Stendahl (Philadelphia: Fortress Press, 1967), p. 83; Franz Mussner, "'Christus (ist) des Gesetzes Ende zur Gerechtigkeit für jeden, der glaubt' (Röm 10,4)," in *Paulus--Apostat oder Apostel? Jüdische und christliche Antworten*, with contributions by Markus Barth, Jochanan Bloch, Josef Blank et al., Foreword by Franz Henrich (Regensburg: Verlag Friedrich Pustet, 1977), pp. 31-44; Anders Nygren, *Commentary on Romans*, trans. Carl C. Rasmussen (London: SCM Press, 1952), pp. 379-80; Herman Ridderbos, *Paul: An Outline of His Theology*, trans. John Richard de Witt (Grand Rapids: Wm. B. Eerdmans Publishing Co., 1975), pp. 137, 155-56; William Sanday and Arthur C. Headlam, *A Critical and Exegetical Commentary on the Epistle to the Romans*, ICC, 5th ed. (Edinburgh: T. & T. Clark, 1902), p. 284; Sanders, *Paul and Palestinian Judaism*, p. 550; Heinrich Schlier, *Der Römerbrief*, HTKNT, Bd. 6 (Freiburg: Herder, 1977), p. 311; Hans Wilhelm Schmidt, *Der Brief des Paulus an die Römer*, THkNT, Bd. 6 (Berlin: Evangelische Verlagsanstalt, 1962), p. 175; Hans Joachim Schoeps, *Paul: The Theology of the Apostle in the Light of Jewish Religious History*, trans. Harold Knight (Philadelphia: Westminster Press, 1974), p. 171; Peter Stuhlmacher, *Gerechtigkeit Gottes bei Paulus*, FRLANT, Hft. 87 (Göttingen: Vandenhoeck & Ruprecht, 1965), p. 93; John F. Walvoord, "Law in the Epistle to the Romans," *Bibliotheca Sacra* 94 (1937):286 and apparently at first Ulrich Wilckens, "Die Bekehrung des Paulus als religionsgeschichtliches Problem," in *Rechtfertigung als Freiheit: Paulusstudien* (Neukirchen-Vluyn: Neukirchener Verlag, 1974), pp. 14-15.

Though this list could be expanded many times over, it is sufficient to demonstrate the widespread support of this particular interpretation of the verse at hand.

[7]"'Das Ende des Gesetzes': Über Ursprung und Ansatz der paulinischen Theologie," *ZTK* 67 (1970):30.

⁸For a discussion of the difference between these two ways of viewing the end of the law and the references in scholarly literature, see Luz, *Geschichtsverständnis*, pp. 143-44.

⁹See Nygren, *Romans*, p. 380.

¹⁰So van Dülmen, *Gesetzes*, pp. 126, 185-218; Käsemann, *Römer*, pp. 270-71 and Kertelge, *"Rechtfertigung,"* p. 97, n. 171.

¹¹So Fitzmyer, "Paul and the Law," p. 75 and Schoeps, *Paul*, p. 171.

¹²So Wilckens, "Die Bekehrung des Paulus," pp. 14-15.

¹³So Stuhlmacher, *Das paulinische Evangelium: I. Vorgeschichte*, FRLANT, Hft. 95 (Göttingen: Vandenhoeck & Ruprecht, 1968), pp. 74-75 and the literature cited there.

¹⁴So Sanders, *Paul and Palestinian Judaism*, p. 550.

¹⁵Actually the word νόμος does not appear at all in this context. However, Andrew John Bandstra typically argues that "what is said here of Moses and his ministry can also be said to pertain, *mutatis mutandis*, to the law." *The Law and the Elements of the World: An Exegetical Study in Aspects of Paul's Teaching* (Kampen: J. H. Kok, 1964), p. 79. See also 3:3, 6-7, 15.

¹⁶So Ernest Bernard Allo, *Saint Paul Seconde Épître aux Corinthiens*, ÉtBib, 2d ed. (Paris: J. Gabalda, 1956), pp. 88, 90-91; C. K. Barrett, *A Commentary on the Second Epistle to the Corinthians*, HNTC (New York: Harper & Row, 1973), pp. 118-21; Bultmann, *Der zweite Brief an die Korinther*, ed. Erich Dinkler, KExKNT, Sonderband (Göttingen: Vandenhoeck & Ruprecht, 1976), pp. 86, 88-89 and Luz, *Geschichtsverständnis*, pp. 145-46.

By way of clarification we should point out that Allo (Ibid., p. 90) and Bultmann (Ibid., p. 88) regard τοῦ καταργουμένου (3:13) not as a reference to the old covenant but to the vanishing glory on Moses' face. Allo, however, maintains a secondary reference to the law.

¹⁷So Barrett, Ibid., p. 118; Bultmann, Ibid., p. 90 and Luz, Ibid.

¹⁸So Bultmann, Ibid.

¹⁹So Barrett, *Second Corinthians*, p. 121.

²⁰So Allo, *Seconde Corinthiens*, pp. 88, 90.

²¹So Mussner, *Der Galaterbrief*, HTKNT, Bd. 9 (Freiburg: Herder, 1974), p. 178. Ernest De Witt Burton speaks of the statutes of the law. *A Critical and Exegetical Commentary on the Epistle to the Galatians*, ICC, 1st ed. (Edinburgh: T. & T. Clark, 1921), p. 130. Likewise, J. B. Lightfoot refers to

the ordinances of the law. *Saint Paul's Epistle to the Galatians*, 10th ed. (London: Macmillan & Co., 1900), p. 117.

[22] So Hans Lietzmann, *An die Galater*, HNT, Bd. 10, Aufl. 4 (Tübingen: J. C. B. Mohr, 1971), p. 17 and Schlier, *Der Brief an die Galater*, KExKNT, Abt. 7, Aufl. 10 (Göttingen: Vandenhoeck & Ruprecht, 1949), pp. 59-60.

[23] *Römer*, 86.

[24] "Die Offenbarung des Zornes Gottes. Röm 1-3," in *Das Ende des Gesetzes: Paulusstudien*, Gesammelte Aufsätze, Bd. 1, BEvT, Bd. 16, Aufl. 2 (Munich: Chr. Kaiser Verlag, 1958), p. 32.

[25] *Evangelium und neues Gesetz in der ältesten Christenheit bis auf Marcion*, Studia theologica Rheno-Traiectina, vol. 5 (Utrecht: Kemink en Zoon, 1960), p. 71.

[26] *The Epistle to the Romans*, trans. Harold Knight (London: Lutterworth Press, 1961), p. 169. See also Althaus (*Römer*, p. 64), who speaks of the end of the order of the law.

[27] *Galater*, pp. 126-27. So also Mussner, *Galaterbrief*, p. 260 and Albrecht Oepke, *Der Brief des Paulus an die Galater*, THkNT, Bd. 9, Aufl. 2 (Berlin: Evangelische Verlagsanstalt, 1957), p. 88. Interestingly, these three exegetes all connect this verse with Rom 10:4.

[28] *Galatians*, p. 168. See also Wang, "Law," pp. 209-210.

[29] *A Commentary on the First Epistle to the Corinthians*, HNTC (New York: Harper & Row, 1968), p. 212. Italics his. Archibald Robertson and Alfred Plummer think Paul's remark shows how completely he had broken with Judaism. *A Critical and Exegetical Commentary on the First Epistle of St Paul to the Corinthians*, ICC, 2d ed. (Edinburgh: T. & T. Clark, 1914), p. 191. So also Bläser, *Gesetz*, pp. 226-27.

[30] *Römer*, p. 179.

[31] "*Rechtfertigung*," p. 212.

[32] Wang, "Law," pp. 187-189.

[33] *Romains*, pp. 162-63. So also, Sanday and Headlam who understand "law" in a more general sense. *Romans*, pp. 172-73.

[34] *Antinomismus*, pp. 43-44.

[35] *Galatians*, p. 140. So also Wang, "Law," p. 209. Lagrange perceives this aspect of the abolition of the law only in germinal form here. *Saint Paul Épître aux Galates*, ÉtBib, 2d ed. (Paris: J. Gabalda, 1950), p. 74.

³⁶*Antinomismus*, p. 51.

³⁷*Adam und Christus: Exegetisch-religionsgeschichtliche Untersuchung zu Röm. 5,12-21 (1. Kor. 15)*, WMANT, Bd. 7 (Neukirchen: Kreis Moers, 1962), p. 249, n. 3. So also Schlier, *Römerbrief*, p. 177. See also Walter Grundmann, "Gesetz, Rechtfertigung und Mystik bei Paulus: Zum Problem der Einheitlichkeit der paulinischen Verkündigung," *ZNW* 32 (1933):58-59.

³⁸So Joseph Huby, *Saint Paul Épître aux Romains*, ed. Stanislas Lyonnet, Verbum Salutis, 10 (Paris: Beauchesne et Ses Fils, 1957), p. 199 and Lagrange, *Romains*, p. 112.

³⁹"Law," p. 79. So also Bläser, *Gesetz*, p. 52; Burton, *Galatians*, p. 189; Lagrange, Ibid., pp. 82-83; Mussner, *Galaterbrief*, p. 246; Oepke, *Galater*, p. 81 and Schlier, *Galater*, p. 108.

⁴⁰Ibid., p. 257. So also Fesperman, Ibid., pp. 109-110; Oepke, Ibid., p. 88 and Schlier, Ibid., pp. 125-26.

⁴¹*Romains*, p. 164. See also Kuss, *Der Römerbrief*, 3 Lieferungen (Regensburg: Verlag Friedrich Pustet, 1957-78), 2:438.

⁴²"ΕΝΝΟΜΟΣ ΧΡΙΣΤΟΥ," in *Studia Paulina in honorem Johannis de Zwaan septuagenarii*, ed. J. N. Sevenster and W. C. van Unnik (Haarlem: Erven F. Bohn, 1953), p. 99.

⁴³Ibid., pp. 103-110. See also Bandstra, *Law*, pp. 111-14; Lucien Cerfaux, *The Christian in the Theology of St. Paul*, trans. Lilian Soiron (New York: Herder & Herder, 1967), pp. 443-66; Kuss, "Nomos bei Paulus," pp. 223-25; Longenecker, *Paul*, pp. 188-90; Mussner, *Galaterbrief*, p. 285; Beda Rigaux, "Law and Grace in Pauline Eschatology," *Louvain Studies* 2 (1969):330, 332; Heinz Schürmann, "'Das Gesetz des Christus' (Gal 6,2): Jesu Verhalten und Wort als letztgültige sittliche Norm nach Paulus," in *Neues Testament und Kirche: Für Rudolf Schnackenburg*, ed. Joachim Gnilka (Freiburg: Herder, 1974), pp. 282-300 and Stuhlmacher, *Gerechtigkeit Gottes*, pp. 96-97.

While Bläser recognizes the connection between the "law of Christ" and the words of Jesus, he emphasizes more strongly the interiorization of this "law." *Gesetz*, pp. 234-43. Similarly Bandstra, Ibid., pp. 108-111 and Stanislas Lyonnet, "St. Paul: Liberty and Law," *The Bridge*, 1962, pp. 238-51.

⁴⁴*Paul*, pp. 29, 171-73. See also Birger Gerhardsson, *Memory and Manuscript: Oral Tradition and Written Transmission in Rabbinic Judaism and Early Christianity*, trans. Eric J. Sharpe, Acta Seminarii Neotestamentici Upsaliensis, 22 (Lund: C. W. K. Gleerup, 1961), p. 310.

⁴⁵Ibid., pp. 198-99.

⁴⁶So Bandstra, *Law*, pp. 101-6; Markus Barth, "Exegetische Anfragen an das Gesetzesverständnis Luthers und Barths," in *Promissio und Bund: Gesetz und Evangelium bei Luther und Barth*, Bertold Klappert, Forschungen zur systematischen und ökumenischen Theologie, Bd. 34 (Göttingen: Vandenhoeck & Ruprecht, 1976), p. 256; Bläser, *Gesetz*, pp. 173-81; Ragnar Bring, "Paul and the Old Testament: A Study of the Ideas of Election, Faith and Law in Paul with Special Reference to Romans 9:30-10:30[sic]," *Studia Theologica* 25 (1971):41-52; "Die Gerechtigkeit Gottes und das alttestamentliche Gesetz: Eine Untersuchung von Röm. 10,4," in *Christus und das Gesetz: Die Bedeutung des Gesetzes des Alten Testaments nach Paulus und sein Glauben an Christus* (Leiden: E. J. Brill, 1969), pp. 35-72; C. E. B. Cranfield, "St. Paul and the Law," *SJT* 17 (1964):48-53; *IDB*, s.v. "Law in the NT," by W. D. Davies, 3:100; cf. *Paul and Rabbinic Judaism: Some Rabbinic Elements in Pauline Theology*, rev. ed. (New York: Harper & Row, 1967), p. 69; Felix Flückiger, "Christus, des Gesetzes τέλος," *TZ* 11 (1955):153-57; George E. Howard, "Christ the End of the Law: The Meaning of Romans 10:4ff.," *JBL* 88 (1969): 331-37; Peter von der Osten-Sacken, *Römer 8 als Beispiel paulinischer Soteriologie*, FRLANT, Bd. 112 (Göttingen: Vandenhoeck & Ruprecht, 1975), pp. 250-56; Joseph Sickenberger, *Die Briefe des Heiligen Paulus an die Korinther und Römer*, Die Heilige Schrift des Neuen Testaments, Bd. 6, Aufl. 4. (Bonn: Peter Hanstein Verlagsbuchhandlung, 1932), pp. 257-58; Wang, "Law," pp. 144-58 and so eventually Wilckens, "Was heisst bei Paulus: 'Aus Werken des Gesetzes wird kein Mensch gerecht'?" in *Rechtfertigung als Freiheit*, pp. 100-101.

Drawing an analogy to the rabbinic concept of the *k e l a l*, Karl Barth prefers to use such terms as "common denominator," "sum" or "substance" to translate τέλος. *Church Dogmatics*, ed. G. W. Bromiley and T. F. Torrance, 4 vols. in 13 (Edinburgh: T. & T. Clark, 1936-70), vol. 2/2: *The Doctrine of God*, trans. G. W. Bromiley, J. C. Campbell, Iain Wilson et al. (1957):244-47.

⁴⁷So John W. Drane, *Paul: Libertine or Legalist? A Study in the Theology of the Major Pauline Epistles* (London: S.P.C.K., 1975), p. 133.

⁴⁸"Das Gesetz des Glaubens," *TZ* 10 (1954):415.

⁴⁹ΤΕΛΕΙΟΣ, p. 143, n. 59.

⁵⁰"Gesetzesverständnis," p. 49. See also Ernst Fuchs, *Die Freiheit des Glaubens: Römer 5-8 ausgelegt*, BEvT, Bd. 14 (Munich: Chr. Kaiser Verlag, 1949), p. 85; Jüngel, *Paulus und Jesus*, p. 61; Eduard Lohse, "ὁ νόμος τοῦ πνεύματος τῆς ζωῆς: Exegetische Anmerkungen zu Röm 8,2," in *Neues Testament und christliche Existenz: Festschrift für Herbert Braun zum 70. Geburtstag am 4. Mai 1973*, ed. Hans Dieter Betz and Luise Schottroff (Tübingen: J. C. B. Mohr, 1973), pp. 286-87; von der Osten-Sacken, *Römer 8*, pp. 226-27 and Schmidt, *Römer*, p. 136.

⁵¹"Law," pp. 65-66.

⁵²See Lohse, "Röm 8,2," p. 284; von der Osten-Sacken, *Römer 8*, pp. 232-34; Henning Paulsen, *Überlieferung und Auslegung in Römer 8*, WMANT, Bd. 43 (Neukirchen-Vluyn: Neukirchener Verlag, 1974), pp. 63-66; Ridderbos, *Paul*, pp. 279-80; Schmidt, *Römer*, pp. 137-38 and Sickenberger, *Korinther und Römer*, p. 236.

⁵³*St Paul and the Church of Jerusalem* (Cambridge, England: University Press, 1925), p. 122, n. 54. See also Davies, *Paul and Rabbinic Judaism*, p. 70 and Schoeps, *Paul*, pp. 198-99.

⁵⁴*Die konkreten Einzelgebote in der paulinischen Paränese: Ein Beitrag zur neutestamentlichen Ethik* (Gütersloh: Gütersloher Verlagshaus Gerd Mohn, 1961), p. 96. See further Ridderbos, *Paul*, pp. 279, 285-86.

⁵⁵*A Commentary on the First Epistle to the Corinthians*, trans. James W. Leitch, bibliography and references by James W. Dunkly, ed. George W. MacRae, Hermeneia (Philadelphia: Fortress Press, 1975), p. 126.

⁵⁶So Karl Barth, *A Shorter Commentary on Romans*, trans. D. H. van Daalen (London: SCM Press, 1959), p. 126; Cranfield, "Law," p. 49 and Flückiger, "Christus, des Gesetzes τέλος," p. 156.

⁵⁷*Paulus*, p. 260.

⁵⁸For details see Lieselotte Mattern, *Das Verständnis des Gerichtes bei Paulus*, Abhandlungen zur Theologie des Alten und Neuen Testaments, Bd. 47 (Zurich: Zwingli Verlag, 1966), pp. 123-24.

⁵⁹See Bläser, *Gesetz*, p. 196; Wilfred Joest, *Gesetz und Freiheit: Das Problem des Tertius usus legis bei Luther und die neutestamentliche Parainese*, Aufl. 3 (Göttingen: Vandenhoeck & Ruprecht, 1961), pp. 165-85 and Ridderbos, *Paul*, pp. 178-80.

⁶⁰*Law*, p. 110. See further Bläser, Ibid., pp. 242-43; van Dülmen, *Gesetzes*, pp. 225-30; Hahn, "Gesetzesverständnis," p. 51; von der Osten Sacken, *Römer 8*, p. 257 and Ridderbos, Ibid., p. 282.

⁶¹Ibid., p. 61 and also pp. 225-30. See further Bandstra, Ibid.; Bläser, Ibid., p. 242 and Ridderbos, Ibid.

⁶²"Gesetzesverständnis," p. 62, n. 98. See also Markus Barth, "Die Stellung des Paulus zu Gesetz und Ordnung," *EvT* 33 (1973):516; van Dülmen, Ibid., pp. 66-68, 218-25; Jüngel, *Paulus und Jesus*, p. 61; von der Osten-Sacken, *Römer 8* p. 259; Schlier, *Galater*, pp. 200-201 and Schrage, *Einzelgebote*, pp. 99-100, 238. See further Irene Beck's elaborate treatment of this subject. "Altes und Neues Gesetz: Eine Untersuchung über die Kompromisslosigkeit des paulinischen Denkens," *MüTZ* 15 (1964):127-42.

[63] So, e.g., Markus Barth, Ibid., p. 522; Hahn, Ibid., p. 57; von der Osten-Sacken, Ibid. and Schrage, Ibid., pp. 99-100.

[64] *St Paul and the Church of Jerusalem*, p. 122, n. 54.

[65] So, e.g. Markus Barth, "Gesetz und Ordnung," p. 516 and Schrage, *Einzelgebote*, p. 238 (cf. pp. 100-102).

[66] So Barrett, *A Commentary on the Epistle to the Romans*, HNTC (New York: Harper & Row, 1957), pp. 197-98; Pierre Benoit, "La loi et la croix d' après saint Paul (Rom. vii,7-viii,4)," *Revue Biblique* 47 (1938):502; Bruce, "Paul and the Law of Moses," p. 264; Démann, "Moses und das Gesetz bei Paulus," p. 256; Drane, *Paul*, p. 133; Hans Hellbardt, "Christus, das Telos des Gesetzes," *EvT* 3 (1936):331-46; Joest, *Gesetz und Freiheit*, p. 138; Kuss, *Romerbrief*, 3:751-53; Leenhardt, *Romans*, p. 266, n.*; Henrik Ljungman, *Pistis: A Study of Its Presuppositions and Its Meaning in Pauline Use*, trans. W. F. Salisbury, Acta Reg. Societatis Humaniorum Litterarum Lundiensis, 64 (Lund: C. W. K. Gleerup, 1964), pp. 102-3; Ernst Lohmeyer, *Grundlagen paulinischer Theologie*, Beiträge zur historischen Theologie, 1 (Tübingen: J. C. B. Mohr, 1929), pp. 63-69; Kurt Stalder, *Das Werk des Geistes in der Heiligung bei Paulus* (Zurich: EVZ-Verlag, 1962), pp. 351-57 and Verweijs, *Evangelium und neues Gesetz*, pp. 64-65.

[67] So Bandstra, *Law*, pp. 105-6; Bring, "Röm. 10,4," p. 43; Du Plessis, ΤΕΛΕΙΟΣ, pp. 142-43 and Ladd, "Paul and the Law," p. 58.

[68] See, e.g., Bandstra, Ibid., p. 106; Barrett, *Romans*, p. 198; Benoit, "La loi et la croix," p. 502; Démann, "Moses und das Gesetz bei Paulus," p. 256; Joest, *Gesetz und Freiheit*, p. 138; Ladd, Ibid.; Leenhardt, *Romans*, p. 266, n. * and Stalder, *Das Werk des Geistes*, p. 352.

[69] *Paul*, p. 133.

[70] See, e.g., Althaus, *Gebot und Gesetz: Zum Thema "Gesetz und Evangelium"*, Beiträge zur Förderung christlicher Theologie, Bd. 46, Hft. 2 (Gütersloh: C. Bertelsmann Verlag, 1952); Bandstra, Ibid., pp. 75-114; Beck, "Altes und neues Gesetz"; Bornkamm, "Gesetzesverständnis," p. 111; Bultmann, *Theology of the New Testament*, trans. Kendrick Grobel, 2 vols. in 1 (New York: Charles Scribner's Sons, 1951-55), 1:268, 341; Burton, *Galatians*, pp. 447-60; Hans F. von Campenhausen, *The Formation of the Christian Bible*, trans. J. A. Baker (Philadelphia: Fortress Press, 1972), p. 33; van Dülmen, *Gesetzes*, pp. 218-30; Paul Feine, *Das gesetzesfreie Evangelium des Paulus nach seinem Werdegang dargestellt* (Leipzig: J. C. Hinrichs, 1899), p. 222; Hahn, "Gesetzesverständnis," p. 62, n. 98; Cristoph Haufe, "Die Stellung des Paulus zum Gesetz," *TLZ* 91 (1966):171-78; Joest, Ibid., p. 140; Jüngel, *Paulus und Jesus*, p. 61; Kertelge, *"Rechtfertigung"*, pp. 202-6; Kuss, "Nomos bei Paulus," pp. 210-27; Ladd, "Paul and the Law," pp. 65-67; Lohse, "Röm 8,2," pp. 286-87; Longenecker, *Paul*,

pp. 144-53; T. W. Manson, "Jesus, Paul, and the Law," in *Judaism and Christianity*, 3 vols. (London: Sheldon Press, 1937-38), vol. 3: *Law and Religion*, ed. Erwin I. J. Rosenthal (1938):136; Mauer, *Gesetzeslehre*, p. 53; Ridderbos, *Paul*, pp. 278-88; Schlier, *Der Brief an die Galater*, KExKNT, Abt. 7, Aufl. 12 (Göttingen: Vandenhoeck & Ruprecht, 1962), pp. 176-88; Schrage, *Einzelgebote*, pp. 93-102, 228-38; Charles A. Anderson Scott, *Christianity according to St. Paul* (Cambridge, England: University Press, 1927), pp. 41-46; Gottlieb Söhngen, *Gesetz und Evangelium: Ihre Analoge Einheit: Theologisch, philosophisch, staatsbürgerlich* (Freiburg: Verlag Karl Alber, 1957), pp. 37-39, 83-85; R. McL. Wilson, "Nomos: The Biblical Signification of Law," *SJT* 5 (1952):44-45.

[71] Ibid.

[72] *Paul*, pp. 144-53. For an explanation of these terms, see Ibid., pp. 122-27.

[73] *Galatians*, pp. 447-60.

[74] *Gebot und Gesetz*.

[75] *Einzelgebote*, pp. 232-33.

[76] *Gerechtigkeit Gottes*, pp. 96-97.

[77] *Gesetzes*, pp. 223-25. See also Beck, "Altes und neues Gesetz," p. 135.

[78] "Gesetz."

[79] "St. Paul and the Law," p. 67.

[80] "Nomos bei Paulus," pp. 221-23.

[81] "Paulus und das Alte Testament," in *Studien zur Geschichte und Theologie der Reformation: Festschrift für Ernst Bizer*, ed. Luise Abrahowski and J. F. Gerhard Goeters (Neukirchen-Vluyn: Neukirchener Verlag, 1969), p. 55.

[82] "Matices del término 'ley' en las cartas de San Pablo," *Estudios Eclesiásticos* 49 (1974):46.

[83] So, e.g., Beck, "Altes und neues Gesetz," p. 142; Bultmann, *Theology*, 1:344; Burton, *Galatians*, p. 458; van Dülmen, *Gesetzes*, pp. 225-30 and Ladd, "Paul and the Law," p. 66.

[84] So, e.g., von Campenhausen, *Bible*, pp. 29-30; Ladd, Ibid., p. 67; Ridderbos, *Paul*, p. 284 and Schrage, *Einzelgebote*, p. 231.

[85] *Paul and His Interpreters: A Critical History*, trans. W. Montgomery (London: Adam & Charles Black, 1912), pp. 246-47.

[86] *Christianity according to St Paul*, pp. 42, 45.

Notes: Chapter I

[87]"The Law, Jews and Gentiles--A Jewish Perspective," *Lutheran Quarterly* 21 (1969):414.

[88]See pp. 25-27.

[89]*Paul and Rabbinic Judaism*, p. 72 and *Torah in the Messianic Age and/or the Age to Come*, JBL Monograph Series, vol. 7 (Philadelphia: Society of Biblical Literature, 1952), p. 84. So also Longenecker, *Paul*, pp. 184-87.

[90]*Paul and Rabbinic Judaism*, p. 144. In addition, see Howard M. Teeple, who also connects the concept of a new law with the idea of a new Moses. *The Mosaic Eschatological Prophet*, JBL Monograph Series, vol. 10 (Philadelphia: Society of Biblical Literature, 1957), pp. 110-11.

But more can be said here. Drawing on those Jewish traditions which equate Torah with Wisdom, Davies holds that Paul's identification of Christ with Wisdom means he understood Christ in his person as well as his words to be the New Torah. Ibid., pp. 147-76.

[91]Ibid., p. 73.

[92]"Torah and Paul," in *God's Christ and His People: Studies in Honour of Nils Alstrup Dahl*, ed. Jacob Jervell and Wayne A. Meeks (Oslo: Universitetsvorlaget, 1977), pp. 132-40. See also idem., "Torah and Christ," *Interp* 29 (1975):372-90 and *IDB*, Supplementary Volume, s.v. "Torah," pp. 909-11.

[93]*La notion de nomos dans le Pentateuque grec*, preface by Ignace de la Potterie, AnBib, 52 (Rome: Biblical Institute Press, 1973).

[94]"Torah and Paul," p. 137. Italics his.

[95]*Gesetz und Geschichte: Untersuchungen zur Theologie der jüdischen Apokalyptik und der pharisäischen Orthodoxie*, WMANT, Bd. 3 (Neukirchen: Neukirchener Verlag, 1960).

[96]"Torah and Paul," p. 138.

[97]See W. Feyerabend, "Über den Schluss des 3. Kapitels im Briefe an die Römer," *Neue kirchliche Zeitschrift* 3 (1892): 409-20 and Lohse, "'Wir richten das Gesetz auf!' Glaube und Thora im Römerbrief," in *Treue zur Thora: Beiträge zur Mitte des christlich-jüdischen Gesprachs: Festschrift für Günther Harder zum 75. Geburtstag*, ed. Peter von der Osten-Sacken, Veröffentlichungen aus dem Institut Kirche und Judentum bei der Kirchlichen Hochschule Berlin, Hft. 3 (Berlin: Institut Kirche und Judentum, 1977), pp. 65-71. In his recent monograph on the development in Paul's attitude toward the law, Hans Hübner singles out Rom 3:31 for special treatment. *Das Gesetz bei Paulus: Ein Beitrag zum Werden der paulinischen Theologie*, FRLANT, Bd. 119 (Göttingen: Vandenhoeck & Ruprecht, 1978), pp. 118-29.

CHAPTER II

ROMANS 3:31 AS A *CRUX INTERPRETUM*

[1]*Marcion: Das Evangelium vom fremden Gott: Eine Monographie zur Geschichte der Grundlegung der katholischen Kirche. Neue Studien zu Marcion* (Darmstadt: Wissenschaftliche Buchgesellschaft, 1960), p. 104 [Beilagen].

[2]*The Epistle of Paul to the Romans*, Moffatt New Testament Commentary (London: Hodder & Stoughton, 1932), p. 63. Italics his.

[3]*Bible*, p. 33.

[4]*Paul*, p. 183.

[5]*Romans*, 1:125.

[6]Ibid. See also Luz, *Geschichtsverständnis*, p. 172 and Schlier, *Römerbrief*, p. 119.

[7]So Cranfield, *A Critical and Exegetical Commentary on the Epistle to the Romans*, ICC, 2 vols. (Edinburgh: T. & T. Clark, 1975-), vol. 1: *Introduction and Commentary on Romans I-VIII* (1975), 1:223 and Murray, Ibid., 1:127 respectively. See also Charles Hodge, *Commentary on the Epistle to the Romans*, new rev. ed. (New York: A. C. Armstrong & Son, 1896), p. 159; Luz, Ibid., p. 177 and Nygren, *Romans*, p. 167.

[8]*Römer*, p. 36. See further Luz, Ibid., p. 171. Though understanding νόμος here as Scripture, Dodd concedes to this argument when he declares: "His [Paul's] Greek readers, however could not be expected to bear in mind that 'Law' meant *Torah*, and that *Torah* had a wider sense; and in the sense which 'Law' has borne in most of this discussion it is confusing and misleading to say that *we uphold the Law*, unless by that is meant that the moral principles which underlie the precepts of the Law are, in fact, fulfilled by those who rely on divine grace." *Romans*, p. 64. Words in brackets mine. Italics his.

[9]"Notes au Commentaire de Père Huby," in *Romains*, Joseph Huby, p. 582.

[10]*Geschichtsverständnis*, p. 171.

[11]"Römer 4 und die Idee der Heilsgeschichte," in *Rekonstruktion und Interpretation: Gesammelte Aufsätze zum Neuen Testament*, BEvT, Bd. 50 (Munich: Chr. Kaiser Verlag, 1969), p. 166.

¹²*Romans*, 1:223. See also Hodge, *Romans*, p. 159 and Murray, *Romans*, 1:125.

¹³Ibid.

¹⁴*Notes on Epistles of St Paul from Unpublished Commentaries* (London: Macmillan & Co., 1895), p. 275. So also apparently Nils A. Dahl, "The Missionary Theology in the Epistle to the Romans," in *Studies in Paul: Theology for the Early Christian Mission*, assisted by Paul Donahue (Minneapolis: Augsburg Publishing House, 1977), pp. 83, 85.

¹⁵"Toposforschung und Torahinterpretation bei Paulus und Jesus," *NTS* 24 (1978):478-79.

¹⁶"Über den Schluss des 3. Kapitels im Briefe an die Römer," pp. 409-13, 415-17. See also Mauer, *Gesetzeslehre*, p. 91 and Stalder, *Das Werk des Geistes*, p. 269.

¹⁷*TDNT*, s.v. "ἵστημι," 7:649.

¹⁸"Gesetzesverständnis," p. 111.

¹⁹"Law," p. 282.

²⁰*Römer*, p. 36. See further Bandstra, *Law*, p. 100.

²¹*Romans*, p. 166.

²²"Altes und neues Gesetz," pp. 136-37. For other possible references see Luz, *Geschichtsverständnis*, p. 172, n. 140.

²³*Gottes Gerechtigkeit: Ein Kommentar zum Römerbrief*, Aufl. 2 (Stuttgart: Calwer Verlag, 1952), pp. 156-57.

²⁴*Romans*, 1:126.

²⁵*Notes*, p. 275.

²⁶"Missionary Theology," pp. 83, 85.

²⁷"Paul and the New Testament Ethic in the Thought of John Knox," in *Christian History and Interpretation: Studies Presented to John Knox*, ed. W. R. Farmer, C. F. D. Moule and R. R. Niebuhr (Cambridge, England: University Press, 1967), pp. 282-83.

²⁸So van Dülmen, *Gesetzes*, p. 88; Klein, "Römer 4," p. 150 and Schlier, *Römerbrief*, p. 119. Cf. Luz, *Geschichtsverständnis*, p. 173. See also Wilckens, *Der Brief an die Römer*, Evangelisch-Katholischer Kommentar zum Neuen Testament, Bd. 6/1 (Zurich: Benziger Verlag, 1978), 1:249. But cf. Ibid., 1:250.

²⁹"Toposforschung und Torahinterpretation," p. 479.

³⁰"Notes," p. 582.

[31] *Critical and Exegetical Hand-Book to the Epistle to the Romans*, trans. John C. Moore and Edwin Johnson, rev. and ed. by William P. Dickson, with a Preface and Supplementary Notes by Timothy Dwight (New York: Funk & Wagnalls, 1884), p. 144.

[32] E.G., von der Osten-Sacken, *Römer 8*, p. 247, n. 7 and Wilckens, "Zu Römer 3,21-4,25. Antwort an G. Klein," in *Rechtfertigung als Freiheit*, p. 53.

[33] "Zur Gedankenführung in den paulinischen Briefen," in *Studia Paulina in honorem Johannis de Zwaan septuagenarii*, ed. J. N. Sevenster and W. C. van Unnik (Haarlem: Erven F. Bohn, 1953), p. 147.

[34] *Memory and Manuscript*, p. 287. See also Gustaf Dalman, *Jesus-Jeshua: Studies in the Gospels*, trans. Paul P. Levertoff (London: S.P.C.K., 1929), pp. 57-58; David Daube, "'Ye Have Heard--But I Say Unto You,'" in *The New Testament and Rabbinic Judaism*, Jordan Lectures in Comparative Religion, 2 (London: Athlone Press, 1956), p. 60 and Michel, *Römer*, p. 97.

[35] See von der Osten-Sacken's fairly detailed formulation of this argument. *Römer 8*, pp. 245-50.

[36] See pp. 29-30 above.

[37] *Romans*, p. 96.

[38] Cf. Barrett, *Romans*, pp. 84, 86; Karl Barth, *Romans*, p. 48; Bläser, *Gesetz*, p. 37; Jules Cambier, *L' Évangile de Dieu selon l' Épître aux Romains: Exégèse et Théologie biblique*, Studia Neotestamentica, Studia 3, 3 tomes (Brussels: Desclée de Brouwer, 1967-), t. 1: *L' Évangile de la Justice et de la Grâce* (1967), 1:159; Dodd, *Romans*, pp. 63-65; Friedrich, "Das Gesetz des Glaubens," pp. 416-17; Gerhardsson, *Memory and Manuscript*, pp. 287-88; Gronemeyer, *Antinomismus*, pp. 117-18; Hahn, "Gesetzesverständnis," pp. 37-41; Huby, *Romains*, pp. 163-65; Hübner, *Gesetz*, pp. 123-24; Jeremias, "Die Gedankenführung in Röm 4: Zum paulinischen Glaubensverständnis," in *Foi et Salut selon S. Paul (Épître aux Romains 1,16): Colloque Oecumenique a l' Abbaye de S. Paul hors les murs, 16-21 avril 1968*, with the collaboration of S. Agourides, J. J. von Allmen, L. Arnaldich et al., AnBib, 42 (Rome: Pontifical Biblical Institute, 1970), pp. 51-52; Kasemann, *Römer*, pp. 97-98; *The Interpreter's Bible*, ed. George Arthur Buttrick, 12 vols. (New York: Abingdon-Cokesbury Press, 1951-57), vol. 9: *The Epistle to the Romans*, by John Knox (1954):437-38; Kuss, "Nomos bei Paulus," pp. 222-23; Lagrange, *Romains*, pp. 80-81; Leenhardt, *Romans*, p. 112; Lietzmann, *Einführung in die Textgeschichte der Paulusbriefe an die Römer*, HNT, Bd. 8, Aufl. 5 (Tübingen: J. C. B. Mohr, 1971), p. 52; Lohse, "Glaube und Thora im Römerbrief"; "Röm 8,2," pp. 280-83; Meyer, *Romans*, p. 145; Michel, *Römer*, p. 97; von der Osten-Sacken, *Römer 8*, pp. 247-48; Schmidt, *Römer*, pp. 75-76; Sickenberger, *Korinther und Römer*, p. 202; Wilckens, "Die Rechtfertigung Abrahams nach Römer 4," in *Rechtfertigung als Freiheit*, pp. 42-43 and *Römer*, 1:250.

[39] As we have already seen, Jeremias treats some of Paul's rhetorical questions under the rubric of "objections." "Zur Gedankenführung in den paulinischen Briefen," pp. 146-48. Here we hope to advance upon Jeremias' treatment of these texts.

Studies on Pauline style and rhetoric are sorely lacking. Among those presently available we found the following somewhat helpful: Bultmann, *Der Stil der paulinischen Predigt und die kynisch-stoische Diatribe*, FRLANT, Bd. 13 (Göttingen: Vandenhoeck & Ruprecht, 1910); James Hope Moulton, *A Grammar of New Testament Greek*, 4 vols. (Edinburgh: T. & T. Clark, 1908-76), vol. 4: *Style*, by Nigel Turner (1976):80-100; Norbert Schneider, *Die rhetorische Eigenart der paulinischen Antithese*, HUT, Bd. 11 (Tübingen: J. C. B. Mohr, 1970); Johannes Weiss, "Beiträge zur paulinischen Rhetorik," in *Theologische Studien: Professor D. Bernhard Weiss zu seinem 70. Geburtstage dargebracht*, by C. R. Gregory, A. von Harnack, M. W. Jacobus et al. (Göttingen: Vandenhoeck & Ruprecht, 1897), pp. 165-247 and Paul Wendland, "Philo und die kynisch-stoische Diatribe," in *Beiträge zur Geschichte der griechischen Philosophie und Religion*, ed. Paul Wendland and Otto Kern (Berlin: G. Reimer, 1895), pp. 1-75. For additional bibliography see Schneider, Ibid., pp. 126-34.

Recently, Hans Dieter Betz and Wilhelm Wuellner have undertaken to analyze Galatians and Romans respectively from the standpoint of rhetoric. See "The Literary Composition and Function of Paul's Letter to the Galatians," *NTS* 21 (1975): 353-79 and "Paul's Rhetoric or Argumentation in Romans: An Alternative to the Donfried-Karris Debate over Romans," *CBQ* 38 (1976):330-51.

[40] E.g., Rom 2:21-23; 6:2b-3; 10:14-15a; 11:15; 1 Cor 4:21; 15:12; 2 Cor 6:14-16a.

[41] E.g., Rom 3:1, 9, 27, 29; 4:3, 9; 7:24; 10:18, 19; 1 Cor 3:5; Gal 3:19; 4:30.

[42] The dependent use of μὴ γένοιτο, in which it is usually combined with a dative subject and a complementary infinitive, is not a matter of concern in this inquiry.

[43] The Lucan use of absolute μὴ γένοιτο does not concern us, as it does not follow the pattern of Paul's usage, i.e., question negated by μὴ γένοιτο. A possible exception might be Gal 2:17, on which see p. 51, n. 108 below.

[44] So Adolf Bonhöffer, *Epiktet und das Neue Testament*, Religionsgeschichtliche Versuche und Vorarbeiter, Bd. 10 (Giessen: Alfred Töpelmann, 1911), p. 138. As Bonhöffer also points out, the absolute use of μὴ γένοιτο cannot be documented prior to Paul. It does occur, however, subsequent to Paul and Epictetus in Lucian, Achilles Tatius and Aristaenetus.

[45] The most likely exception to the presence of such a false inference in questions negated by μὴ γένοιτο is 1 Cor 6:15. See Burton, *Galatians*, p. 126; Lagrange, *Galates*, p. 50 and Oepke, *Galater*, p. 60. On this see the discussion below,

Notes: Chapter II   141

p. 57. Burton also thinks that Rom 11:1 could be another exception. Ibid. On this see p. 49, n. 101.

⁴⁶So F. Blass and A. Debrunner, *A Greek Grammar of the New Testament and Other Early Christian Literature*, trans. and rev. by Robert W. Funk (Chicago: University of Chicago Press, 1961), par. 384 and Burton, *Syntax of the Moods and Tenses in New Testament Greek*, 3d ed. (Chicago: University of Chicago Press, 1898), p. 79.

⁴⁷See Bultmann, *Stil*, p. 67; Jeremias, "Zur Gedankenführung in den paulinischen Briefen," pp. 146-48 and Weiss, "Rhetorik," pp. 220-21, 228, 230-33, 238, 240.

⁴⁸Although Epictetus (ca. A.D. 50-120) did not write down his philosophical discourses, they were apparently preserved to a fairly faithful degree by his pupil, Flavius Arrian, in the second century A.D. So W. A. Oldfather, trans., *Epictetus: The Discourses as Reported by Arrian, the Manual, and Fragments*, Loeb Classical Library, 2 vols. (London: W. Heinemann, 1926-28), 1 (1926):xii-xiii. The citations from Epictetus in what follows are taken from Oldfather's Greek text and English translation.

⁴⁹*Discourses* 1.1.13; 1.2.35; 1.5.10; 1.8.15; 1.9.32; 1.10.7; 1.11.23; 1.12.10; 1.19.7; 1.26.6; 1.28.19, 24; 1.29.9; 2.8.2, 26; 2.23.23; 3.1.42, 44; 3.7.4; 3.23.14, 25; 3.24.101, 113; 4.7.26; 4.8.26; 4.11.24, 33, 36. As *Discourses* 3.24.101, 113 do not fit the usual pattern, i.e., question negated by μή γένοιτο, we may disregard them here.

⁵⁰So *Discourses* 1.2.35; 1.8.15; 1.10.7; 1.12.10; 1.19.7; 1.28.19; 1.29.9; 2.23.23; 3.1.44; 3.23.25; 4.11.33. Bonhöffer recognizes this fact but unfortunately cites no examples. *Epiktet und das Neue Testament*, p. 137. Nor does he indicate whether all the occurrences of this expression in Epictetus fit into this pattern.

⁵¹So *Discourses* 1.1.13; 1.5.10; 1.9.32; 1.11.23; 1.28.24; 2.8.2, 26; 3.1.42; 3.7.4; 3.23.14; 4.7.26; 4.8.26; 4.11.24, 35.

⁵²So *Discourses* 1.2.36-37; 1.19.7-10; 2.23.23-47; 3.23.25-26 (μέν); 4.11.33-36 (εἰ μή).

⁵³So *Discourses* 1.8.16; 1.12.10-16.

⁵⁴So *Discourses* 1.28.19-28.

⁵⁵So *Discourses* 1.10.7-13; 1.29.9-15 (no introductory word).

⁵⁶So *Discourses* 3.1.44-45.

⁵⁷So *Discourses* 1.2.36-37; 1.8.16; 3.1.44-45; 3.23.25-26 and *Discourses* 1.10.7-13; 1.12.10-16; 1.19.7-10; 1.28.19-28; 1.29.9-15; 2.23.23-47; 4.11.33-36 respectively.

⁵⁸So *Discourses* 1.2.35-37; 1.8.15-16; 3.1.44-45.

⁵⁹So *Discourses* 1.10.7; 1.19.7; 1.28.19; 1.29.9; 2.23.23; 4.11.33 and *Discourses* 1.12.10; 3.23.25 respectively. The composite nature of the *Discourses* may account for the difficulty one sometimes experiences in determining how far Epictetus carries the clarification of his μὴ γένοιτο. To this extent the *Discourses* differ from Paul's flowing discourse in Romans and elsewhere.

⁶⁰See also *Discourses* 1.5.10; 1.9.32; 1.11.23; 2.8.26; 3.1.42; 3.7.4; 4.7.26; 4.8.26; 4.11.35 and cf. Lucian, *Dialogues of the Gods* 1.2; *Dialogues of the Courtesans* 13.4; Achilles Tatius, *The Adventures of Leucippe and Clitophon* 5.18.4.

⁶¹See *Discourses* 1.5.10; 1.9.32; 1.28.24; 2.8.2; 2.8.26; 3.1.42; 4.8.26; 4.11.24.

⁶²So *Discourses* 1.28.24; 3.1.42; 4.8.26.

⁶³While Paul may intend to represent this question as proceeding from an imaginary Jewish opponent (cf. 2:17-29), it could also come from a knowledgeable Gentile who is following the apostle's discourse closely. Or Paul may not have a specific person or group in mind. His use of questions or objections may simply be an indirect way of warding off false conclusions which could be drawn from his statements. This may also be said of those questions negated by μὴ γένοιτο. See Bultmann, *Stil*, p. 68.

Actually, this phenomenon of intermittent questions or objections interrupting one's discourse is characteristic of what is commonly called the "Cynic-Stoic diatribe." See Bultmann, Ibid., pp. 10-19. Whether or not the "diatribe" can be called a literary genre (*Gattung*), it is evident from a reading of Epictetus' *Discourses*, for example, that at the pre-literary stage there existed a style of speaking or teaching which often contained elements of a dialogue with sporadic questions and objections. For a definition of the "diatribe," see Wendland, "Philo," pp. 3-4.

⁶⁴So Paul J. Achtemeier, "St. Paul, Accommodation or Confrontation," (Th.D. dissertation, Union Theological Seminary in New York, 1957), p. 243. For further discussion on the specific meaning of the "oracles," see J. W. Doeve, "Some Notes with Reference to τὰ λόγια τοῦ θεοῦ in Romans 3.2," in *Studia Paulina in honorem Johannis de Zwaan septuagenarii*, ed. J. N. Sevenster and W. C. van Unnik (Haarlem: Erven F. Bohn, 1953), pp. 111-23.

⁶⁵So Käsemann, *Römer*, p. 74.

⁶⁶Though Cranfield (*Romans*, 1:180) contends that ἠπίστησαν and ἀπιστία signify unbelief rather than unfaithfulness, the juxtaposition of these words with τὴν πίστιν τοῦ θεοῦ speaks in favor of the notion of faithlessness or apostasy in relation to God's covenant with Israel (so Bornkamm,

"Theologie als Teufelskunst. Rm. 3,1-9," in *Geschichte und Glaube*, 2:143 and Käsemann, Ibid., p. 73).

[67] Cf. Epictetus, *Discourses* 3.1.44.

[68] The imperative γινέσθω should probably be supplied with πᾶς δὲ ἄνθρωπος ψεύστης contrary to the RSV, "though every man be false." So Achtemeier, "St. Paul, Accommodation or Confrontation," p. 245. This statement (3:4b) is probably an allusion to Ps 115:2 [LXX]. With Paul's use of "every man" the discussion seems to take on a more general form. Perhaps, as Schlier suggests, the Jews are used typically of humanity. *Römerbrief*, p. 94, n. 7.

[69] The infinitive κρίνεσθαι can be either passive or middle. If passive, it refers to God's being judged. If middle, it refers to God's contending in a lawsuit. So Cranfield, *Romans*, 1:182, n. 4.

[70] Oepke recognizes this pattern clearly when he says: "Der immer stark rhetorische Aufbau des Zshgs ist überall, wo sie vorkommt, ziemlich der gleiche: 1. paul Voraussetzung (Rm 3,3f u 3,5f mit εἰ aus dem Vorhergehenden aufgenommen), 2. daraus scheinbar logisch sich ergebende, sachlich jedoch abzulehnende dialektisch-gegnerische Folgerung (etwas anders nur 1 Kr 6,15) in Frageform, 3. Ablehnung der Folgerung, 4. präzisierte Gegenbehauptung oder wenn mit γάρ angeknüpft (Rm 9,14f; 11,1; Gl 3,21), Begründung der Ablehnung." *Galater*, p. 60.

[71] Weiss notices this fact when he refers to the positive thought which is juxtaposed to the negative one. "Rhetorik," pp. 220-21. See also Schlier, *Römerbrief*, p. 93.

[72] So Bornkamm, "Rm. 3,1-9," p. 144.

[73] So, e.g., Althaus, *Römer*, p. 29; Dahl, "Missionary Theology," p. 85; Dodd, *Romans*, pp. 44, 46; Knox, *Romans*, pp. 421-22 and Weiss, "Rhetorik," p. 220.

[74] The reference to God's inflicting wrath (ὀργή) shows that Paul's thought regresses at least to Rom. 2 if not to 1:18.

[75] Cf. Epictetus, *Discourses* 1.10.7-13; 1.29.9-15.

[76] See Kuss, *Römerbrief*, 1:103-4; Lagrange, *Romains*, p. 66 and Schlier, *Römerbrief*, p. 95.

[77] So Cranfield, *Romans*, 1:185.

[78] Many manuscripts read εἰ γάρ instead of εἰ δέ. The choice between the two readings is a difficult one. If we adopt the former with Cranfield (Ibid., 1:185, n. 3), then 3:7 would appear to be an additional grounding for the false inference raised in 3:5. If we adopt the latter, then 3:7 stands in an adversative relation to 3:6 as a reply to it.

⁷⁹On this problem see Cranfield, Ibid., 1:185-87.

⁸⁰So Cranfield, Ibid., 1:187.

⁸¹So Käsemann, *Römer*, p. 78.

⁸²So Jeremias, "Zur Gedankenführung in den paulinischen Briefen," pp. 146-47 and Weiss, "Rhetorik," p. 220.

⁸³So Jeremias, Ibid., p. 147 and Weiss, Ibid.

⁸⁴Weiss' assertion (Ibid.) that the relative clause ὧν . . . ἐστιν (3:8b) functions instead of μὴ γένοιτο in answer to 3:7-8a cannot be maintained, for the form τί and the content of 3:7 exclude such a possibility.

⁸⁵*Romans*, 1:99.

⁸⁶On the structure of Paul's argument in this text and in 6:15; 7:7, 13, see Dahl, "Missionary Theology," pp. 82-83.

⁸⁷So Cranfield, *Romans*, 1:296.

⁸⁸So Cranfield, Ibid., 1:316.

⁸⁹So Cranfield, Ibid., 1:319.

⁹⁰So Barrett, *Romans*, p. 131. However, Cranfield understands ὑπὸ νόμον in the sense of standing under the condemnation of the law. Ibid., 1:320.

⁹¹Ibid., 1:321.

⁹²The use of ἤ (7:1) indicates Paul is giving a second analogy for their consideration. So Barrett, *Romans*, p. 135.

⁹³The ὥστε (7:12) seems to draw out the results of Paul's exposition (7:7-11).

⁹⁴So Cranfield, *Romans*, 1:341.

⁹⁵So Cranfield, Ibid., 1:354-55; Eichholz, *Paulus*, p. 255; Krister Stendahl, "The Apostle Paul and the Introspective Conscience of the West," *HTR* 56 (1963):211-12 and Werner Georg Kümmel, *Römer 7 und das Bild des Menschen im Neuen Testament: Zwei Studien*, Theologische Bücherei, Bd. 53 (Munich: Chr. Kaiser Verlag, 1974), pp. 57-58.

On the other hand, Käsemann apparently denies a close connection between Rom 7:14-25 and 7:13. See *Römer*, p. 189.

⁹⁶So Barrett, *Romans*, p. 146.

⁹⁷While Bultmann contends 7:25b is a marginal gloss now incorporated into the text ("Glossen im Römerbrief," *TLZ* 72 [1947]:197-202) and Friedrich Müller rearranges this verse and 8:1 to get the following sequence, 7:22-23, 25b, 24-25a; 8:2, 1, 3 ("Zwei Marginalien im Brief des Paulus an die Römer,"

ZNW 40 [1941]:249-54), Dahl recently argues that 7:25b is a delayed conclusion which refers back to and clarifies the statements in 7:5-6. "Missionary Theology," p. 85.

[98] On the relationship between Rom 7 and 8 see especially von der Osten-Sacken's recent treatment. *Römer 8*, pp. 188-244.

[99] So Barrett, *Romans*, pp. 180-81. On the other hand, some understand the first occurrence of "seed" in a purely physical sense, making "children" a theological rather than a physical term. So Murray, *Romans*, 2:10 and Schlier, *Römerbrief*, p. 290.

[100] So Barrett, Ibid., p. 185.

[101] Burton suggests that this question may not be a false inference from the preceding discussion. However, he does not elaborate on this point. *Galatians*, p. 126.

[102] So Barrett, *Romans*, p. 209.

[103] Presumably the law in its promise of righteousness (see 9:31) or simply righteousness (see 10:3).

[104] So Barrett, *Romans*, p. 212.

[105] Connected with ἐξ ἐθνῶν and contrasted with φύσει Ἰουδαῖοι, the word ἁμαρτωλοί apparently designates the Gentiles as "sinners" because they do not possess nor keep the law as the Jews. See Schlier, *Galater*, Aufl. 10, p. 53.

[106] So Burton understands and translates. *Galatians*, pp. 119, 123.

[107] As earlier (2:15), the term ἁμαρτωλοί, following the emphatic καὶ αὐτοί, which refers back to 2:15, probably indicates those who do not keep the law. Schlier, however, argues it should be understood in an absolute rather than a relative sense. *Galater*, p. 59, n. 1.

[108] On the debate about the accenting and understanding of αρα, cf. Burton (*Galatians*, p. 126, n.*), who prefers ἄρα, with Lightfoot (*Galatians*, p. 117), who prefers ἆρα.
C. F. D. Moule argues that 2:17 is not a question. *An Idiom-Book of New Testament Greek*, 2d ed. (Cambridge, England: University Press, 1971), p. 196. But this is hardly likely as the pattern of Paul's use of μὴ γένοιτο shows. So Burton, Ibid., pp. 125-26.

[109] See Betz, "In Defense of the Spirit: Paul's Letter to the Galatians as a Document of Early Christian Apologetics," in *Aspects of Religious Propaganda in Judaism and Early Christianity*, ed. E. Schüssler Fiorenza, University of Notre Dame Center for the Study of Judaism and Christianity in Antiquity, 2 (Notre Dame: University of Notre Dame Press, 1976), pp. 105-7; Jan Lambrecht, "The Line of Thought in Gal. 2.14b-21," *NTS*

24 (1978):491; Oepke, *Galater*, p. 61 and Ridderbos, *The Epistle of Paul to the Churches of Galatia*, NICNT (Grand Rapids: Wm. B. Eerdmans Publishing Co., 1953), p. 101.

For other interpretations, see the discussions in Burton, Ibid., pp 127-30; John Eadie, *A Commentary on the Greek Text of the Epistle of Paul to the Galatians* (Edinburgh: T. & T. Clark, 1894; reprint ed., Grand Rapids: Zondervan Publishing House, n.d.), pp. 174-77; Klein, "Individualgeschichte und Weltgeschichte bei Paulus: Eine Interpretation ihres Verhältnisses im Galaterbrief," in *Rekonstruktion und Interpretation*, pp. 185-90; Lagrange, *Galates*, pp. 48-50; Lambrecht, Ibid., pp. 485-89; Lightfoot, Ibid., pp. 116-17; Mussner, *Galaterbrief*, pp. 176-77 and Schlier, *Galater*, pp. 58-59.

[110] So Burton, Ibid., p. 127 and Schlier, Ibid. Cf. Rom 3:3, 5.

[111] See Ridderbos, *Galatia*, pp. 102-3 and Schlier, Ibid., p. 59. Cf. Gal 3:21; Rom 9:14-15; 11:1. To the contrary, Lambrecht contends that γάρ here has the function of continuation and of slight opposition. "Gal. 2.14b-21," pp. 491-93, 495.

[112] The "I" form here (and in 2:19) is general or typical, approximating the "we" (2:17). So Schlier, Ibid. Burton, however, regards the "I" form here as a tactful way of describing Peter's behavior at Antioch but in 2:19 as an emphatic way of depicting Paul's personal experience. *Galatians*, pp. 130, 132.

[113] Thus Ridderbos takes this verse to refer to "the building up and the breaking down of self-righteousness on the basis of the works of the law." *Galatia*, p. 102. As we have already seen, others find here a reference to the abrogation of certain prohibitions of the law, the abolition of the law as a dividing wall between Jews and Gentiles or the nullification of the law as a way of salvation. See p. 9 above.

[114] So Schlier, *Galater*, p. 59.

[115] So Klein, "Individualgeschichte und Weltgeschichte," p. 199 and Schlier, Ibid.

[116] So Eadie, *Galatians*, pp. 183-84. Cf. Rom 7:4 and see Schlier, Ibid., pp. 62-63.

[117] Cf. Rom 6:1-11.

[118] Though the apostle's discussion about Christ as the "seed" (3:16) is somewhat parenthetical here, it is surely a necessary preparation for 3:19c.

[119] So Burton, *Galatians*, p. 188; Eadie, *Galatians*, p. 264; Lightfoot, *Galatians*, pp. 144-45 and Schlier, *Galater*, p. 107.

Notes: Chapter II

[120] So Eadie, Ibid., p. 269 and Schlier, Ibid., p. 114.

[121] So Burton, *Galatians*, p. 190. Similarly Mussner, *Galaterbrief*, p. 250.

[122] So Eadie, *Galatians*, p. 270; Lightfoot, *Galatians*, pp. 146-47 and Ridderbos, *Galatia*, p. 140. For additional interpretations see Burton, Ibid., pp. 191-92 and Eadie, Ibid., pp. 271-74.

[123] So Oepke, *Galater*, p. 84 and Schlier, *Galater*, p. 116.

[124] Burton thinks this problem is suggested by the whole argument from 3:10, but especially from 3:15 onward. *Galatians*, p. 192. Schlier, however, would limit the background of the question to 3:19b-20. Ibid., p. 120.

[125] So Burton, Ibid., p. 194. As in the case of 2:18, so also here Lambrecht denies that 3:21cd, etc. are a grounding or explanation for Paul's μὴ γένοιτο. "Gal. 2.14b-21," p. 492.

[126] By "Scripture" Paul could imply a specific passage as Deut 27:26 (cf. Gal 3:10) or Ps 143:2 (Gal 2:16). Schlier understands Scripture in general. *Galater*, p. 121.
As 3:23-24 show, the Scripture's confinement of humanity under sin is parallel to its confinement under the law.

[127] So Burton, *Galatians*, p. 196. Cf. Rom 3:9, 19.

[128] See Eadie, *Galatians*, p. 279 and Schlier, *Galater*, p. 105.

[129] So Eadie, Ibid., pp. 289-90; Lightfoot, *Galatians*, p. 165 and Schlier, Ibid., p. 131.

[130] So Allo, *Saint Paul Première Épître aux Corinthiens*, ÉtBid, 2d ed. (Paris: J. Gabalda, 1956), p. 141.

[131] So Barrett, *First Corinthians*, p. 144 and Conzelmann, *First Corinthians*, p. 108. Otherwise, Allo, Ibid., pp. 141-42.

[132] Personal translation. So Barrett, Ibid., p. 146 and Jerome Murphy-O'Connor, "Corinthian Slogans in 1 Cor. 6:12-20," *CBQ* 40 (1978):394-95. Conzelmann apparently limits the Corinthian slogan to 6:13a. Ibid., p. 110.

[133] So Barrett, Ibid., pp. 146-47; Conzelmann, Ibid. and Murphy-O'Connor, Ibid., p. 395.

[134] So Barrett, Ibid., pp. 147-48; Conzelmann, Ibid. and Murphy-O'Connor, Ibid.

[135] See p. 33, n. 45 above.

¹³⁶So Conzelmann, *First Corinthians*, p. 111. Otherwise Lambrecht, who holds that 6:16 does not explain the μὴ γένοιτο of 6:15c but the interrogative clause of 6:15b. "Gal. 2.14b-21," p. 486, n. 7.

¹³⁷Personal translation. So Murphy-O'Connor, "1 Cor. 6:12-20," p. 393.

¹³⁸See pp. 39-41 above.

¹³⁹We exclude 1 Cor 6:15 from this summary, as it does not fit the usual pattern of Pauline usage and, therefore, is not related to Rom 3:31 which, as we will eventually show, does conform to this pattern.

¹⁴⁰Cf. p. 38, ns. 52-56 above.

¹⁴¹Cf. p. 38, n. 57 above.

¹⁴²See pp. 41-44 above.

¹⁴³While Weiss has recognized this point with regard to Rom 6:1, 15; 7:7; 9:14 ("Rhetorik," pp. 228, 230, 238), Dahl has perceived it with respect to Rom 6:1, 15; 7:7, 13; 9:14; 11:1, 11; Gal 3:21 ("Missionary Theology," pp. 82-84; "The Future of Israel," and "Contradictions in Scripture," in *Studies in Paul*, pp. 144, 149-50 and pp. 173-74 respectively).

¹⁴⁴Schmidt is close to the truth when he calls Rom 3:31 both the conclusion to the exposition of Rom 3 and the transition to Rom 4. *Römer*, pp. 75-76.

CHAPTER III

THE EXEGESIS OF ROMANS 3:21-4:25

¹So Cranfield, *Romans*, 1:195-96 and Schlier, *Römerbrief*, p. 99.

²So van Dülmen, *Gesetzes*, pp. 82-83 and Käsemann, *Römer*, p. 81.

³So Cranfield, *Romans*, 1:196-97.

⁴So George Foot Moore, *Judaism in the First Centuries of the Christian Era, the Age of the Tannaim*, 3 vols. (Cambridge: Harvard University Press, 1927-30), 1:263. See also Bläser, *Gesetz*, p. 31 and Eichholz, *Paulus*, pp. 241-42.

In his recent study on νόμος in the Greek Pentateuch, Laurent Monsengwo Pasinya comes to a bold conclusion that challenges previous scholarly findings about the meaning of the Greek νόμος. He argues that νόμος was not simply a comprehensive term for laws during the period in which the Pentateuch was translated into Greek. Rather his analysis of the Greek sources indicates it could mean the manifestation of God, the symbol of the polis and of the cosmos, as well as the incarnation of the king. Thus he asserts that νόμος became the hinge on which the whole life of the Greek society pivoted, i.e., the relations of the world of the gods with that of people, as well as the relations of people among themselves and with the universe. In Greek Antiquity, according to Monsengwo Pasinya, νόμος was the term which denoted "religion." *La notion de nomos*, p. 201. Moreover, he argues that the same is true in the case of the Jewish Torah. It was the term that designated the totality of those teachings which govern the relations of people with God and with themselves. Hence, according to Monsengwo Pasinya, Torah summed up in itself the covenant and synthesized the whole religion of Israel. Ibid. In view of his findings he faults C. H. Dodd with an inadequate analysis of the use of νόμος in the Septuagint and with adopting a too restricted and incomplete understanding of it. Ibid., p. 202. (Dodd had argued that the use of νόμος to translate "Torah" in the Septuagint had given a misleading legalistic tone to much of the OT. "The Law," in *The Bible and the Greeks* [London: Hodder & Stoughton, 1935], pp. 33-34, 41). In conclusion, Monsengwo Pasinya states that νόμος, as a translation of Torah, has a global content in the Pentateuch; it does not denote the individual laws nor the legislative part of the covenant only, nor the doctrinal part only, but the entirety of these. It signifies the divine revelation composed of both doctrinal as well as legislative elements. Therefore, it does not depict the divine revelation as directing or commanding but as teaching and instructing. Ibid., p. 203.

⁵So Murray, *Romans*, 1:109-110.

⁶So Wilckens contends: "Dass νόμος und νόμος--zumal in *einem* Satzgefüge zusammengeordnet--ein und dieselbe Tora meinen, ist unmöglich zu bestreiten. Gewiss stehen sie in verschiedener Funktion: 'Ohne Gesetz', das heisst: abseits des Werke fordernden und zum Heil bzw. Unheil anrechnenden Kriteriums des endzeitlichen Gerichtes; zusammen mit den 'Propheten' dagegen hat dasselbe Gesetz die Funktion des 'Zeugen' der Glaubensgerechtigkeit." "Römer 3,21-4,25," pp. 53-54. Italics his.

⁷While some understand δικαιοσύνη as a status of righteousness before God (cf. 3:20; see Klein, "Gottes Gerechtigkeit als Thema der neuesten Paulus-Forschung," in *Rekonstruktion und Interpretation*, p. 232), others interpret it as God's claim (*Recht*) over his creation which manifests itself in saving power (see Käsemann, *Römer*, p. 86).

⁸So von der Osten-Sacken, *Römer 8*, p. 246. See also Hahn, "Gesetzesverständnis," p. 37, n. 27 and Wilckens, "Römer 4," p. 42.

⁹So *TDNT*, s.v. "μάρτυς," by Hermann Strathmann, 4:496.

¹⁰So Friedrich, "Das Gesetz des Glaubens," pp. 409-410; Hahn, "Gesetzesverständnis," p. 40; Lohse, "Glaube und Thora im Römerbrief," p. 65; von der Osten-Sacken, *Römer 8*, pp. 246-47 and Wilckens, "Römer 3,21-4,25," pp. 53-54.

¹¹Nonetheless, Friedrich tries to find it portrayed in the OT cult (see 3:24-25) or in the Shema (see 3:29-30; cf. Deut 6:4). Ibid., pp. 412-15. But he also finds this witness of the law in the Pentateuchal stories about Abraham (see Rom 4). Ibid., pp. 414, 416.

¹²As we hope to demonstrate, this witness of the law to righteousness by faith is embodied in Paul's treatment of Abraham (Rom 4). Otto Michel thinks Paul specifically anticipates Rom 4 by his reference (3:21b) to the law (so 4:3 = Gen 15:6) or the prophets (so 4:7 = Ps 32:1-2). *Römer*, p. 90.

¹³So Meyer, *Romans*, p. 129.

¹⁴George E. Howard argues that πίστις here means "faithfulness," i.e., the faithfulness of Christ. "On the 'Faith of Christ,'" *HTR* 60 (1967):464. However, see Käsemann (*Römer*, p. 87) who supports the meaning that we have attached to the word in this context.

¹⁵On the relationship of this clause to the preceding verses, see Cranfield, *Romans*, 1:205.

Notes: Chapter III

[16] So Käsemann, *Römer*, p. 88. For surveys of the discussion about the presence of a pre-Pauline formula in this verse and in vv. 25-26, see Herbert Koch, *Römer 3,21-31 in der Paulusinterpretation der letzten 150 Jahre* (Göttingen: By the author, 1971), pp. 107-34; Hans-Jürgen van der Minde, *Schrift und Tradition bei Paulus: Ihre Bedeutung und Funktion im Römerbrief*, Paderborner Theologische Studien, Bd. 3 (Munich: Verlag Ferdinand Schöningh, 1976), pp. 58-64 and Stuhlmacher, "Zum neueren Exegesis von Röm 3,24-26," in *Jesus und Paulus: Festschrift für Werner Georg Kümmel zum 70. Geburtstag*, ed. E. Earle Ellis and Erich Grässer (Göttingen: Vandenhoeck & Ruprecht, 1975), pp. 315-33.

[17] While some (so, e.g., Nygren, *Romans*, pp. 156-58) argue that ἱλαστήριον refers to the "mercy-seat," an object of temple furniture, others debate whether it entails the notion of "expiation" (so, e.g., Dodd, *Romans*, pp. 54-55) or "propitiation" (so, e.g., Cranfield, *Romans*, 1:214-18).

[18] So Käsemann, *Römer*, p. 91. Otherwise, Cranfield, Ibid., 1:211-12.

[19] These verses (3:25b-26) have also become a focal point for gaining a proper understanding of the concept of God's righteousness. While some as Käsemann (Ibid., p. 94) understand this concept primarily in terms of God's claim (*Recht*) over his creation, others as Klein ("Gottes Gerechtigkeit," p. 230), take it to refer to the result of God's justifying activity, i.e., a righteous status before God.

[20] So Cranfield, *Romans*, 1:219 and Käsemann, Ibid., p. 95. For a somewhat different understanding of what this boasting entails, see Wilckens, *Römer*, 1:246-47.

[21] So Friedrich, "Das Gesetz des Glaubens," p. 415. Otherwise, Blass and Debrunner, *Grammar*, par. 298(2). However, they admit that such is its meaning in 1 Cor 15:35, the only other occurrence of the word in Paul.

[22] For references see Cranfield, *Romans*, 1:219, n. 5.

[23] So Friedrich, "Das Gesetz des Glaubens," p. 408.

[24] So Käsemann, *Römer*, p. 95; Lietzmann, *Römer*, p. 52; Luz, *Geschichtsverständnis*, p. 173 and Schlier, *Römerbrief*, p. 116.

[25] "Das Gesetz des Glaubens," p. 402.

[26] *Römerbrief*, 1:176.

[27] "Das Gesetz des Glaubens," pp. 404-5. Barrett also admits this argument but interprets νόμος as "religious system." *Romans*, p. 83.

[28] See Hahn, "Gesetzesverständnis," pp. 45-49; Lohse, "Röm 8,2," and von der Osten-Sacken, *Römer 8*, pp. 209-20, 226-30.

²⁹"Das Gesetz des Glaubens," pp. 404, 409.

³⁰Ibid., p. 415. So also Lohse, "Röm 8,2," pp. 281-82.

³¹*Romans*, 1:220.

³²"Abraham in den paulinischen Hauptbriefen," *MüTZ* 17 (1966):64.

³³*Römer 8*, p. 245. See further Hübner, *Gesetz*, pp. 118-19.

³⁴"Gesetzesverständnis," p. 41.

³⁵*Römer*, 1:247.

³⁶So Friedrich, "Das Gesetz des Glaubens," pp. 409-410. Cf. Rom 8:2 where the equally compact expressions, "the law of the Spirit of life in Christ Jesus" and "the law of sin and death," can also be defined by reference to the preceding context, the former by reference to 7:10, 12, 14, 22, 25, the latter by reference to 7:7-12 and 7:13-25. See von der Osten-Sacken, *Römer 8*, pp. 226-31 and Wilckens, *Römer*, 1:245. However, this approach is disputed. See Cranfield, *Romans*, 1:375-76.

³⁷Unless we understand νόμος here in the broader sense of the entire OT (cf. 3:19), Paul does not carry forward his use of the expression, "the law and the prophets." This abandonment of the reference to the "prophets" may be occasioned by Paul's predominant concern with the νόμος, here apparently embracing the whole Pentateuch as in 3:21.

³⁸So Käsemann understands πίστεως in this verse. *Römer*, p. 95.

³⁹Von der Osten-Sacken's argument that the phrase "law of faith" is not simply a reiteration of 3:21 but actually means that the law as a witness to God's righteousness has come to validity through faith seems to rely too heavily on his interpretation of 3:31 and 8:2. *Römer 8*, p. 245, n. 1. Of course, it is true, as he says, that the law in its witness to righteousness by faith (3:21b-22) is validated when one appropriates by faith the righteousness which comes through Christ's redemptive work (3:24-26).

⁴⁰As Schneider argues, the contrast here is not between νόμος and νόμος but between the attached genitives, ἔργων and πίστεως. *Paulinischen Antithese*, p. 98.

⁴¹Accepting γάρ instead of οὖν with Bruce M. Metzger, *A Textual Commentary on the Greek New Testament: A Companion Volume to the United Bible Societies' Greek New Testament*, (Third Edition) (London: United Bible Societies, 1971), p. 509.

⁴²So Cranfield, *Romans*, 1:220-21.

Notes: Chapter III

[43] Ibid., 1:221.

[44] Personal translation. For the reasons see Cranfield, Ibid., 1:222.

[45] So Klein, "Römer 4," p. 166; Luz, *Geschichtsverständnis*, p. 173 and Murray, *Romans*, 1:126.

[46] So Walvoord, "Law," p. 282. But Bläser has shown it is impossible to determine the reference of νόμος on the basis of the presence or absence of the article as Walvoord does. *Gesetz*, pp. 1-22.

[47] So Bläser, Ibid., p. 193; Cranfield, *Romans*, 1:223, n. 4; Friedrich, "Das Gesetz des Glaubens," pp. 415-16; Leenhardt, *Romans*, p. 112; Meyer, *Romans*, pp. 144-45; Sanday and Headlam, *Romans*, p. 96 and Wilckens, "Römer 4," pp. 42-43. Von der Osten-Sacken insists one should not attempt to define precisely the meaning of νόμος (whether Pentateuch or Mosaic law) in 3:21, 27, 31 but let the issue hang in suspense. *Römer 8*, p. 246.

[48] So Dodd, *Romans*, p. 64; Gronemeyer, *Antinomismus*, p. 118; Huby, *Romains*, pp. 163-64; Käsemann, *Römer*, p. 97; Lagrange, *Romains*, p. 80 and Lietzmann, *Römer*, p. 52.

[49] So Barrett, *Romans*, pp. 84, 86 and Ernst Kühl, "Stellung und Bedeutung des alttestamentlichen Gesetzes im Zusammenhang der paulinischen Lehre," *Theologische Studien und Kritiken* 67 (1894):128. Such an understanding of νόμος seems unlikely in view of the context which refers clearly to the OT law in one sense or another.

[50] So apparently Beck, "Altes und neues Gesetz," pp. 132, n. 14, 135-37. She relates 3:31 to 3:27 where Paul speaks of the "law of faith." Cf 8:2; Gal 6:2; 1 Cor 9:21. According to Beck this "law of faith" or "law of the Spirit" is the OT law in its fulfilment in faith which works through love. Ibid., p. 135. Again, such an understanding of νόμος seems unlikely here in view of the context. So Cambier, *Romains*, 1:159.

[51] At the same time Dodd's claim that Paul's Greek readers could not be aware that νόμος meant Torah and that Torah had a wider range of meaning than the legal one also falls to the ground in the light of the context. See p. 27, n. 8 above. Moreover, Dodd's argument weakens in view of Monsengwo Pasinya's findings. See p. 65, n. 4 above.

[52] *Gesetz*, pp. 1-22.

[53] Cf. 3:19, 21b; 4:6-8. The presence of Ps 32:1-2 (Rom 4:6-8) might support this contention. However, it plays a secondary role in Rom 4, Gen 15:6 (the Pentateuch) being the primary text.

[54] See p. 31, n. 34 above.

⁵⁵E.g., b. Aboth 4.9: "R. Jonathan said: Whoever fulfils (form of קום) the Torah out of [a state of] poverty, his end [will be] to fulfil (form of קום) it out of [a state of] wealth; and whoever discards (form of בטל) the Torah out of [a state of] wealth, his end [will be] to discard (form of בטל) it out of [a state of] poverty."; b. Menaḥoth 99b: "Resh Laḳish said: There are times [99b] when the suppression (form of בטל) of the Torah may be the foundation (form of קום) of the Torah, for it is written, '*Which thou didst break*': The Holy One, blessed be He, said to Moses, 'Thou didst well to break'!" and b. Sanhedrin 90a: "Our Rabbis taught: If one prophesies so as to eradicate a law of the Torah, he is liable [to death]; partially to confirm (form of קום) and partially to annul (form of בטל) it,--R. Simeon exempts him." Italics theirs. Words in brackets theirs. Words in parentheses mine. Citations are taken from *The Babylonian Talmud*, gen. ed. Isidore Epstein, 35 vols. (London: Soncino Press, 1935-52). See further p. Megillah 70d. For a favorable analysis of the evidence, see Dalman, *Jesus-Jeshua*, pp. 58-61.

⁵⁶As Hübner (*Gesetz*, p. 121) points out, Wilhelm Bacher does not even mention בטל under the exegetical terminology of either the Tannaim or the Amoraim, nor does he regard בטל as a negative counterpart to קום. See *Die exegetische Terminologie der jüdischen Traditionsliteratur*, 2 Teile, 1. T.: *Die bibelexegetische Terminologie der Tannaiten*; 2. T.: *Die bibel- und traditionsexegetische Terminologie der Amoräer* (Leipzig: J. C. Hinrichs, 1899-1905; reprint ed. Darmstadt: Wissenschaftliche Buchgesellschaft, 1965), s.v. "קים," 1:170-71; 2:186-89. More importantly, Hübner (Ibid., p. 122) notes further that those cases in which בטל and קום appear together in rabbinic literature are really not concerned with the exegesis of the law. Thus, b. Aboth 4.9, e.g., deals with the study of the law not the interpretation of the law.

⁵⁷For additional evidence see Bacher, Ibid.; Joseph Bonsirven, *Exégèse rabbinique et exégèse paulinienne*, Bibliothèque de Théologie Historique (Paris: Beauchesne et Ses Fils, 1939), pp. 21, 32, 69, 71-74, 96-97, 111, 202-5, 342 and *A Dictionary of the Targumim, the Talmud Babli and Yerushalmi, and the Midrashic Literature*, comp. Marcus Jastrow, 2 vols. (London: Luzac, 1903), s.v. "קום," 2:1330-31.

⁵⁸So Walter Bauer, *A Greek-English Lexicon of the New Testament and Other Early Christian Literature*, trans. and adapted from the 4th rev. and augmented German ed., 1952, by William F. Arndt and F. Wilbur Gingrich (Chicago: University of Chicago Press, 1957), s.v. "καταργέω," p. 418 and *TDNT*, s.v. "καταργέω," by Gerhard Delling, 1:453.

⁵⁹So Bauer, Ibid., s.v. "ἵστημι," pp. 382-83 and *TDNT*, s.v. "ἵστημι," by Walter Grundmann, 7:649.

⁶⁰See p. 61 above.

⁶¹See pp. 59-61 above.

[62]*Romains*, p. 164. Despite Klein's misgivings (see "Römer 4" and "Exegetische Probleme in Römer 3,21-4,25. Antwort an U. Wilckens," in *Rekonstruktion und Interpretation*, pp. 170-79), we must agree in principle with those who argue that Paul is concerned to show a *heilsgeschichtliche Kontinuität* here. See Berger, "Abraham"; Bornkamm, *Paul*, trans. D. M. G. Stalker (New York: Harper & Row, 1971), pp. 148-49; Christian Dietzfelbinger, *Paulus und das Alte Testament: Die Hermeneutik des Paulus untersucht an seiner Deutung der Gestalt Abrahams*, Theologische Existenz Heute, n. F. 95 (Munich: Chr. Kaiser Verlag, 1961); Goppelt, "Paul und Heilsgeschichte: Conclusions from Romans 4 and 1 Corinthians 10:1-13," *Interp* 21 (1967):315-26; Käsemann, "The Faith of Abraham in Romans 4," in *Perspectives on Paul*, trans. Margaret Kohl (Philadelphia: Fortress Press, 1971), pp. 79-101; Wilckens, "Römer 4" and "Römer 3,21-4,25." For a survey of scholarly discussion of Heilsgeschichte as it relates to Paul's treatment of Abraham, see Fred Dale Layman, "Paul's Use of Abraham: An Approach to Paul's Understanding of History" (Ph.D. dissertation, University of Iowa, 1972), especially pp. 293-97.

In a quite different approach Bruce Edward Schein recently contends that Paul introduces Abraham here as a model for prospective converts. "Abraham Our Father" (Ph.D. dissertation, Yale University, 1973), pp. 234-88.

[63]The inner coherence that Rom 4 displays has led exegetes to inquire about its possible existence before the composition of this epistle. Accordingly, since Otto Michel's suggestion (*Römer*, p. 98) that Rom 4 was originally an independent midrash on Abraham, other scholars have undertaken to analyze and locate it in its context in Romans.

Peder Borgen regards it as similar to a homiletic pattern found also in the Gospel of John and in Philonic exegesis. *Bread from Heaven: An Exegetical Study of the Concept of Manna in the Gospel of John and the Writings of Philo*, Supplements to Novum Testamentum, 10 (Leiden: E. J. Brill, 1965), pp. 46-61. The three main characteristics of this pattern are: First, there is a correspondence between the opening and closing parts of the homily (cf. 4:3 and 4:22). As a result, the closing statement sums up points of the homily (see 4:22). Second, besides the main OT quotation there is at least one subordinate OT citation (cf. 4:3, 9, 22 with 4:7-8, 17-18). Finally, words from the principal OT text are paraphrased or quoted in the homily (see 4:3, 9, 22). Ibid., p. 47.

Agreeing with Borgen's analysis, E. Earle Ellis considers this chapter "a (?pre-formed) expository piece" that Paul employs as the concluding text of a larger midrash (Rom 1:17-4:25). "Exegetical Patterns in 1 Corinthians and Romans," in *Grace upon Grace: Essays in Honor of Lester J. Kuyper*, ed. James I. Cook (Grand Rapids: Wm. B. Eerdmans Publishing Co., 1975), pp. 139-41.

Robin Scroggs carries this process one step further when he argues that Rom 1:16-4:25 and 9:1-11:36 form one of two self-contained homilies in Rom 1-11 (the other being Rom 5-8). According to Scroggs, this exegetical homily, now disjoined by Rom 5-8, deals with the meaning of Israel's history, taking the form of a narration of the events of Heilsgeschichte. "Paul as Rhetorician: Two Homilies in Romans 1-11," in *Jews*,

Greeks and Christians: Religious Cultures in Late Antiquity. Essays in Honor of William David Davies, ed. Robert Hamerton-Kelly and Robin Scroggs, Studies in Judaism in Late Antiquity, 21 (Leiden: E. J. Brill, 1976), pp. 275-81, 289-92. Finally, Hans-Jürgen van der Minde finds in Rom 4 a pre-Pauline midrash (basically vv. 3, 11-13, 16-18c) which the apostle has subsequently redacted for his own purposes in Romans. *Schrift und Tradition bei Paulus*, pp. 78-86.

It is not within the scope of this investigation to interact with these different approaches. However, the tendency observed in some of them to view Rom 4 as an independent exposition on Abraham neatly inserted into the epistle at the appropriate point could offer one explanation for what some scholars consider the rough transition between Rom 3:31 and 4:1. See above and pp. 76-77 below.

[64]So Cranfield (*Romans*, 1:223) against Meyer, who argues that οὖν here is clearly inferential yet introduces the proof for Rom 3:31. *Romans*, p. 152. But Cranfield's attempt to relate Rom 4:1 strictly to 3:27 creates a problem in itself, because it practically compels us to skip over the immediately preceding verses, especially 3:31, treating them as parenthetical.

[65]See pp. 58-59 above.

[66]See Blass and Debrunner, *Grammar*, par. 366(2).

[67]Otherwise Jeremias, "Röm 4," p. 52 and Luz, *Geschichtsverständnis*, p. 174, n. 146.

[68]See Bauer, *Lexicon*, s.v. "οὖν," p. 597 and H. E. Dana and Julius R. Mantey, *A Manual Grammar of the Greek New Testament* (New York: Macmillan Co., 1927), pp. 252-58. Bauer calls τί οὖν ἐροῦμεν a rhetorical transition formula. Ibid., s.v. "εἶπον," p. 225. Though he denies the connection with Rom 3:31, Murray still regards οὖν as transitional here declaring that it "intimates advance to consideration of what the example of Abraham establishes." *Romans*, 1:127. Cf. the use of οὖν in 4:10 where Dana and Mantey describe it as "emphatic." Ibid., pp. 255-56.

[69]*Discourses* 1.28.19-20a: οὐδενὶ οὖν διαφέρει ἄνθρωπος πελαργοῦ;--μὴ γένοιτο· ἀλλὰ τούτοις οὐ διαφέρει. τίνι οὖν διαφέρει;--Ζήτει καὶ εὑρήσεις, ὅτι ἄλλῳ διαφέρει, etc. Admittedly, the question following the counter-assertion in Epictetus is more closely tied to it verbally than Rom 4:1 is to 3:31c. Moreover, the argument that the new question (Rom 4:1) does not seem suitably related to the categorical assertion (3:31c) also loses much of its force when we observe this parallel in Epictetus and recognize that Rom 4 begins as a deliberation on what Paul has just said. Against Murray, *Romans*, 1:125.

[70]So, e.g., Sanday and Headlam, *Romans*, p. 99.

[71]*Römer*, p. 53. This reading could explain the absence of εὑρηκέναι in the other manuscripts by accidental

omission because of homoioarchon. Cf. ἐροῦμεν and εὑρηκέναι. So Metzger, *Textual Commentary*, p. 509. In this case the transposition of εὑρηκέναι after ἡμῶν would probably be due to scribal reinsertion after accidental omission (so Lietzmann, Ibid.) or else to intentional change (so Käsemann, *Römer*, p. 99). Once this transposition occurred, εὑρηκέναι was associated with κατὰ σάρκα and the sense of the question was destroyed. In reaction to this new sense εὑρηκέναι was removed to prevent the misunderstanding that justification by faith is a fleshly affair. So Lietzmann, Ibid. Thus the shorter reading came into being. The substitution of πατέρα for προπάτορα is more likely since the latter is the more difficult reading, occurring nowhere else in the NT and only once in the LXX (3 Macc 2:21). So Metzger, Ibid., p. 510.

[72] So Luz, *Geschichtsverständnis*, p. 174, n. 148.

[73] So Michel, *Römer*, p. 99. Cranfield ties κατὰ σάρκα even more closely to ἡμῶν. *Romans*, 1:227.

[74] So Berger, "Abraham," p. 68.

[75] *Römer*, p. 99.

[76] "Römer 4," p. 38, n. 15. Some, however, understand this verse as intended to represent the objections of a fictitious Jewish opponent. So Kuss, *Römerbrief*, 1:179-80; Luz, *Geschichtsverständnis*, p. 174; Sanday and Headlam, *Romans*, pp. 97-98 and Schmidt, *Römer*, pp. 76-77. If such were the case, one might construe the question in the following manner: If what you say about your message of faith's establishing the law is true, then what shall we say Abraham our forefather according to the flesh has found? For if Abraham was justified by works, he has grounds for boasting (4:1-2a). When the question is put in this way, the verb εὑρίσκειν refers to striving after works. So Schmidt, Ibid., p. 77. Paul would answer: But not before God (4:2b) and then proceed to cite God's verdict on Abraham from Scripture (4:3).

[77] Contrary to Berger ("Abraham," p. 65), it is quite conceivable Paul has in mind here and in the following verses the works of the law. On the one hand, the correspondence between 4:2-3 and 3:27-28 indicates this. On the other hand, Paul's discussion of circumcision (4:9-12) and of the relationship between faith and law (4:13-16) substantiates it. As the Sirach text above shows, Judaism presumed Abraham's knowledge of the Torah and his performance of its works. See Schein, "Abraham," pp. 70-71. Berger himself admits that vv. 4-8 relate to the situation under the law.

[78] So Käsemann, *Römer*, p. 99. Otherwise, Klein, "Römer 4," p. 151, n. 25.

[79] So Cranfield, *Romans*, 1:228. Against Schlier, *Römerbrief*, p. 123 and Schmidt, *Römer*, p. 77.

[80] Jubilees stresses this point at length (11:15-23:10) and Gen 26:5 would certainly support this assumption.

On the Jewish estimation of Abraham, especially as it relates to Rom 4:2-3, see Martin Dibelius, *James: A Commentary on the Epistle of James*, rev. Heinrich Greeven, trans. Michael A. Williams, ed. Helmut Koester, Hermeneia (Philadelphia: Fortress Press, 1976), pp. 168-74; Dietzfelbinger, *Paulus und das Alte Testament*; Erwin Ramsdell Goodenough, *By Light, Light: The Mystic Gospel of Hellenistic Judaism* (New Haven: Yale University Press, 1935), pp. 137, 142-43; *TDNT*, s.v. "'Αβραάμ," by Joachim Jeremias; James Raymond Lord, "Abraham: A Study in Ancient Jewish and Christian Interpretation" (Ph.D. dissertation, Duke University, 1968), pp. 64-221; Samuel Sandmel, *Philo's Place in Judaism: A Study of Conceptions of Abraham in Jewish Literature* (Cincinnati: Hebrew Union College Press, 1956); Schein, "Abraham," pp. 19-92; Otto Schmitz, "Abraham im Spätjudentum und im Urchristentum," in *Aus Schrift und Geschichte: Theologische Abhandlungen Adolf Schlatter zu seinem 70. Geburtstage dargebracht von Freunden und Schülern*, ed. Karl B. Bornhäuser (Stuttgart: Calwer Vereinsbuchhandlung, 1922), pp. 99-116 and Hermann L. Strack and Paul Billerbeck, *Kommentar zum Neuen Testament aus Talmud und Midrasch*, 6 vols. in 7 (Munich: Beck, 1922-61), 3:186-201.

On the estimation of Abraham in early Christianity, see Jeremias, Ibid.; Lord, Ibid., pp. 222-28; Schein, Ibid., pp. 93-317 and Schmitz, Ibid., pp. 116-23.

[81] However, we cannot agree with Cranfield that Rom 4 presents the case of Abraham primarily in order to confirm the statement that boasting has been excluded (3:27). *Romans*, 1:224. Boasting is a secondary motif. So Sanday and Headlam, *Romans*, p. 98.

[82] So Friedrich, "Das Gesetz des Glaubens," p. 416. As in Gal 4:21, Paul could just as easily have written νόμος as γραφή. In fact, at Gal 4:30 Paul does change to the term γραφή, while still referring to the law (the Pentateuch). In a similar manner Paul moves from the term νόμος (Rom 3:31) to the term γραφή (Rom 4:3). As in Rom 3:21, 27, 31 and 4:1-25, so also in Gal 4:21, we encounter one and the same law, though viewed from different perspectives. On the one hand, it witnesses to the reception of the promise by faith; on the other hand, it and its works threaten to assume dominance in the spiritual lives of the willing Galatians. See von der Osten-Sacken, *Römer 8*, p. 247. Cf. also Gal 3:22-23 where the law and the Scripture have the same negative function of imprisoning humanity in its sin.

[83] From this point forward one should note how the law is excluded from the acquisition of righteousness (so vv. 2, 4-6, 9-10, 13-16) but still witnesses (as Scripture) to righteousness by faith (so vv. 3, 9, 22-24).

[84] So Barrett, "Abraham," in *From First Adam to Last: A Study in Pauline Theology* (New York: Charles Scribner's Sons, 1962), p. 32.

On the meaning of πίστις in its Genesis context against the background of the rest of the OT, see Gerhard von Rad,

"Faith Reckoned as Righteousness," in *The Problem of the Hexateuch and Other Essays*, trans. E. W. Trueman Dicken, introduction by Norman W. Porteous (Edinburgh: Oliver & Boyd, 1966), pp. 125-30.
On the use of Gen 15:6 in the NT, see Hahn, "Genesis 15,6 im Neuen Testament," in *Probleme biblischer Theologie. Gerhard von Rad zum 70. Geburtstag*, ed. Hans Walter Wolff (Munich: Chr. Kaiser Verlag, 1971), pp. 90-107 and the literature cited there.

[85] Notably Paul does not mention Abraham's great "works" reported in Genesis (see chaps. 17-18, 22). On this see Schein, "Abraham," pp. 247-48. Moreover, he does not tie Abraham's faith (Gen 15:6) to his call, his obedience or his "sacrifice" of Isaac. On this see Dietzfelbinger, *Paulus und das Alte Testament*, pp. 13-19.

[86] The concepts of working or not working apparently refer to the attempt or, conversely, the refusal to establish a claim on God on the basis of one's works. Certainly Paul does not reject the works (of the law) per se nor want to imply that Abraham did no good works. So Cranfield, *Romans*, 1:232, n. 2.

[87] So Cranfield, Ibid., 1:232; Anthony Tyrrell Hanson, *Studies in Paul's Technique and Theology* (London: S.P.C.K., 1974), pp. 53-62; Käsemann, "Romans 4," pp. 84-85 and Schein, "Abraham," pp. 250-52. Otherwise Meyer, *Romans*, pp. 157-58; Sanday and Headlam, *Romans*, p. 101 and Schmidt, *Römer*, p. 78.

[88] So Ex 23:7 (MT); cf. Prov 17:15; 24:24; Is 5:23. But see Ex 23:7 (LXX): καὶ οὐ δικαιώσεις τὸν ἀσεβῆ ἕνεκεν δώρων and Cranfield's comment. Ibid., 1:232, n. 1.

[89] For what appear on the surface to be exceptions to this view, see Siegfried Schulz, "Zur Rechtfertigung aus Gnaden in Qumran und bei Paulus," *ZTK* 56 (1959):155-85. But see Bornkamm, *Paul*, p. 139; Herbert Braun, *Qumran und das Neue Testament*, 2 Bde. (Tübingen: J. C. B. Mohr, 1966), 2:165-72, 229-35 and Walter Grundmann, "The Teaching of Righteousness of Qumran and the Question of Justification by Faith in the Theology of the Apostle Paul," in *Paul and Qumran: Studies in New Testament Exegesis*, ed. Jerome Murphy-O'Connor (Chicago: Priory Press, 1968), pp. 85-114. E. P. Sanders rejects the prevalent understanding of Judaism represented by these scholars as well as Schluz's "Pauline" interpretation of the Qumran texts. *Paul and Palestinian Judaism*, pp. 287-98, 305-312.

[90] So Gerhardsson, *Memory and Manuscript*, p. 287; Jeremias, "Paulus als Hillelit," in *Neotestamentica et Semitica: Studies in Honor of Matthew Black*, ed. E. Earle Ellis and Max Wilcox (Edinburgh: T. & T. Clark, 1969), pp. 92-93; "Zur Gedankenführung in den paulinischen Briefen," pp. 149-51 and Vielhauer, "Paulus und das Alte Testament," p. 36, n. 15.
For the rabbinic evidence see Bacher, *Terminologie*, s.v. "שָׁוָה גְּזֵרָה," 1:13-16; 2:27 and Samuel Rosenblatt, *The*

Interpretation of the Bible in the Mishnah (Baltimore: John Hopkins Press, 1935), pp. 28-29.

[91] For other instances where Paul quotes OT passages in series or in combination partly on the basis of the presence of a similar word, see Rom 9:25-26, 33; 11:8-9; 15:9-12; 1 Cor 3:19-20; 15:54-55. For an evaluation of these cases see Michel, *Paulus und seine Bibel* (Gütersloh: C. Bertelsmann, 1929; reprint ed. Darmstadt: Wissenschaftliche Buchgesellschaft, 1972), pp. 85-87 and Ellis, *Paul's Use of the Old Testament* (Edinburgh: Oliver & Boyd, 1957), p. 50. Moreover, Ellis cautions against overemphasizing the presence of the rabbinic principles of *a fortiori* and *gezerah shawah* in Rom 4-5. Ibid., p. 46.

[92] Certainly we cannot say that "faith reckoned as righteousness" is here defined simply in terms of the "non-reckoning of sin" as a *gezerah shawah* would imply.

[93] From unpublished manuscript entitled, "Halakic Midrash. Hermeneutical Systems of Hillel and the Tannaim."

[94] *TDNT*, s.v. "λογίζομαι," 4:292.

[95] Jeremias insists that in 4:9-12 Paul engages in another *gezerah shawah*, Gen 15:6 explaining Ps 32:1-2. "Zur Gedankenführung in den paulinischen Briefen," p. 150. So also Barrett, *Romans*, pp. 89-90; Cranfield, *Romans*, 1:235 and Schlier, *Römerbrief*, p. 126. But this assertion must face the same objections raised above. How does Gen 15:6 now clarify the meaning of λογίζεσθαι in Ps 32:1-2?

[96] *Paulus und das Alte Testament*, pp. 12-13. Von der Osten-Sacken speaks in a similar fashion. *Römer 8*, pp. 247-48. On the connection of Abraham's circumcision with the law in Jewish thought, see Schein, "Abraham," pp. 67-70.

[97] On the rabbinic calculations see Strack and Billerbeck, *Kommentar*, 3:203.

[98] Taking περιτομῆς as a genitive of apposition with Michel, *Römer*, p. 104. Paul apparently derives the term σημεῖον from the Genesis account where circumcision is called the σημεῖον διαθήκης (17:11). See Berger, "Abraham," p. 67. Klein accuses the apostle of a "völlig analogielose Usurpation des vorgegebenen alttestamentlichen Textes." "Römer 4," p. 154. Otherwise, Wilckens, "*Römer 3,21-4,25*," p. 62, n. 13 and Karl Heinrich Rengstorf, *TDNT*, s.v. "σημεῖον," 7:258.

[99] So Gottfried Fitzer, *TDNT*, s.v. "σφραγίς," 7:949 and G. W. H. Lampe, *The Seal of the Spirit: A Study in the Doctrine of Baptism and Confirmation in the New Testament and the Fathers* (London: Longmans, Green & Co., 1951), p. 91.

[100] Understanding δι' ἀκροβυστίας as referring to physical uncircumcision and denoting the outward circumstances of Gentile Christians with Cranfield, *Romans*, 1:237, n. 1. On the other hand, Berger argues that this phrase designates the

character of the faith that brings one into kinship with Abraham and so interprets πάντων as including both Jewish and Gentile Christians. "Abraham," p. 69. According to Berger, his approach has the merit of explaining the absence of a second εἰς τὸ λογισθῆναι αὐτοῖς δικαιοσύνην at the end of v. 12. Cf. Rom 2:25-29. Against Berger see Klein, "Römer 3,21-4,25," p. 179, n. 14 and van der Minde, *Schrift und Tradition bei Paulus*, p. 72, n. 16.

Furthermore, it is doubtful that δι' ἀκροβυστίας should be connected with εἰς τὸ εἶναι αὐτὸν πατέρα as Luz does: "damit er Vater der Glaubenden sei durch die Vorhaut." *Geschichtsverständnis*, p. 175. The phrase is more closely tied to τῶν πιστευόντων.

[101] See Mt 3:9; Lk 3:8; 13:6; 19:9; Jn 8:33, 39. For Christian opposition to this notion, see Mt 3:9; Lk 3:8; Mt 8:11 and parallels; Lk 16:19-31. For additional evidence and discussion, see Jeremias, "'Αβραάμ;" Schein, "Abraham," pp. 93-191 and Schmitz, "Abraham."

[102] For the rabbinic evidence on whether a proselyte could call Abraham his "father," see Strack and Billerbeck, *Kommentar*, 3:211.

[103] Contrary to the usual understanding of the phrase, Berger argues that ἡ πίστις ἡ ἐν τῇ ἀκροβυστίᾳ (4:11b; cf. 4:12b) designates an attribute of faith not actual uncircumcision. "Abraham," p. 68, n. 38.

[104] So Käsemann, *Römer*, p. 108.

[105] So Blass and Debrunner, *Grammar*, par. 276(3); Cranfield, *Romans*, 1:237-38; Klein, "Römer 4," p. 156, n. 42; Kuss, *Römerbrief*, 1:186; Luz, *Geschichtsverständnis*, p. 175 and Schlier, *Römerbrief*, p. 128. Cf. Berger, "Abraham," pp. 68-69. Van der Minde's solution, based on his reconstruction of the *Vorlage*, still leaves us with the problem of the "superfluous" τοῖς at the level of the Pauline redaction. *Schrift und Tradition bei Paulus*, pp. 81-83.

[106] "Abraham 'père en circoncision' des Gentils," in *Recueil Lucien Cerfaux: Études d' Exégèse et d' Histoire Religieuse Réunies a l' Occasion de Son Soixante-dixième Anniversaire*; Bibliotheca Ephemeridum Theologicarum Lovaniensium, 6-7, 18; 3 tomes (Gembloux: J. Duculot, 1954-62), 2:335. So also Cambier, *Romains*, 1:171. Though Käsemann agrees substantially with Cerfaux, he seems to understand the first group as the Jews generally, the second as the Jewish Christians. *Römer*, p. 108.

[107] Against Cerfaux see Luz, *Geschichtsverständnis*, pp. 175-76, n. 156.

[108] So Berger, "Abraham," p. 68.

[109] See Dietzfelbinger, *Paulus und das Alte Testament*, p. 13, n. 28.

[110] "Das Gesetz des Glaubens," p. 416. Similarly Hahn, "Gesetzesverständnis," pp. 40-41.

[111] For discussions of the understanding of this inheritance in the OT and in Judaism, see Cranfield, Romans, 1:239 and Schein, "Abraham," pp. 84-90.

[112] So Dietzfelbinger, Paulus und das Alte Testament, p. 19 and Käsemann, Römer, p. 112. On the various ways in which the apostle uses this term in his writings, see Schein, Ibid., pp. 267-74. On the other hand, Michel argues that "seed" here refers to Christ as in the case of Gal 3:16. Römer, pp. 105-6.

[113] Ibid., p. 36.

[114] So Cranfield, Romans, 1:238. Both the preceding context and vv. 14-16 show that Paul is not considering "law" in some general sense. Against Sanday and Headlam, Romans, p. 110.

[115] So Schlier, Römerbrief, p. 129.

[116] So Johannes Schneider, TDNT, s.v. "παράβασις," 5:739-40.

[117] Taking διὰ τοῦτο as a backward rather than a forward reference. So Käsemann, Römer, p. 113 against Cranfield, Romans, 1:241.

[118] Supplying the implicit concept of κληρονομία from 4:14 with Käsemann, Ibid. Others supply ἐπαγγελία from 4:13 or think Paul has in mind something like God's plan of salvation. So Barrett, Romans, p. 95.

[119] Taking the expressions, οὐ τῷ ἐκ τοῦ νόμου μόνον and ἀλλὰ καὶ τῷ ἐκ πίστεως (4:16d) as denoting Jewish and Gentile Christians respectively. So Althaus, Römer, pp. 44-45; Kuss, Römerbrief, 1:189 and van der Minde, Schrift und Tradition bei Paulus, p. 84.

Others argue that these expressions refer to Jews and Christians (Jewish and Gentile) respectively. So Klein, "Römer 4," pp. 160-61 and Michel, Römer, pp. 107-8. Among other things, they contend that, if one understands the phrase ὁ ἐκ τοῦ νόμου as indicating Jewish Christians, then a contradiction would arise between 4:16d and 4:14, where οἱ ἐκ νόμου are excluded from the inheritance, and between 4:16d and 4:12, where the Jews participate in Abraham's faith along with the Gentiles.

But in opposition to this approach one should note that the intervening statement (4:16a) presupposes faith on the part of the seed which is ὁ ἐκ τοῦ νόμου (4:16d). The reference of οἱ ἐκ νόμου has not changed, only the circumstances in which they appear. Against Cranfield, Romans, 1:242-43. In the former instance (4:14) those who possess and perform the works of the law were viewed in opposition to faith; in the latter (4:16d) they are viewed as "seed" and "heirs" after having themselves come to faith. The Jewish Christians remain οἱ ἐκ νόμου (cf. 1 Cor 7:17-24) and as such share the promised inheritance; the Gentile Christians are described in the appropriate term, οἱ ἐκ πίστεως 'Αβραάμ, in contrast to the Jewish ones. Moreover, if we understand πᾶν τὸ σπέρμα as representing believers generally (so Schlier, *Römerbrief*, p. 131), any interpretation which regards οἱ ἐκ τοῦ νόμου as non-believing Jews would force upon this word a double meaning within the same clause. Against Klein, Ibid., p. 161, with van Dülmen, *Gesetzes*, p. 94, n. 77.

Finally, Käsemann (Ibid.) and Wilckens (*Römer*, 1:271-72) argue that, strictly speaking, these expressions (4:16d) refer to Jewish Christians who possess both characteristics mentioned here, i.e., the law and the faith of Abraham. (They do admit a loose reference to Gentile Christians also.) However, as in 4:12b, the second τῷ before ἐκ πίστεως 'Αβραάμ seems to deny this possibility.

[120] So Barrett, *Romans*, p. 96.

[121] So Blass and Debrunner, *Grammar*, par. 294(2).

[122] So Cranfield, *Romans*, 1:243 and Kuss, *Römerbrief*, 1:190.

[123] *Römer*, p. 114.

[124] For the evidence see Cranfield, *Romans*, 1:244-45 and Käsemann, Ibid., pp. 114-15.

[125] So Dietzfelbinger, *Paulus und das Alte Testament*, p. 26.

[126] So Barrett, *Romans*, p. 97.

[127] Taking εἰς τό as expressing result. So Cranfield, *Romans*, 1:246 and Käsemann, *Römer*, p. 116.

[128] Omitting the negative οὐ with Metzger, *Textual Commentary*, p. 510.

[129] *Romans*, 1:247. Philo also evaluated Gen 17:17 in a positive manner in the light of Gen 15:4, 6. See *De mutatione nominum* 175-80. See further Schein, "Abraham," pp. 80-81.

[130] So Cranfield, Ibid., 1:249.

[131] So Nygren, *Romans*, p. 182.

[132] So Cranfield, *Romans*, 1:250.

[133] So Cranfield, Ibid.

[134] Note the correspondence between the present tense participle μαρτυρουμένη (3:21b) and the present validity implied in δι' ἡμᾶς (4:24). Thus van der Minde declares that

the entire Abraham story (4:1-22) stands under the theme of "witness." *Schrift und Tradition bei Paulus*, p. 102. See also Wilckens, "Römer 3,21-4,25," pp. 70-71.

[135] The phrase μέλλει λογίζεσθαι may be understood as a reference to the present assurance of justification (so Cranfield, *Romans*, 1:250) or to the future judgment (so Käsemann, *Römer*, p. 120).

[136] "Apokalyptik und Typologie bei Paulus," *TLZ* 89 (1964):333. So also Käsemann, "Romans 4," pp. 95-99. Otherwise, Luz, *Geschichtsverständnis*, p. 180, n. 174 and Vielhauer, "Paulus und das Alte Testament," p. 41.

[137] For a discussion and evaluation of the treatment of this verse in recent literature, see van der Minde, *Schrift und Tradition bei Paulus*, pp. 90-99.

[138] So van der Minde, Ibid., p. 98.

[139] Von der Osten-Sacken urges that the full meaning of Rom 3:31 and its exposition in Rom 4 can only be appreciated when one realizes that the establishment of the law through faith is synonymous with Paul's confession (1:18-3:20) that all have sinned and lack the glory of God (3:23). He explains that, while Rom 3:19-20 depict this confession as a judgment based on the law itself, 3:21-22 view it as a judgment of faith which results from the revelation of God's righteousness apart from the law. Perceived by faith, this revelation assigns to the law the function of pronouncing universal guilt and thus excluding itself as a means of salvation. Therefore, according to von der Osten-Sacken, when Paul (Rom 4) introduces the positive proof that the law itself witnesses to faith as the bearer of salvation, what he has said earlier about the law (1:18-3:20) is confirmed at the same time. As a result he concludes: "Die Aussagen in Röm. 1,18-3,20 und Röm. 4 stehen deshalb, vermittelt durch den Abschnitt 3,21-31, im Verhältnis der Komplementarität zueinander. Sie explizieren die beiden Dimensionen des Wortes Gottes (Thora als 'Gesetz' und 'Verheissung'), die ante Christum auseinandertreten, im Evangelium bzw. beim Glaubenden jedoch zu seinem Heil zusammenfallen." *Römer 8*, p. 249. See also Ibid., pp. 248-50; Bornkamm, "Gesetzesverständnis," p. 111; Hahn, "Gesetzesverständnis," p. 41 and Lohse, "Glauben und Thora im Römerbrief," pp. 65-66.

While one would not deny the basic truth of von der Osten-Sacken's statements, it should be said that this establishment of the law in its negative sense is certainly not the primary intention of Paul's expositions in Rom 4. In addition, when he proceeds to interpret Rom 3:31 in the light of his understanding of Rom 8:2-4, von der Osten-Sacken (Ibid., pp. 249-50) seems to suggest an identification of the terms ἱστάνειν (3:31) and πληροῦν (8:4) which is not warranted by Pauline usage.

CHAPTER IV

ROMANS 10:4 ONCE MORE

[1] Unavailable was Mary Ann Getty's extensive treatment of this text, "Christ Is the End of the Law: Romans 10:4 in Its Context" (Ph.D. dissertation, Catholic University of Louvain, 1975), which is now undergoing revision for eventual publication.

[2] See Bauer, *Lexicon*, s.v. "τέλος," pp. 818-20; *TDNT*, s.v. "τέλος," by Gerhard Delling, 8:49-56 and Henry George Liddell and Robert Scott, *A Greek-English Lexicon*, new ed. rev. and augmented by Henry Stuart Jones and Roderick McKenzie, 2 vols. in 1 (Oxford: Clarendon Press, 1925-40), s.v. "τέλος," pp. 1772-74. However, some still appeal to linguistic arguments. So, e.g., Flückiger, "Christus, des Gesetzes τέλος," pp. 153-54; Luz, *Geschichtsverständnis*, pp. 140-41; Murray, *Romans*, 2:49 and Sanday and Headlam, *Romans*, p. 285.

[3] But cf. Sanday and Headlam, Ibid., p. 284.

[4] See p. 8 above.

[5] See p. 8 above.

[6] See p. 8 above.

[7] See p. 14 above.

[8] See p. 19 above.

[9] See p. 19 above. With regard to such mediating approaches, we must agree with Käsemann that they practically render the message of the NT unintelligible. *Römer*, p. 270.

[10] So Luz, *Geschichtsverständnis*, pp. 140-41, Michel, *Römer*, p. 224 and Murray, *Romans*, 2:49.

[11] So Luz, Ibid., p. 141.

[12] So Luz, Ibid. and Murray, *Romans*, 2:50.

[13] So Käsemann, *Römer*, p. 270; Luz, Ibid., pp. 145-56 and Mussner, "Röm 10,4," pp. 33-34.

[14] So von der Osten-Sacken, *Römer 8*, p. 252.

[15] So von der Osten-Sacken, Ibid., pp. 252-53.

[16] So Bandstra, *Law*, pp. 102-5; Karl Barth, *Church Dogmatics*, 2/2:245; Bring, "Röm. 10,4," pp. 49-55; Cranfield, "Law," pp. 49-50; Flückiger, "Christus, des Gesetzes τέλος," p. 155; Howard, "Romans 10:4ff.," pp. 335-37 and Wang, "Law," pp. 149-51.

[17] So Flückiger, Ibid., pp. 154-55 and von der Osten-Sacken, *Römer 8*, p. 255.

[18] So Barth, *Church Dogmatics*, 2/2:244 and Flückiger, Ibid., p. 155.

[19] So Bandstra, *Law*, p. 101 and Wang, "Law," p. 148. For additional objections see Bring, "Röm. 10,4," pp. 35-72; Flückiger, Ibid., pp. 153-56; Howard, "Romans 10:4ff.," pp. 331-37 and Wang, Ibid., pp. 144-58.

[20] So Bläser, *Gesetz*, pp. 173-77; Bring, Ibid., p. 46; Flückiger, Ibid., p. 154 and Wilckens, "'Aus Werken des Gesetzes,'" p. 100.

[21] See p. 96 and n. 16 above.

[22] So Bläser, *Gesetz*, p. 179; von der Osten-Sacken, *Römer 8*, p. 255 and Wang, "Law," p. 146.

[23] So Cranfield, "Law," p. 49; Flückiger, "Christus, des Gesetzes τέλος," p. 156 and von der Osten-Sacken, Ibid., pp. 250, 256.

[24] So Käsemann, *Römer*, p. 270.

[25] So van Dülmen, *Gesetzes*, pp. 126, 185-218.

[26] So Käsemann, *Römer*, p. 270. For additional objections see Jüngel, *Paulus und Jesus*, p. 52 and Murray, *Romans*, 2:49-50.

[27] So Cranfield, "Some Notes on Romans 9:30-33," in *Jesus und Paulus: Festschrift für Werner Georg Kümmel zum 70. Geburtstag*, ed. E. Earle Ellis and Erich Grässer (Göttingen: Vandenhoeck & Ruprecht, 1975), p. 35. Käsemann appropriately labels the entire section, "Israels Schuld und Fall." Ibid., p. 264.

[28] See Cranfield, Ibid., pp. 35-36 and Käsemann, Ibid., p. 265.

[29] So Cranfield, Ibid., p. 38 and Käsemann, Ibid.

[30] So von der Osten-Sacken, *Römer 8*, pp. 252-53.

[31] So Murray (*Romans*, 2:43) and Sanday and Headlam (*Romans*, p. 279), who understand it as "principle," "rule" or "order" on the analogy of Rom 3:27; 7:21, 23; 8:2.

Notes: Chapter IV

³²Luz's apparent attempt to interpret νόμος δικαιοσύνης as "die Gerechtigkeit des Gesetzes" as though the Greek read δικαιοσύνη ἐκ νόμου (cf. 10:5) is unacceptable. *Geschichtsverständnis*, p. 157. So also the RSV, "the righteousness which is based on the law."

³³So Huby, *Romains*, p. 360 and Lagrange, *Romains*, p. 249. Schlier combines this approach with the following one. *Römerbrief*, p. 307.

³⁴Apparently some understand this function of promising righteousness particularly in terms of the law's witness to righteousness (cf. 3:21). So Käsemann, *Römer*, p. 265. See also Cranfield, "Romans 9:30-33," pp. 37-38.

Others seem to view this function as the law's promise of righteousness to those who keep or fulfil it (cf. 10:5). So Lietzmann, *Römer*, p. 94 and Michel, *Römer*, p. 219, n. 4. See also von der Osten-Sacken, *Römer 8*, p. 252, n. 25.

³⁵So Barrett, *Romans*, p. 193; Gronemeyer, *Antinomismus*, p. 123; Schmidt, *Römer*, p. 172 and Wang, "Law," p. 143. For other approaches similar to the three we have mentioned, see Bläser, *Gesetz*, pp. 173, 177; Bring, "Röm. 10,4," p. 46; van Dülmen, *Gesetzes*, p. 125, n. 167; Flückiger, "Christus, des Gesetzes τέλος," p. 154; Hahn, "Gesetzesverständnis," pp. 49-50; Ladd, "Law," p. 50; Ljungman, *Pistis*, p. 104; Stalder, *Das Werk des Geistes*, p. 350 and Stuhlmacher, *Gerechtigkeit Gottes*, p. 92.

³⁶With Käsemann, *Römer*, p. 265.

³⁷See Käsemann, Ibid.

³⁸So Cranfield, "Romans 9:30-33," p. 39 and von der Osten-Sacken, *Römer 8*, p. 253.

³⁹Although not original, the alternative reading which adds δικαιοσύνης after the second occurrence of νόμος (9:31) accurately represents what Paul says in an economy of words.

⁴⁰So von der Osten-Sacken, *Römer 8*, p. 253.

⁴¹We should logically supply διώκειν and νόμος δικαιοσύνης from the preceding verse (9:31). So Cranfield, "Romans 9:30-33," p. 39. Käsemann's interpolation of the verb "to live" (*Römer*, p. 264) and Barrett's substitution of δικαιοσύνη for νόμος (*Romans*, p. 193) are unwarranted.

⁴²The conjunction ὡς represents the subjective attitude of the Jews who held that ἐξ ἔργων was a legitimate method by which they might pursue and attain to the "law of righteousness." So Sanday and Headlam, *Romans*, p. 280.

⁴³Though not original, the alternative reading which adds νόμου after ἔργων correctly represents the source of these works. Cf. 3:20, 28; Gal 2:16; 3:2, 5, 10.

[44] So von der Osten-Sacken, *Römer 8*, p. 253.

[45] Against van Dülmen, *Gesetzes*, p. 125.

[46] So Käsemann, *Römer*, p. 265.

[47] So Cranfield, "Romans 9:30-33," p. 40 and Lagrange, *Romains*, p. 250.

[48] See Cranfield, Ibid., p. 41.

[49] Käsemann thinks this conflation may be pre-Pauline in origin. *Römer*, p. 267. Cf. 1 Pet 2:6, 8.

[50] See Cranfield, "Romans 9:30-33," p. 42 and Karlheinz Müller, *Anstoss und Gericht: Eine Studie zum jüdischen Hintergrund des paulinischen Skandalon-Begriffs*, Studien zum Alten und Neuen Testament, Bd. 19 (Munich: Kösel-Verlag, 1969), pp. 75-78.

[51] See Gustav Stählin, *TDNT*, s.v. "προσκόπτω," 6:754-56 and "σκάνδαλον," 7:352-54.

[52] On the possible messianic interpretation of the "stone" (Is 28:16) in pre-Christian times, see Müller, *Anstoss und Gericht*, pp. 78-79 and Jeremias, *TDNT*, s.v. "λίθος," 4:272-73.

[53] See Cranfield, "Romans 9:30-33," p. 42; Jeremias, Ibid., 4:276; Käsemann, *Römer*, p. 266 and Müller, Ibid., pp. 80-83.

[54] So von der Osten-Sacken, *Römer 8*, p. 254.

[55] So Cranfield, "Romans 9:30-33," pp. 42-43 and von der Osten-Sacken, Ibid., pp. 253-54.

[56] So Käsemann, *Römer*, p. 267 and Luz, *Geschichtsverständnis*, pp. 30-33.

[57] So Bultmann, *TDNT*, s.v. "γινώσκω," 1:707.

[58] In the light of 10:3b and Phil 3:9 some scholars understand ἡ δικαιοσύνη τοῦ θεοῦ as the gift of a righteous status before God. So Barrett, *Romans*, pp. 196-97; Klein, "Gottes Gerechtigkeit," pp. 232-33; Lietzmann, *Römer*, p. 95 and Michel, *Römer*, p. 223.
But others interpret it as God's claim over his creation which manifests itself in his saving power. So Käsemann, *Römer*, p. 269; Christian Müller, *Gottes Gerechtigkeit und Gottes Volk: Eine Untersuchung zu Römer 9-11*, FRLANT, Hft. 86 (Göttingen: Vandenhoeck & Ruprecht, 1964), pp. 72-75 and Stuhlmacher, *Gerechtigkeit Gottes*, p. 93.
Kertelge sees a double orientation of the concept of God's righteousness in this verse. The first occurrence refers to God's righteousness as a gift to the individual (genitive of origin), the second to God's righteousness as an expression of

Notes: Chapter IV

his saving will and activity (subjective genitive). *"Rechtfertigung"*, p. 96. See further J. A. Ziesler, *The Meaning of Righteousness in Paul: A Linguistic and Theological Enquiry*, SNTS Monograph Series, 20 (Cambridge, England: University Press, 1972), pp. 205-6.

[59] See Kertelge, Ibid., p. 95, n. 161.

[60] So Schlier, *Römerbrief*, p. 310.

[61] In view of 9:32-33 and 10:4, Kertelge (*"Rechtfertigung"*, p. 98) and Leenhardt (*Romans*, p. 265) assert that Christ appears here as the personified righteousness of God which Israel has rejected.

[62] So von der Osten-Sacken, *Römer 8*, p. 254.

[63] See Mussner, "Röm 10,4," pp. 35-37.

[64] So von der Osten-Sacken, *Römer 8*, pp. 254-55.

[65] On the analogy of Paul's use of the expression τὸν νόμον τελεῖν (Rom 2:27; cf. Jas 2:8), von der Osten-Sacken prefers to translate τέλος as "fulfilment" (*Erfüllung*). *Römer 8*, p. 252.

[66] In light of the thematic statement (9:31) Stuhlmacher's assertion that νόμος here is no longer the document of election but the Mosaic Torah (cf. 10:5) cannot be accepted. *Gerechtigkeit Gottes*, p. 93.

[67] The prepositional phrase εἰς δικαιοσύνην should be related to the entire statement τέλος γὰρ νόμου Χριστός. So Käsemann, *Römer*, p. 270. The preposition εἰς may be understood as consecutive ("so that"), final ("in order that") or even as referential ("as far as righteousness is concerned"). See Hodge, *Romans*, p. 529.

[68] Notably Paul reiterates in Rom 10:4 those positive connections between the law and Christ/righteousness/faith that he affirms in 9:31-33 as the following diagram shows:

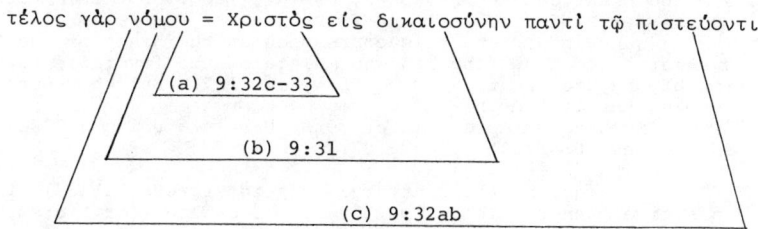

τέλος γὰρ νόμου = Χριστὸς εἰς δικαιοσύνην παντὶ τῷ πιστεύοντι
(a) 9:32c-33
(b) 9:31
(c) 9:32ab

(a) One attains to the *law* through faith in *Christ*.
(b) The *law* promises (or demands) *righteousness*.
(c) One attains to the *law* through *faith* alone.

⁶⁹Paul's emphasis on faith underlines the universal accessibility of the righteousness which the law promises and which becomes a reality in Christ (9:32-33). The Jews, on the other hand, limited salvation to the works of the law and tried to establish their own righteousness in this manner (9:32; 10:3). See Howard, "Romans 10:4ff.," pp. 336-37.

⁷⁰So Metzger argues that it has early and diversified support, that copyists would more likely have moved ὅτι to a position immediately after γράφει and that ποιεῖν τὴν ἐκ νόμου δικαιοσύνην is non-Pauline language. In this case τὴν δικαιοσύνην would function as an "accusative of specification," i.e., "For Moses writes concerning the righteousness, etc." *Textual Commentary*, p. 524.

⁷¹Moreover, if Metzger were right, this would be the only instance of Paul's use of γράφειν with the accusative of specification.

⁷²See, e.g., Käsemann, *Römer*, pp. 272-73.

⁷³So Bandstra, *Law*, pp. 104-5; Karl Barth, *Church Dogmatics*, 2/2:245 and Cranfield, "Law," p. 49. See, however, the criticism of Bandstra by Wang, "Law," pp. 151-53 and Ridderbos, *Paul*, p. 156, n. 156.

⁷⁴So Bring, "Röm. 10,4," p. 54; Flückiger, "Christus, des Gesetzes τέλος," p. 155; Howard, "Romans 10:4ff.," pp. 336-37 and Wang, Ibid., pp. 155-58. See the criticism of Bring by Wang, Ibid., pp. 154-55.

⁷⁵So von der Osten-Sacken, *Römer 8*, p. 255 and apparently Bläser, *Gesetz*, p. 180. Cf. Cranfield, "Law," p. 50, n. 1.

⁷⁶To interpret this ποιεῖν in some Christian sense, e.g., as the exercise of faith (so Bring, "Röm. 10,4," p. 54 and Flückiger, "Christus, des Gesetzes τέλος," p. 155) seems contrary to Pauline theology (cf. 2:17; Gal 3:12; Phil. 3:6, 9). In addition, one should note that when Paul applies Deut 30:14 to the Christian faith (10:8), he deliberately omits from the citation the phrase καὶ ἐν ταῖς χερσίν σου αὐτὸ ποιεῖν. See van der Minde, *Schrift und Tradition bei Paulus*, p. 112.
Wang interprets this expression on the basis of the OT covenant concept as "the man who maintains the favorable relationship by keeping the law." "Law," p. 157. But what does "keeping the law" mean?
Howard, moreover, interprets 10:5 in a universal sense. See "Romans 10:4ff.," pp. 336-37.

⁷⁷Bring, on the contrary, even interprets Gal 3:12 in a positive manner. Ibid., pp. 59-62. See Wang's criticism. Ibid., p. 154.

⁷⁸Bring, however, denies the connection between Phil 3:6 and Rom 10:5. Ibid., pp. 53-54.

[79] That the particle δέ can indicate contrast (without the μέν . . . δέ construction) goes without saying. See Bauer, *Lexicon*, s.v. "δέ," p. 170.

[80] Käsemann detects here the contrast between γράμμα (γράφει, 10:5) and πνεῦμα (λέγει, 10:6) familiar elsewhere in Paul (2:29; 7:6; 2 Cor 3:6). "The Spirit and the Letter," in *Perspectives on Paul*, pp. 155-66.

[81] So Käsemann, *Römer*, p. 273. Ridderbos, however, denies that Moses is viewed here as promoting the righteousness based on the law. Rather he argues: "What Paul means to say is this, that he who strives after the righteousness that is by the law is then bound to the word of Moses, that is, to do what the law demands." *Paul*, p. 156.

[82] Thus Dan O. Via, Jr. contends that "Paul speaks in this fashion because he sees righteousness by faith to be an Old Testament structure of meaning as well as a Christian one." "A Structuralist Approach to Paul's Old Testament Hermeneutic," *Interp* 28 (1974):212. At the same time Via draws our attention to Rom 4.

[83] It is conceivable that this modification and interpretation of Deut 30:12-14 comes to Paul in whole or in part from prior Christian exegesis. Cf. Jn 1:51; 3:13; 6:62; 1 Pet 3:19; Eph 4:8. So Käsemann, *Römer*, pp. 276-77. Whatever the case may be, Paul achieves his exegetical designs through the use of this text.

[84] A reminiscence of Ps 106:26[LXX] may have facilitated this change.

[85] Matthew Black relates this interpretative procedure to Jewish *pesher* exegesis with its actualizing "this is that" and insertion of interpretative sections into the OT text. "The Christological Use of the Old Testament in the New Testament," *NTS* 18 (1971-72):8-9. So also Käsemann, *Römer*, pp. 271-72. See 9:7 and cf. 1QpHab 11:17-12:10; CD 7:14-21. Bonsirven compares Paul's method to what he calls the "distributive exegesis" of the rabbis. *Exégèse rabbinique et exégèse paulinienne*, pp. 42-46, 306-7.

[86] For differing views of how Paul might have been able to interpret Deut 30:12-14 with reference to Christ, see Arnold M. Goldberg, "Torah aus der Unterwelt? Eine Bemerkung zu Röm 10,6-7," *Biblische Zeitschrift* 14 (1970):127-31; Jan Heller, "Himmel- und Höllenfahrt nach Römer 10, 6-7," *EvT* 32 (1972):478-86; Lyonnet, "Saint Paul et l' exégèse juive de sons temps. A propos de Rom., 10:6-8," in *Mélanges bibliques redigés en l' honneur de André Robert*, Travaux de l' Institut catholique de Paris, 4 (Paris: Bloud et Gay, 1957), pp. 494-506; M. Jack Suggs, "'The Word Is Near You': Romans 10:6-10 within the Purpose of the Letter," in *Christian History and Interpretation: Studies Presented to John Knox*, ed. W. R. Farmer, C. F. D. Moule and R. R. Niebuhr (Cambridge, England: University Press, 1967), pp. 304-311 and Via, "Paul's Old Testament Hermeneutic," pp. 215-20.

[87] The notion of "bringing Christ down from heaven" apparently points to Christ in his ascension rather than his incarnation. Note the parallel between 10:6-7 and 10:9. So Käsemann, *Römer*, p. 276. Otherwise Barrett, *Romans*, p. 199.

[88] Paul interprets this question in the sense of Ps 70:20[LXX] and Wisdom 16:13. So Käsemann, Ibid., p. 275.

[89] So Käsemann, Ibid., p. 278 and Schlier, *Römerbrief*, p. 312.

[90] So Käsemann, Ibid.

[91] See van der Minde, *Schrift und Tradition bei Paulus*, pp. 112-15 and the literature cited there. Käsemann, among others, suggests its connection with the administration of baptism in the early church. Ibid., p. 279.

[92] So Käsemann, Ibid.

[93] So Käsemann, Ibid. and Schlier, *Römerbrief*, p. 314.

[94] See Lagrange, *Romains*, p. 259; Murray, *Romans*, 2:57; Sanday and Headlam, *Romans*, p. 291 and Schlier, Ibid.

[95] The verb πιστεύειν denotes acceptance of the Christian message and also obedience. Cf. 10:9, 16. So Käsemann, *Römer*, p. 281.

[96] Paul has both abbreviated and pluralized the OT text (MT and LXX) so that it now refers to the messengers of the gospel.

[97] So Käsemann, *Römer*, pp. 282-83. Otherwise Schlier, *Römerbrief*, p. 318.

[98] These words originally applied to the heavens and the firmament. See Ps 18:1-4[LXX].

[99] However, Käsemann interprets γινώσκειν here as "acknowledge" (*anerkennen*). *Römer*, p. 284.

[100] So Käsemann, Ibid.; Murray, *Romans*, 2:62-64 and Sanday and Headlam, *Romans*, pp. 299-300.
Others interpret Paul's argument to mean that if the "foolish" Gentiles have understood, how much more the knowledgeable Jews. So Althaus, *Römer*, p. 111; Lagrange, *Romains*, p. 262 and Michel, *Römer*, p. 232.
Moreover, according to Schlier, Israel's knowledge is revealed in their jealousy of the Gentiles who have converted to Christ (10:19). *Römerbrief*, p. 319.

[101] By substituting ὑμᾶς for αὐτούς, Paul contemporizes the OT text so that it addresses the Jews of his time. As 11:11-32 show, this passage is programmatic for Paul's understanding of his apostolic mission in relation to Israel.

¹⁰²Paul has reordered the clauses in this text and switched the participles ἐπερωτῶσιν and ζητοῦσιν. Originally referring to Israel, these words now apply to the Gentiles.

¹⁰³By applying this citation to Israel, for whom it was originally intended, the apostle contrasts it sharply with the preceding text (Is 65:1) which he reapplied to the Gentiles.

¹⁰⁴In his initial statement (10:5) Paul views the law in a narrower sense, in terms of its commandments and prohibitions; in his second (10:6-8) he regards the law in its entirety as a witness along with the prophets. So Dahl, "The Future of Israel," p. 148. See also Käsemann, *Römer*, p. 273.

¹⁰⁵So Käsemann, Ibid., p. 277.

¹⁰⁶Against those exegetes mentioned on p. 105, ns. 73-74 above.

¹⁰⁷Against Bläser, *Gesetz*, p. 180; van Dülmen, *Gesetzes*, p. 125 and van der Minde, *Schrift und Tradition bei Paulus*, p. 109. Cf. Phil 3:6.

¹⁰⁸Thus E. P. Sanders argues in this connection that what is wrong with the law is that it rests on works but salvation, according to Paul, can only be by faith. *Paul and Palestinian Judaism*, p. 483, n. 37.

¹⁰⁹A point aptly stressed by Howard, "Romans 10:4ff.," p. 336.

¹¹⁰Von der Osten-Sacken seems to view Rom 10:5 as a grounding for 10:3 and 10:6-8 as a grounding for 10:4. *Römer 8*, p. 255.

¹¹¹"Law," p. 50, n. 1.

¹¹²But cf. Gal 3:24 and see von der Osten-Sacken, *Römer 8*, p. 256.

CONCLUSION

¹So Mussner, "Röm 10,4," p. 37 and van Dülmen, *Gesetzes*, p. 126 respectively.

SELECTED BIBLIOGRAPHY

Commentaries

Allo, Ernest Bernard. *Saint Paul Première Épître aux Corinthiens.* ÉtBib. 2d ed. Paris: J. Gabalda, 1956. 515 pp.

_____. *Saint Paul Seconde Épître aux Corinthiens.* ÉtBib. 2d ed. Paris: J. Gabalda, 1956. 387 pp.

Althaus, Paul. *Der Brief an die Römer.* Das Neue Testament Deutsch, Bd. 6. Aufl. 11. Göttingen: Vandenhoeck & Ruprecht, 1970. 159 pp.

Barrett, C. K. *A Commentary on the Epistle to the Romans.* HNTC. New York: Harper & Row, 1957. 294 pp.

_____. *A Commentary on the First Epistle to the Corinthians.* HNTC. New York: Harper & Row, 1968. 410 pp.

_____. *A Commentary on the Second Epistle to the Corinthians.* HNTC. New York: Harper & Row, 1973. 353 pp.

Barth, Karl. *A Shorter Commentary on Romans.* Translated by D. H. van Daalen. London: SCM Press, 1959. 188 pp.

Bultmann, Rudolf. *Der zweite Brief an die Korinther.* Edited by Erich Dinkler. KExKNT, Sonderband. Göttingen: Vandenhoeck & Ruprecht, 1976. 270 pp.

Burton, Ernest De Witt. *A Critical and Exegetical Commentary on the Epistle to the Galatians.* ICC. 1st ed. Edinburgh: T. & T. Clark, 1921. 541 pp.

Cambier, Jules. *L' Évangile de Dieu selon l' Épître aux Romains: Exégèse et Théologie biblique.* Studia Neotestamentica, Studia 3. 3 tomes. Brussels: Desclée de Brouwer, 1967-. T. 1: *L' Évangile de la Justice et de la Grâce*, 1967. 444 pp.

Conzelmann, Hans. *A Commentary on the First Epistle to the Corinthians.* Translated by James W. Leitch. Bibliography and references by James W. Dunkly. Edited by George W. MacRae. Hermeneia. Philadelphia: Fortress Press, 1975. 323 pp.

Cranfield, C. E. B. *A Critical and Exegetical Commentary on the Epistle to the Romans.* ICC. 2 vols. Edinburgh:

T. & T. Clark, 1975-. Vol. 1: *Introduction and Commentary on Romans I-VIII*, 1975. 444 pp.

Dibelius, Martin. *James: A Commentary on the Epistle of James*. Revised by Heinrich Greeven. Translated by Michael A. Williams. Edited by Helmut Koester. Hermeneia. Philadelphia: Fortress Press, 1976. 285 pp.

Dodd, C. H. *The Epistle of Paul to the Romans*. Moffatt New Testament Commentary. London: Hodder & Stoughton, 1932. 246 pp.

Eadie, John. *A Commentary on the Greek Text of the Epistle of Paul to the Galatians*. Edinburgh: T. & T. Clark, 1894; reprint ed., Grand Rapids: Zondervan Publishing House, n.d. 480 pp.

Gaugler, Ernst. *Der Römerbrief*. Prophezei Schweizerisches Bibelwerk für die Gemeinde. 2 Teile. Zurich: Zwingli-Verlag, 1945-52.

Hodge, Charles. *Commentary on the Epistle to the Romans*. New rev. ed. New York: A. C. Armstrong & Son, 1896. 716 pp.

Huby, Joseph. *Saint Paul Épître aux Romains*. Edited by Stanislas Lyonnet. Verbum Salutis, 10. Paris: Beauchesne et Ses Fils, 1957. 643 pp.

The Interpreter's Bible. Edited by George Arthur Buttrick. 12 vols. New York: Abingdon-Cokesbury Press, 1951-57. Vol. 9: *The Epistle to the Romans*, by John Knox, 1954.

Käsemann, Ernst. *An die Römer*. HNT, Bd. 8a. Tübingen: J. C. B. Mohr, 1973. 407 pp.

Kuss, Otto. *Der Römerbrief*. 3 Lieferungen. Regensburg: Verlag Friedrich Pustet, 1957-78.

Lagrange, Marie Joseph. *Saint Paul Épître aux Galates*. ÉtBib. 2d ed. Paris: J. Gabalda, 1950. 175 pp.

_____. *Saint Paul Épître aux Romains*. ÉtBib. Paris: J. Gabalda, 1950. 403 pp.

Leenhardt, Franz J. *The Epistle to the Romans*. Translated by Harold Knight. London: Lutterworth Press, 1961. 389 pp.

Lietzmann, Hans. *Einführung in die Textgeschichte der Paulusbriefe an die Römer*. HNT, Bd. 8. Aufl. 5. Tübingen: J. C. B. Mohr, 1971. 134 pp.

_____. *An die Galater*. HNT, Bd. 10. Aufl. 4. Tübingen: J. C. B. Mohr, 1971. 48 pp.

Bibliography

Lightfoot, J. B. *Notes on Epistles of St Paul from Unpublished Commentaries*. London: Macmillan & Co., 1895. 336 pp.

―――. *Saint Paul's Epistle to the Galatians*. 10th ed. London: Macmillan & Co., 1900. 384 pp.

Meyer, Heinrich August Wilhelm. *Critical and Exegetical Hand-Book to the Epistle to the Romans*. Translated by John C. Moore and Edwin Johnson. Revised and edited by William P. Dickson. With a Preface and Supplementary Notes by Timothy Dwight. New York: Funk & Wagnalls, 1884. 588 pp.

Michel, Otto. *Der Brief an die Römer*. KExKNT, Abt. 4. Aufl. 10. Göttingen: Vandenhoeck & Ruprecht, 1955. 357 pp.

Murray, John. *The Epistle to the Romans*. NICNT. 2 vols. Grand Rapids: Wm. B. Eerdmans Publishing Co., 1959-65.

Mussner, Franz. *Der Galaterbrief*. HTKNT, Bd. 9. Freiburg: Herder, 1974. 425 pp.

Nygren, Anders. *Commentary on Romans*. Translated by Carl C. Rasmussen. London: SCM Press, 1952. 457 pp.

Oepke, Albrecht. *Der Brief des Paulus an die Galater*. THkNT, Bd. 9. Aufl. 2. Berlin: Evangelische Verlagsanstalt, 1957. 176 pp.

Ridderbos, Herman. *The Epistle of Paul to the Churches of Galatia*. NICNT. Grand Rapids: Wm. B. Eerdmans Publishing Co., 1953. 238 pp.

Robertson, Archibald and Alfred Plummer. *A Critical and Exegetical Commentary on the First Epistle of St Paul to the Corinthians*. ICC. 2d ed. Edinburgh: T. & T. Clark, 1914. 424 pp.

Sanday, William and Arthur C. Headlam. *A Critical and Exegetical Commentary on the Epistle to the Romans*. ICC. 5th ed. Edinburgh: T. & T. Clark, 1902. 450 pp.

Schlatter, Adolf. *Gottes Gerechtigkeit: Ein Kommentar zum Römerbrief*. Aufl. 2. Stuttgart: Calwer Verlag, 1952. 411 pp.

Schlier, Heinrich. *Der Brief an die Galater*. KExKNT, Abt. 7. Aufl. 10. Göttingen: Vandenhoeck & Ruprecht, 1949. 211 pp.

―――. *Der Brief an die Galater*. KExKNT, Abt. 7. Aufl. 12. Göttingen: Vandenhoeck & Ruprecht, 1962. 287 pp.

―――. *Der Römerbrief*. HTKNT, Bd. 6. Freiburg: Herder, 1977. 455 pp.

Schmidt, Hans Wilhelm. *Der Brief des Paulus an die Römer.*
    ThkNT, Bd. 6. Berlin: Evangelische Verlagsanstalt,
    1962. 278 pp.

Sickenberger, Joseph. *Die Briefe des Heiligen Paulus an die
    Korinther und Römer.* Die Heilige Schrift des Neuen
    Testamentes, Bd. 6. Aufl. 4. Bonn: Peter Hanstein
    Verlagsbuchhandlung, 1932. 333 pp.

Wilckens, Ulrich. *Der Brief an die Römer.* Evangelisch-
    Katholischer Kommentar zum Neuen Testament, Bd. 6/1.
    Zurich: Benziger Verlag, 1978. 337 pp.

Monographs

Althaus, Paul. *Gebot und Gesetz: Zum Thema "Gesetz und
    Evangelium".* Beiträge zur Förderung christlicher
    Theologie, Bd. 46, Hft. 2. Gütersloh: C. Bertels-
    mann Verlag, 1952. 39 pp.

Bandstra, Andrew John. *The Law and the Elements of the World:
    An Exegetical Study in Aspects of Paul's Teaching.*
    Kampen: J. H. Kok, 1964. 209 pp.

Barth, Karl. *Church Dogmatics.* Edited by G. W. Bromiley and
    T. F. Torrance. 4 vols. in 13. Edinburgh: T. & T.
    Clark, 1936-70. Vol. 2/2: *The Doctrine of God.*
    Translated by G. W. Bromiley, J. C. Campbell, Iain
    Wilson et al., 1957.

Bläser, Peter. *Das Gesetz bei Paulus.* NTA, Bd. 19, Hfte. 1-2.
    Münster: Aschendorffsche Verlagsbuchhandlung, 1941.
    252 pp.

Bonhöffer, Adolf. *Epiktet und das Neue Testament.* Religions-
    geschichtliche Versuche und Vorarbeiter, Bd. 10.
    Giessen: Alfred Töpelmann, 1911. 412 pp.

Bonsirven, Joseph. *Exégèse rabbinique et exégèse paulinienne.*
    Bibliothèque de Théologie Historique. Paris: Beau-
    chesne et Ses Fils, 1939. 405 pp.

Borgen, Peder. *Bread from Heaven: An Exegetical Study of the
    Concept of Manna in the Gospel of John and the Writings
    of Philo.* Supplements to Novum Testamentum, 10.
    Leiden: E. J. Brill, 1965. 217 pp.

Bornkamm, Günther. *Paul.* Translated by D. M. G. Stalker.
    New York: Harper & Row, 1971. 260 pp.

Brandenburger, Egon. *Adam und Christus: Exegetisch-
    religionsgeschichtliche Untersuchung zu Röm. 5, 12-21
    (1. Kor. 15).* WMANT, Bd. 7. Neukirchen: Kreis Moers,
    1962. 302 pp.

Braun, Herbert. *Qumran und das Neue Testament.* 2 Bde. Tübingen: J. C. B. Mohr, 1966.

Bultmann, Rudolf. *Der Stil der paulinischen Predigt und die kynisch-stoische Diatribe.* FRLANT, Bd. 13. Göttingen: Vandenhoeck & Ruprecht, 1910. 109 pp.

_____. *Theology of the New Testament.* Translated by Kendrick Grobel. 2 vols. in 1. New York: Charles Scribner's Sons, 1951-55.

von Campenhausen, Hans F. *The Formation of the Christian Bible.* Translated by J. A. Baker. Philadelphia: Fortress Press, 1972. 342 pp.

Cerfaux, Lucien. *The Christian in the Theology of St. Paul.* Translated by Lilian Soiron. New York: Herder & Herder, 1967. 568 pp.

Conzelmann, Hans. *An Outline of the Theology of the New Testament.* Translated by John Bowden. New York: Harper & Row, 1969. 373 pp.

Dalman, Gustaf. *Jesus-Jeshua: Studies in the Gospels.* Translated by Paul P. Levertoff. London: S.P.C.K., 1929. 256 pp.

Davies, W. D. *Paul and Rabbinic Judaism: Some Rabbinic Elements in Pauline Theology.* Rev. ed. New York: Harper & Row, 1967. 392 pp.

_____. *Torah in the Messianic Age and/or the Age to Come.* JBL Monograph Series, vol. 7. Philadelphia: Society of Biblical Literature, 1952. 99 pp.

Dietzfelbinger, Christian. *Paulus und das Alte Testament: Die Hermeneutik des Paulus untersucht an seiner Deutung der Gestalt Abrahams.* Theologische Existenz Heute, n. F. 95. Munich: Chr. Kaiser Verlag, 1961. 41 pp.

Drane, John W. *Paul: Libertine or Legalist? A Study in the Theology of the Major Pauline Epistles.* London: S.P.C.K., 1975. 194 pp.

van Dülmen, Andrea. *Die Theologie des Gesetzes bei Paulus.* Stuttgarter biblische Monographien, Bd. 5. Stuttgart: Verlag Katholisches Bibelwerk, 1968. 282 pp.

Du Plessis, Paul Johannes. ΤΕΛΕΙΟΣ: *The Idea of Perfection in the New Testament.* Theologische Academie uitgaande van de Johannes Calvijn stichting te Kampen. Kampen: J. H. Kok, [1959]. 255 pp.

Eichholz, Georg. *Die Theologie des Paulus im Umriss.* Neukirchen-Vluyn: Neukirchener Verlag, 1972. 322 pp.

Ellis, E. Earle. *Paul's Use of the Old Testament.* Edinburgh: Oliver & Boyd, 1957. 204 pp.

Feine, Paul. *Das gesetzesfreie Evangelium des Paulus nach seinem Werdegang dargestellt.* Leipzig: J. C. Hinrichs, 1899. 232 pp.

Fuchs, Ernst. *Die Freiheit des Glaubens: Römer 5-8 ausgelegt.* BEvT, Bd. 14. Munich: Chr. Kaiser Verlag, 1949. 123 pp.

Gerhardsson, Birger. *Memory and Manuscript: Oral Tradition and Written Transmission in Rabbinic Judaism and Early Christianity.* Translated by Eric J. Sharpe. Acta Seminarii Neotestamentici Upsaliensis, 22. Lund: C. W. K. Gleerup, 1961. 379 pp.

Goodenough, Erwin Ramsdell. *By Light, Light: The Mystic Gospel of Hellenistic Judaism.* New Haven: Yale University Press, 1935. 436 pp.

Goppelt, Leonard. *Theologie des Neuen Testaments.* Edited by Jürgen Roloff. Göttinger theologische Lehrbücher. 2 Teile. Göttingen: Vandenhoeck & Ruprecht, 1975-76. 2. T.: *Vielfalt und Einheit des apostolischen Christuszeugnisses,* 1976.

Grafe, Eduard. *Die paulinische Lehre vom Gesetz nach den vier Hauptbriefen.* Aufl. 2. Leipzig: J. C. B. Mohr, 1893. 33 pp.

Gronemeyer, Reimer. *Zur Frage nach dem paulinischen Antinomismus: Exegetisch-systematische Überlegungen mit besonderer Berücksichtigung der Forschungsgeschichte im 19. Jahrhundert.* Hamburg: By the author, 1970. 252 pp.

Hanson, Anthony Tyrrell. *Studies in Paul's Technique and Theology.* London: S.P.C.K., 1974. 329 pp.

von Harnack, Adolf. *Marcion: Das Evangelium vom fremden Gott: Eine Monographie zur Geschichte der Grundlegung der katholischen Kirche. Neue Studien zu Marcion.* Darmstadt: Wissenschaftliche Buchgesellschaft, 1960. 235, 455[Beilagen], 28 pp.

Hübner, Hans. *Das Gesetz bei Paulus: Ein Beitrag zum Werden der paulinischen Theologie.* FRLANT, Bd. 119. Göttingen: Vandenhoeck & Ruprecht, 1978. 195 pp.

Joest, Wilfred. *Gesetz und Freiheit: Das Problem des Tertius usus legis bei Luther und die neutestamentliche Parainese.* Aufl. 3. Göttingen: Vandenhoeck & Ruprecht, 1961. 240 pp.

Jüngel, Eberhard. *Paulus und Jesus: Eine Untersuchung zur Präzisierung der Frage nach dem Ursprung der Christologie.* HUT, Bd. 2. Tübingen: J. C. B. Mohr, 1962. 319 pp.

Kertelge, Karl. *"Rechtfertigung" bei Paulus: Studien zur Struktur und zum Bedeutungsgehalt des paulinischen Rechtfertigungsbegriffs.* NTA, n. F., Bd. 3. Münster: Verlag Aschendorff, 1967. 335 pp.

Knox, Wilfred L. *St Paul and the Church of Jerusalem.* Cambridge, England: University Press, 1925. 396 pp.

Koch, Herbert. *Römer 3,21-31 in der Paulusinterpretation der letzten 150 Jahre.* Göttingen: By the author, 1971. 160 pp.

Kümmel, Werner Georg. *Römer 7 und das Bild des Menschen im Neuen Testament: Zwei Studien.* Theologische Bücherei, Bd. 53. Munich: Chr. Kaiser Verlag, 1974. 233 pp.

Lampe, G. W. H. *The Seal of the Spirit: A Study in the Doctrine of Baptism and Confirmation in the New Testament and the Fathers.* London: Longmans, Green & Co., 1951. 340 pp.

Ljungman, Henrik. *Pistis: A Study of Its Presuppositions and Its Meaning in Pauline Use.* Translated by W. F. Salisbury. Acta Reg. Societatis Humaniorum Litterarum Lundiensis, 64. Lund: C. W. K. Gleerup, 1964. 122 pp.

Lohmeyer, Ernst. *Grundlagen paulinischer Theologie.* Beiträge zur historischen Theologie, 1. Tübingen: J. C. B. Mohr, 1929. 235 pp.

Longenecker, Richard N. *Paul, Apostle of Liberty.* New York: Harper & Row, 1964. 310 pp.

Luz, Ulrich. *Das Geschichtsverständnis des Paulus.* BEvT, Bd. 49. Munich: Chr. Kaiser Verlag, 1968. 426 pp.

Mattern, Lieselotte. *Das Verständnis des Gerichtes bei Paulus.* Abhandlungen zur Theologie des Alten und Neuen Testaments, Bd. 47. Zurich: Zwingli Verlag, 1966. 235 pp.

Mauer, Christian. *Die Gesetzeslehre des Paulus nach ihrem Ursprung und in ihrer Entfaltung dargelegt.* Zollikon-Zurich: Evangelischer Verlag, 1941. 107 pp.

Michel, Otto. *Paulus und seine Bibel.* Gütersloh: C. Bertelsmann, 1929; reprint ed., Darmstadt: Wissenschaftliche Buchgesellschaft, 1972. 227 pp.

van der Minde, Hans-Jürgen. *Schrift und Tradition bei Paulus: Ihre Bedeutung und Funktion im Römerbrief.* Paderborner Theologische Studien, Bd. 3. Munich: Verlag Ferdinand Schöningh, 1976. 221 pp.

Monsengwo Pasinya, Laurent. *La notion de nomos dans le Pentateuque grec.* Preface by Ignace de la Potterie, AnBib, 52. Rome: Biblical Institute Press, 1973. 246 pp.

Moore, George Foot. *Judaism in the First Centuries of the Christian Era, the Age of the Tannaim*. 3 vols. Cambridge: Harvard University Press, 1927-30.

Müller, Christian. *Gottes Gerechtigkeit und Gottes Volk: Eine Untersuchung zu Römer 9-11*. FRLANT, Hft. 86. Göttingen: Vandenhoeck & Ruprecht, 1964. 116 pp.

Müller, Karlheinz. *Anstoss und Gericht: Eine Studie zum jüdischen Hintergrund des paulinischen Skandalon-Begriffs*. Studien zum Alten und Neuen Testament, Bd. 19. Munich: Kösel-Verlag, 1969. 143 pp.

Munck, Johannes. *Christ and Israel: An Interpretation of Romans 9-11*. Translated by Ingeborg Nixon. Foreword by Krister Stendahl. Philadelphia: Fortress Press, 1967. 156 pp.

von der Osten-Sacken, Peter. *Römer 8 als Beispiel paulinischer Soteriologie*. FRLANT, Bd. 112. Göttingen: Vandenhoeck & Ruprecht, 1975. 339 pp.

Paulsen, Henning. *Überlieferung und Auslegung in Römer 8*. WMANT, Bd. 43. Neukirchen-Vluyn: Neukirchener Verlag, 1974. 226 pp.

Ridderbos, Herman. *Paul: An Outline of His Theology*. Translated by John Richard de Witt. Grand Rapids: Wm. B. Eerdmans Publishing Co., 1975. 587 pp.

Rössler, Dietrich. *Gesetz und Geschichte: Untersuchungen zur Theologie der jüdischen Apokalyptik und der pharisäischen Orthodoxie*. WMANT, Bd. 3. Neukirchen: Neukirchener Verlag, 1960. 119 pp.

Rosenblatt, Samuel. *The Interpretation of the Bible in the Mishnah*. Baltimore: John Hopkins Press, 1935. 93 pp.

Sanders, E. P. *Paul and Palestinian Judaism: A Comparison of Patterns of Religion*. Philadelphia: Fortress Press, 1977. 627 pp.

Sandmel, Samuel. *Philo's Place in Judaism: A Study of Conceptions of Abraham in Jewish Literature*. Cincinnati: Hebrew Union College Press, 1956. 218 pp.

Schneider, Norbert. *Die rhetorische Eigenart der paulinischen Antithese*. HUT, Bd. 11. Tübingen: J. C. B. Mohr, 1970. 147 pp.

Schoeps, Hans Joachim. *Paul: The Theology of the Apostle in the Light of Jewish Religious History*. Translated by Harold Knight. Philadelphia: Westminster Press, 1974. 303 pp.

Schrage, Wolfgang. *Die konkreten Einzelgebote in der paulinischen Paränese: Ein Beitrag zur neutestamentlichen Ethik*. Gütersloh: Gütersloher Verlagshaus Gerd Mohn, 1961. 320 pp.

Schweitzer, Albert. *Paul and His Interpreters: A Critical History.* Translated by W. Montgomery. London: Adam & Charles Black, 1912. 253 pp.

Scott, Charles A. Anderson. *Christianity according to St. Paul.* Cambridge, England: University Press, 1927. 283 pp.

Söhngen, Gottlieb. *Gesetz und Evangelium: Ihre Analoge Einheit: Theologisch, philosophisch, staatsbürgerlich.* Freiburg: Verlag Karl Alber, 1957. 135 pp.

Stalder, Kurt. *Das Werk des Geistes in der Heiligung bei Paulus.* Zurich: EVZ-Verlag, 1962. 523 pp.

Stuhlmacher, Peter. *Gerechtigkeit Gottes bei Paulus.* FRLANT, Hft. 87. Göttingen: Vandenhoeck & Ruprecht, 1965. 276 pp.

_____. *Das paulinische Evangelium: I. Vorgeschichte.* FRLANT, Hft. 95. Göttingen: Vandenhoeck & Ruprecht, 1968. 313 pp.

Teeple, Howard M. *The Mosaic Eschatological Prophet.* JBL Monograph Series, vol. 10. Philadelphia: Society of Biblical Literature, 1957. 122 pp.

Verweijs, P. G. *Evangelium und neues Gesetz in der ältesten Christenheit bis auf Marcion.* Studia theologica Rheno-Traiectina, vol. 5. Utrecht: Kemink en Zoon, 1960. 382 pp.

Ziesler, J. A. *The Meaning of Righteousness in Paul: A Linguistic and Theological Enquiry.* SNTS Monograph Series, 20. Cambridge, England: University Press, 1972. 254 pp.

Articles in Periodicals and Series

Barth, Markus. "Die Stellung des Paulus zu Gesetz und Ordnung," *EvT* 33 (1973):496-526.

Beck, Irene. "Altes und neues Gesetz: Eine Untersuchung über die Kompromisslosigkeit des paulinischen Denkens," *MüTZ* 15 (1964):127-42.

Benoit, Pierre. "La loi et la croix d' après saint Paul (Rom. vii,7-viii,4)," *Revue Biblique* 47 (1938):481-509.

Berger, Klaus. "Abraham in den paulinischen Hauptbriefen," *MüTZ* 17 (1966):47-89.

Betz, Hans Dieter. "The Literary Composition and Function of Paul's Letter to the Galatians," *NTS* 21 (1975):353-79.

Black, Matthew. "The Christological Use of the Old Testament in the New Testament," *NTS* 18 (1971-72):1-14.

Bring, Ragnar. "Paul and the Old Testament: A Study of the Ideas of Election, Faith and Law in Paul with Special Reference to Romans 9:30-10:30[sic]," *Studia Theologica* 25 (1971):21-60.

Bruce, F. F. "Paul and the Law of Moses," *BJRL* 57 (1975): 259-79.

Bultmann, Rudolf. "Glossen im Römerbrief," *TLZ* 72 (1947): 197-202.

Cranfield, C. E. B. "St. Paul and the Law," *SJT* 17 (1964): 43-68.

Feyerabend, W. "Über den Schluss des 3. Kapitels im Briefe an die Römer," *Neue kirchliche Zeitschrift* 3 (1892): 409-20.

Flückiger, Felix. "Christus, des Gesetzes τέλος," *TZ* 11 (1955): 153-57.

Friedrich, Gerhard. "Das Gesetz des Glaubens," *TZ* 10 (1954): 401-17.

Goldberg, Arnold M. "Torah aus der Unterwelt? Eine Bemerkung zu Röm 10,6-7," *Biblische Zeitschrift* 14 (1970):127-31.

Goppelt, Leonard. "Apokalyptik und Typologie bei Paulus," *TLZ* 89 (1964):321-44.

_____. "Paul and Heilsgeschichte: Conclusions from Romans 4 and 1 Corinthians 10:1-13," *Interp* 21 (1967):315-26.

Grundmann, Walter. "Gesetz, Rechtfertigung und Mystik bei Paulus: Zum Problem der Einheitlichkeit der paulinischen Verkündigung," *ZNW* 32 (1933):52-65.

Hahn, Ferdinand. "Das Gesetzesverständnis im Römer- und Galaterbrief," *ZNW* 67 (1976):29-63.

Haufe, Christoph. "Die Stellung des Paulus zum Gesetz," *TLZ* 91 (1966):171-78.

Hellbardt, Hans. "Christus, das Telos des Gesetzes," *EvT* 3 (1936):331-46.

Heller, Jan. "Himmel- und Höllenfahrt nach Römer 10,6-7," *EvT* 32 (1972):478-86.

Howard, George. "Christ the End of the Law: The Meaning of Romans 10:4ff.," *JBL* 88 (1969):331-37.

_____. "On the 'Faith of Christ,'" *HTR* 60 (1967):459-65.

Kennedy, H. A. A. "St. Paul and the Law," *The Expositor*, 8th Series, 13 (1917):338-66.

Kuhl, Ernst. "Stellung und Bedeutung des alttestamentlichen Gesetzes im Zusammenhang der paulinischen Lehre," *Theologische Studien und Kritiken* 67 (1894):120-46.

Kuss, Otto. "Nomos bei Paulus," *MüTZ* 17 (1966):173-227.

Lambrecht, Jan. "The Line of Thought in Gal. 2.14b-21," *NTS* 24 (1978):484-95.

Lyonnet, Stanislas. "St. Paul: Liberty and Law," *The Bridge*, 1962, pp. 229-51.

Marín, Francisco. "Matices del término 'ley' en las cartas de San Pablo," *Estudios Eclesiásticos* 49 (1974):19-46.

Müller, Friedrich. "Zwei Marginalien im Brief des Paulus an die Römer," *ZNW* 40 (1941):249-54.

Murphy-O'Connor, Jerome. "Corinthian Slogans in 1 Cor 6:12-20," *CBQ* 40 (1978):391-96.

Rigaux, Beda. "Law and Grace in Pauline Eschatology," *Louvain Studies* 2 (1969):329-33.

Sanders, James A. "Torah and Christ," *Interp* 29 (1975):372-90.

Schulz, Siegfried. "Zur Rechtfertigung aus Gnaden in Qumran und bei Paulus," *ZTK* 56 (1959):155-85.

Stendahl, Krister. "The Apostle Paul and the Introspective Conscience of the West," *HTR* 56 (1963):199-215.

Stuhlmacher, Peter. "'Das Ende des Gesetzes': Über Ursprung und Ansatz der paulinischen Theologie," *ZTK* 67 (1970): 14-39.

Via, Dan O., Jr. "A Structuralist Approach to Paul's Old Testament Hermeneutic," *Interp* 28 (1974):201-20.

Walvoord, John F. "Law in the Epistle to the Romans," *Bibliotheca Sacra* 94 (1937):15-30, 281-95.

Wilson, R. McL. "Nomos: The Biblical Signification of Law," *SJT* 5 (1952):36-48.

Wuellner, Wilhelm. "Paul's Rhetoric of Argumentation in Romans: An Alternative to the Donfried-Karris Debate over Romans," *CBQ* 38 (1976):330-51.

_____. "Toposforschung und Torahinterpretation bei Paulus und Jesus," *NTS* 24 (1978):463-83.

Wyschogrod, Michael. "The Law, Jews and Gentiles--A Jewish Perspective," *Lutheran Quarterly* 21 (1969):405-15.

Articles and Essays in Collections

Barrett, C. K. "Abraham." In *From First Adam to Last: A Study in Pauline Theology*. New York: Charles Scribner's Sons, 1962. Pp. 22-45.

Barth, Markus. "Exegetische Anfragen an das Gesetzesverständnis Luthers und Barths." In *Promissio und Bund: Gesetz und Evangelium bei Luther und Barth*. Bertold Klappert. Forschungen zur systematischen und ökumenischen Theologie, Bd. 34. Göttingen: Vandenhoeck & Ruprecht, 1976. Pp. 256-66.

Betz, Hans Dieter. "In Defense of the Spirit: Paul's Letter to the Galatians as a Document of Early Christian Apologetics." In *Aspects of Religious Propaganda in Judaism and Early Christianity*. Edited by E. Schüssler Fiorenza. University of Notre Dame Center for the Study of Judaism and Christianity in Antiquity, 2. Notre Dame: University of Notre Dame Press, 1976. Pp. 99-114.

Bornkamm, Günther. "Die Offenbarung des Zornes Gottes. Röm 1-3." In *Das Ende des Gesetzes: Paulusstudien*. Gesammelte Aufsätze, Bd. 1. BEvT, Bd. 16. Aufl. 2. Munich: Chr. Kaiser Verlag, 1958. Pp. 9-33.

_____. "Theologie als Teufelskunst. Rm. 3,1-9." In *Geschichte und Glaube*. Gesammelte Aufsätze, Bd. 4, T. 2. BEvT, Bd. 53. Munich: Chr. Kaiser Verlag, 1971. Pp. 140-48.

_____. "Wandlungen im alt- und neutestamentlichen Gesetzesverständnis." In *Geschichte und Glaube*. Gesammelte Aufsätze, Bd. 4, T. 2. BEvT, Bd. 53. Munich: Chr. Kaiser Verlag, 1971. Pp. 73-119.

Bring, Ragnar. "Die Gerechtigkeit Gottes und das alttestamentliche Gesetz: Eine Untersuchung von Röm. 10,4." In *Christus und das Gesetz: Die Bedeutung des Gesetzes des Alten Testaments nach Paulus und sein Glauben an Christus*. Leiden: E. J. Brill, 1969. Pp. 35-72.

Bultmann, Rudolf. "Christ the End of the Law." In *Essays, Philosophical and Theological*. Translated by James C. G. Greig. With an Introduction by R. Gregor Smith. The Library of Philosophy and Theology. London: SCM Press, 1955. Pp. 36-66.

Cerfaux, Lucien. "Abraham 'père en circoncision' des Gentils." In *Recueil Lucien Cerfaux: Études d' Exégèse et d' Histoire Religieuse Réunies a l' Occasion de Son Soixante-dixième Anniversaire*. Bibliotheca Ephemeridum Theologicarum Lovaniensieum, 6-7, 18. 3 tomes. Gembloux: J. Duculot, 1954-62. T. 2, pp. 333-38.

Cranfield, C. E. B. "Some Notes on Romans 9:30-33." In *Jesus und Paulus: Festschrift für Werner Georg Kümmel zum 70. Geburtstag.* Edited by E. Earle Ellis and Erich Grässer. Göttingen: Vandenhoeck & Ruprecht, 1975. Pp. 35-43.

Dahl, Nils A. "Contradictions in Scripture." In *Studies in Paul: Theology for the Early Christian Mission.* Assisted by Paul Donahue. Minneapolis: Augsburg Publishing House, 1977. Pp. 159-77.

_____. "The Future of Israel." In *Studies in Paul.* Pp. 137-58.

_____. "The Missionary Theology in the Epistle to the Romans." In *Studies in Paul.* Pp. 70-94.

Daube, David. "'Ye Have Heard--But I Say Unto You.'" In *The New Testament and Rabbinic Judaism.* Jordan Lectures in Comparative Religion, 2. London: Athlone Press, 1956. Pp. 55-62.

Démann, Paul. "Moseş und das Gesetz bei Paulus." In *Moses in Schrift und Überlieferung.* Edited by Fridolin Stier and Eleonore Beck. Kommentare und Beiträge zum Alten und Neuen Testament. Düsseldorf: Patmos Verlag, 1963. Pp. 205-63.

Dodd, C. H. "ΕΝΝΟΜΟΣ ΧΡΙΣΤΟΥ." In *Studia Paulina in honorem Johannis de Zwaan septuagenarii.* Edited by J. N. Sevenster and W. C. van Unnik. Haarlem: Erven F. Bohn, 1953. Pp. 96-110.

_____. "The Law." In *The Bible and the Greeks.* London: Hodder & Stoughton, 1935. Pp. 25-41.

Doeve, J. W. "Some Notes with Reference to τὰ λόγια τοῦ θεοῦ in Romans 3.2." In *Studia Paulina in honorem Johannis de Zwaan septuagenarii.* Edited by J. N. Sevenster and W. C. van Unnik. Haarlem: Erven F. Bohn, 1953. Pp. 111-23.

Ebeling, Gergard. "Reflections on the Doctrine of the Law." In *Word and Faith.* Translated by James W. Leitch. Philadelphia: Fortress Press, 1963. Pp. 247-81.

Ellis, E. Earle. "Exegetical Patterns in 1 Corinthians and Romans." In *Grace upon Grace: Essays in Honor of Lester J. Kuyper.* Edited by James I. Cook. Grand Rapids: Wm. B. Eerdmans Publishing Co., 1975. Pp. 137-42.

Fitzmyer, Joseph A. "Paul and the Law." In *A Companion to Paul: Readings in Pauline Theology.* Edited by Michael J. Taylor. New York: Alba House, 1975. Pp. 73-87.

Grundmann, Walter. "The Teaching of Righteousness of Qumran and the Question of Justification by Faith in the Theology of the Apostle Paul." In *Paul and Qumran: Studies in New Testament Exegesis*. Edited by Jerome Murphy-O'Connor. Chicago: Priory Press, 1968. Pp. 85-114.

Hahn, Ferdinand. "Genesis 15,6 im Neuen Testament." In *Probleme biblischer Theologie. Gerhard von Rad zum 70. Geburtstag*. Edited by Hans Walter Wolff. Munich: Chr. Kaiser Verlag, 1971. Pp. 90-107.

Jeremias, Joachim. "Zur Gedankenführung in den paulinischen Briefen." In *Studia Paulina in honorem Johannis de Zwaan septuagenarii*. Edited by J. N. Sevenster and W. C. van Unnik. Haarlem: Erven F. Bohn, 1953. Pp. 146-54.

_____. "Die Gedankenführung in Röm 4: Zum paulinischen Glaubensverständnis." In *Foi et Salut selon S. Paul (Épître aux Romains 1,16): Colloque Oecumenique a l' Abbaye de S. Paul hors les murs, 16-21 avril 1968*. With the collaboration of S. Agourides, J. J. von Allmen, L. Arnaldich et al. AnBib, 42. Rome: Pontifical Biblical Institute, 1970. Pp. 51-58.

_____. "Paulus als Hillelit." In *Neotestamentica et Semitica: Studies in Honor of Matthew Black*. Edited by E. Earle Ellis and Max Wilcox. Edinburgh: T. & T. Clark, 1969. Pp. 88-94.

Käsemann, Ernst. "The Faith of Abraham in Romans 4." In *Perspectives on Paul*. Translated by Margaret Kohl. Philadelphia: Fortress Press, 1971. Pp. 79-101.

_____. "The Spirit and the Letter." In *Perspectives on Paul*. Pp. 138-66.

Klein, Günter. "Exegetische Probleme in Römer 3,21-4,25. Antwort an U. Wilckens." In *Rekonstruktion und Interpretation. Gesammelte Aufsätze zum Neuen Testament*. BEvT, Bd. 50. Munich: Chr. Kaiser Verlag, 1969. Pp. 170-79.

_____. "Gottes Gerechtigkeit als Thema der neuesten Paulus-Forschung." In *Rekonstruktion und Interpretation*. Pp. 225-36.

_____. "Individualgeschichte und Weltgeschichte bei Paulus: Eine Interpretation ihres Verhältnisses im Galaterbrief." In *Rekonstruktion und Interpretation*. Pp. 180-224.

_____. "Römer 4 und die Idee der Heilsgeschichte." In *Rekonstruktion und Interpretation*. Pp. 145-69.

Ladd, George Eldon. "Paul and the Law." In *Soli Deo Gloria: New Testament Studies in Honor of William Childs Robinson.* Edited by J. McDowell Richards. Richmond: John Knox Press, 1968. Pp. 50-67, 142-46.

Lohse, Eduard. "ὁ νόμος τοῦ πνεύματος τῆς ζωῆς: Exegetische Anmerkungen zu Röm 8,2." In *Neues Testament und christliche Existenz: Festschrift für Herbert Braun zum 70. Geburtstag am 4. Mai 1973.* Edited by Hans Dieter Betz and Luise Schottroff. Tübingen: J. C. B. Mohr, 1973. Pp. 279-88.

_____. "'Wir richten das Gesetz auf!' Glaube und Thora im Römerbrief." In *Treue zur Thora: Beiträge zur Mitte des christlich-jüdischen Gesprächs: Festschrift für Günther Harder zum 75. Geburtstag.* Edited by Peter von der Osten-Sacken. Veröffentlichungen aus dem Institut Kirche und Judentum bei der Kirchlichen Hochschule Berlin, Hft. 3. Berlin: Institut Kirche und Judentum, 1977. Pp. 65-71.

Lyonnet, Stanislas. "Saint Paul et l' exégèse juive de sons temps. A propos de Rom., 10:6-8." In *Mélanges bibliques redigés en l' honneur de André Robert.* Travaux de l' Institut catholique de Paris, 4. Paris: Bloud et Gay, 1957. Pp. 494-506.

Manson, T. W. "Jesus, Paul, and the Law." In *Judaism and Christianity.* 3 vols. London: Sheldon Press, 1937-38. Vol. 3: *Law and Religion.* Edited by Erwin I. J. Rosenthal, 1938. Pp. 125-41.

Mussner, Franz. "'Christus (ist) des Gesetzes Ende zur Gerechtigkeit für jeden, der glaubt' (Röm 10,4)." In *Paulus--Apostat oder Apostel? Jüdische und christliche Antworten.* With contributions by Markus Barth, Jochanan Bloch, Josef Blank et al. Foreword by Franz Henrich. Regensburg: Verlag Friedrich Pustet, 1977. Pp. 31-44.

von Rad, Gerhard. "Faith Reckoned as Righteousness. In *The Problem of the Hexateuch and Other Essays.* Translated by E. W. Trueman Dicken. Introduction by Norman W. Porteous. Edinburgh: Oliver & Boyd, 1966. Pp. 125-30.

Safrai, S. "Religion in Everyday Life." In *The Jewish People in the First Century: Historical Geography, Political History, Social, Cultural and Religious Life and Institutions.* Edited by S. Safrai and M. Stern. Compendia Rerum Iudaicarum ad Novum Testamentum, 1. 2 vols. Assen: Van Gorcum & Co., B.V., 1974-76. Vol. 2, pp. 793-833.

Sanders, James A. "Torah and Paul." In *God's Christ and His People: Studies in Honour of Nils Alstrup Dahl.* Edited by Jacob Jervell and Wayne A. Meeks. Oslo: Universitetsforlaget, 1977. Pp. 132-40.

Schmitz, Otto. "Abraham im Spätjudentum und im Urchristentum." In *Aus Schrift und Geschichte: Theologische Abhandlungen Adolf Schlatter zu seinem 70. Geburtstage dargebracht von Freunden und Schülern*. Edited by Karl B. Bornhäuser. Stuttgart: Calwer Vereinsbuchhandlung, 1922. Pp. 99-123.

Schubert, Paul. "Paul and the New Testament Ethic in the Thought of John Knox." In *Christian History and Interpretation: Studies Presented to John Knox*. Edited by W. R. Farmer, C. F. D. Moule and R. R. Niebuhr. Cambridge, England: University Press, 1967. Pp. 363-88.

Schürmann, Heinz. "'Das Gesetz des Christus' (Gal 6,2): Jesu Verhalten und Wort als letztgültige sittliche Norm nach Paulus." In *Neues Testament und Kirche: Für Rudolf Schnackenburg*. Edited by Joachim Gnilka. Freiburg: Herder, 1974. Pp. 282-300.

Scroggs, Robin. "Paul as Rhetorician: Two Homilies in Romans 1-11." In *Jews, Greeks and Christians: Religious Cultures in Late Antiquity: Essays in Honor of William David Davies*. Edited by Robert Hamerton-Kelly and Robin Scroggs. Studies in Judaism in Late Antiquity, 21. Leiden: E. J. Brill, 1976. Pp. 271-98.

Suggs, M. Jack. "'The Word Is Near You': Romans 10:6-10 within the Purpose of the Letter." In *Christian History and Interpretation: Studies Presented to John Knox*. Edited by W. R. Farmer, C. F. D. Moule and R. R. Niebuhr. Cambridge, England: University Press, 1967. Pp. 289-312.

Stuhlmacher, Peter. "Zum neueren Exegesis von Röm 3,24-26." In *Jesus und Paulus: Festschrift für Werner Georg Kümmel zum 70. Geburtstag*. Edited by E. Earle Ellis and Erich Grässer. Göttingen: Vandenhoeck & Ruprecht, 1975. Pp. 315-33.

Vielhauer, Philipp. "Paulus und das Alte Testament." In *Studien zur Geschichte und Theologie der Reformation: Festschrift für Ernst Bizer*. Edited by Luise Abrahowski and J. B. Gerhard Goeters. Neukirchen-Vluyn: Neukirchener Verlag, 1969. Pp. 33-62.

Weiss, Johannes. "Beiträge zur paulinischen Rhetorik." In *Theologische Studien: Professor D. Bernhard Weiss zu seinem 70. Geburtstage dargebracht*. By C. R. Gregory, A. von Harnack, M. W. Jacobus et al. Göttingen: Vandenhoeck & Ruprecht, 1897. Pp. 165-247.

Wendland, Paul. "Philo und die kynisch-stoische Diatribe." In *Beiträge zur Geschichte der griechischen Philosophie und Religion*. Edited by Paul Wendland and Otto Kern. Berlin: G. Reimer, 1895. Pp. 1-75.

Wilckens, Ulrich. "Die Bekehrung des Paulus als religionsgeschichtliches Problem." In *Rechtfertigung als Freiheit: Paulusstudien*. Neukirchen-Vluyn: Neukirchener Verlag, 1974. Pp. 11-32.

_____. "Die Rechtfertigung Abrahams nach Römer 4." In *Rechtfertigung als Freiheit*. Pp. 33-49.

_____. "Zu Römer 3,21-4,25. Antwort an G. Klein." In *Rechtfertigung als Freiheit*. Pp. 50-76.

_____. "Was heisst bei Paulus: 'Aus Werken des Gesetzes wird kein Mensch gerecht'?" In *Rechtfertigung als Freiheit*. Pp. 77-109.

Primary Texts, Grammars, Dictionaries, Lexicons and Concordances

The Apocrypha and Pseudepigrapha of the Old Testament in English. Edited by R. H. Charles. 2 vols. Oxford: Clarendon Press, 1913.

The Babylonian Talmud. Isidore Epstein, gen. ed. 35 vols. London: Soncino Press, 1935-52.

Bacher, Wilhelm. *Die exegetische Terminologie der jüdischen Traditionsliteratur*. 2 Teile. T. 1: *Die bibelexegetische Terminologie der Tannaiten*. T. 2: *Die bibel- und traditionsexegetische Terminologie der Amoräer*. Leipzig: J. C. Hinrichs, 1899-1905; reprint ed., Darmstadt: Wissenschaftliche Buchgesellschaft, 1965.

Bauer, Walter. *A Greek-English Lexicon of the New Testament and Other Early Christian Literature*. Translated and adapted from the 4th rev. and augmented German ed., 1952, by William F. Arndt and F. Wilbur Gingrich. Chicago: University of Chicago Press, 1957. 909 pp.

Biblia Hebraica. Edited by Rudolf Kittel and Paul Kahle. 3d ed. Stuttgart: Württembergische Bibelanstalt, 1937. 1434 pp.

Blass F. and A. Debrunner. *A Greek Grammar of the New Testament and Other Early Christian Literature*. Translated and revised by Robert W. Funk. Chicago: University of Chicago Press, 1961. 325 pp.

Brown, Francis, S. R. Driver and Charles A. Briggs. *A Hebrew and English Lexicon of the Old Testament*. Oxford: Clarendon Press, 1952. 1126 pp.

Burton, Ernest De Witt. *Syntax of the Moods and Tenses in New Testament Greek*. 3d ed. Chicago: University of Chicago Press, 1898. 215 pp.

Dana, H. E. and Julius R. Mantey. *A Manual Grammar of the Greek New Testament*. New York: Macmillan Co., 1927. 356 pp.

A Dictionary of the Targumim, the Talmud Babli and Yerushalmi, and the Midrashic Literature. Marcus Jastrow, comp. 2 vols. London: Luzac, 1903.

Dupont-Sommer, A. *The Essene Writings from Qumran*. Translated by G. Vermes. Cleveland: World Publishing Co., 1961. 428 pp.

Epictetus: The Discourses as Reported by Arrian, the Manual, and Fragments. Translated by W. A. Oldfather. Loeb Classical Library. 2 vols. London: W. Heinemann, 1926-28.

The Greek New Testament. Edited by Kurt Aland, Matthew Black, Carlo M. Martini et al. 3d ed. New York: American Bible Society, 1975. 918 pp.

Hatch, Edwin and Henry A. Redpath. *A Concordance to the Septuagint and the Other Greek Versions of the Old Testament*. 2 vols. Oxford: Clarendon Press, 1897.

The Interpreter's Dictionary of the Bible. 4 vols. and Supplementary Vol. Vols. 1-4 edited by George Arthur Buttrick; Supplementary Volume edited by Keith Crim. Nashville: Abingdon Press, 1962-76.

Liddell, Henry George and Robert Scott. *A Greek-English Lexicon*. New ed. revised and augmented by Henry Stuart Jones and Roderick McKenzie. 2 vols. in 1. Oxford: Clarendon Press, 1925-40.

Metzger, Bruce M. *A Textual Commentary on the Greek New Testament: A Companion Volume to the United Bible Societies' Greek New Testament (Third Edition)*. London: United Bible Societies, 1971. 775 pp.

Moule, C. F. D. *An Idiom-Book of New Testament Greek*. 2d ed. Cambridge, England: University Press, 1971. 246 pp.

Moulton, James Hope. *A Grammar of New Testament Greek*. 4 vols. Edinburgh: T. & T. Clark, 1908-76. Vol. 4: *Style*, by Nigel Turner, 1976.

Moulton, W. F. and A. S. Geden. *A Concordance to the Greek Testament*. 3d ed. Edinburgh: T. & T. Clark, 1926. 1033 pp.

The New Oxford Annotated Bible with the Apocrypha: Revised Standard Version. Edited by Herbert G. May and Bruce M. Metzger. New York: Oxford University Press, 1977. 1564, 340 pp.

Novum Testamentum Graece. Edited by Erwin Nestle and Kurt Aland. 25th ed. Stuttgart: Württembergische Bibelanstalt, 1968. 670 pp.

Philo. Translated by F. H. Colson and G. H. Whitaker. Loeb Classical Library. 10 vols. Cambridge: Harvard University Press, 1929-71.

Septuaginta. Edited by Alfred Rahlfs. 5th ed. 2 vols. Stuttgart: Württembergische Bibelanstalt, 1952.

Strack, Hermann L. and Paul Billerbeck. *Kommentar zum Neuen Testament aus Talmud und Midrasch*. 6 vols. in 7. Munich: Beck, 1922-61.

The Theological Dictionary of the New Testament. Translated and edited by Geoffrey W. Bromiley. 10 vols. Vols. 1-4 edited by Gerhard Kittel; vols. 5-9 edited by Gerhard Friedrich; vol. 10 compiled by R. E. Pitkin. Grand Rapids: Wm. B. Eerdmans Publishing Co., 1964-76.

Unpublished Materials

Achtemeier, Paul J. "St. Paul, Accommodation or Confrontation." Th.D. dissertation, Union Theological Seminary in New York, 1957. 283 pp.

Fesperman, Francis Irving. "Freedom from the Law: Paul's Doctrine and Its Role in the Early Church." Ph.D. dissertation, Vanderbilt University, 1969. 351 pp.

Getty, Mary Ann. "Christ Is the End of the Law: Romans 10:4 in Its Context." Ph.D. dissertation, Catholic University of Louvain, 1975. 691 pp.

Layman, Fred Dale. "Paul's Use of Abraham: An Approach to Paul's Understanding of History." Ph.D. dissertation, University of Iowa, 1972. 318 pp.

Lord, James Raymond. "Abraham: A Study in Ancient Jewish and Christian Interpretation." Ph.D. dissertation, Duke University, 1968. 328 pp.

Schein, Bruce Edward. "Abraham Our Father." Ph.D. dissertation, Yale University, 1973. 340 pp.

Towner, W. Sibley. Unpublished article, "Halakic Midrash. Hermeneutical Systems of Hillel and the Tannaim."

Wang, Joseph Shou-Jen. "Pauline Doctrine of Law." Ph.D. dissertation, Emory University, 1970. 253 pp.